International and Development Education

The *International and Development Education Series* focuses on the complementary areas of comparative, international, and development education. Books emphasize a number of topics ranging from key international education issues, trends, and reforms to examinations of national education systems, social theories, and development education initiatives. Local, national, regional, and global volumes (single authored and edited collections) constitute the breadth of the series and offer potential contributors a great deal of latitude based on interests and cutting edge research. The series is supported by a strong network of international scholars and development professionals who serve on the International and Development Education Advisory Board and participate in the selection and review process for manuscript development.

SERIES EDITORS
John N. Hawkins
Professor Emeritus, University of California, Los Angeles
Senior Consultant, IFE 2020 East West Center

W. James Jacob
Assistant Professor, University of Pittsburgh
Director, Institute for International Studies in Education

PRODUCTION EDITOR
Heejin Park
Research Associate, Institute for International Studies in Education

INTERNATIONAL EDITORIAL ADVISORY BOARD
Clementina Acedo, *UNESCO's International Bureau of Education, Switzerland*
Ka-Ho Mok, *University of Hong Kong, China*
Christine Musselin, *Sciences Po, France*
Yusuf K. Nsubuga, *Ministry of Education and Sports, Uganda*
Val D. Rust, *University of California, Los Angeles*
John C. Weidman, *University of Pittsburgh*

Institute for International Studies in Education
School of Education, University of Pittsburgh
5714 Wesley W. Posvar Hall, Pittsburgh, PA 15260

Center for International and Development Education
Graduate School of Education & Information Studies, University of California, Los Angeles
Box 951521, Moore Hall, Los Angeles, CA 90095

Titles:
Higher Education in Asia/Pacific: Quality and the Public Good
Edited by Terance W. Bigalke and Deane E. Neubauer

Affirmative Action in China and the U.S.: A Dialogue on Inequality and Minority Education
Edited by Minglang Zhou and Ann Maxwell Hill

Critical Approaches to Comparative Education: Vertical Case Studies from Africa, Europe, the Middle East, and the Americas
Edited by Frances Vavrus and Lesley Bartlett

Curriculum Studies in South Africa: Intellectual Histories & Present Circumstances
Edited by William F. Pinar

Higher Education, Policy, and the Global Competition Phenomenon
Edited by Laura M. Portnoi, Val D. Rust, and Sylvia S. Bagley

The Search for New Governance of Higher Education in Asia
Edited by Ka-Ho Mok

Forthcoming titles:

International Students and Global Mobility in Higher Education: National Trends and New Directions
Edited by Rajika Bhandari and Peggy Blumenthal

Policy Debates in Comparative, International, and Development Education
Edited by John N. Hawkins and William James Jacob

Curriculum Studies in Brazil: Intellectual Histories, Present Circumstances
Edited by William F. Pinar

Increasing Effectiveness of the Community College Financial Model: A Global Perspective for the Global Economy
Edited by Stewart E. Sutin, Daniel Derrico, Rosalind Latiner Raby, and Edward J. Valeau

Access, Equity, and Capacity in Asia Pacific Higher Education
Edited by Deane Neubauer and Yoshiro Tanaka

THE SEARCH FOR NEW GOVERNANCE OF HIGHER EDUCATION IN ASIA

EDITED BY
KA-HO MOK

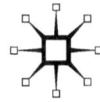

THE SEARCH FOR NEW GOVERNANCE OF HIGHER EDUCATION IN ASIA
Copyright © Ka-Ho Mok, 2010.
Softcover reprint of the hardcover 1st edition 2010 978-0-230-62031-5
All rights reserved.

First published in 2010 by
PALGRAVE MACMILLAN®
in the United States—a division of St. Martin's Press LLC,
175 Fifth Avenue, New York, NY 10010.

Where this book is distributed in the UK, Europe and the rest of the world, this is by Palgrave Macmillan, a division of Macmillan Publishers Limited, registered in England, company number 785998, of Houndmills, Basingstoke, Hampshire RG21 6XS.

Palgrave Macmillan is the global academic imprint of the above companies and has companies and representatives throughout the world.

Palgrave® and Macmillan® are registered trademarks in the United States, the United Kingdom, Europe and other countries.

ISBN 978-1-349-38273-6   ISBN 978-0-230-11155-4 (eBook)
DOI 10.1057/9780230111554

Library of Congress Cataloging-in-Publication Data
   The search for new governance of higher education in Asia / edited by Ka-Ho Mok.
      p. cm.—(International & development education series)

    1. Education, Higher—Asia. 2. Education and globalization—Asia.
  I. Mok, Ka-Ho, 1964–
LA1058.S43 2010
378.5—dc22   2010007418
A catalogue record of the book is available from the British Library.
Design by Newgen Imaging Systems (P) Ltd., Chennai, India.
First edition: August 2010
10 9 8 7 6 5 4 3 2 1

Contents

List of Tables and Figures	vii
List of Acronyms	ix
Series Editors' Introduction	xiii

Introduction: Paradigm Shift or Business as Usual: The Search for New Governance in Higher Education in Asia — 1
Ka-Ho Mok

1. Global Education, Heterarchies, and Hybrid Organizations — 13
   Stephen J. Ball

2. Higher Education Transformation: Some Trends in California and Asia — 29
   John N. Hawkins

3. Changing Governance in China's Higher Education: Some Analyses of the Recent University Enrollment Expansion Policy — 49
   Rui Yang

4. Incorporation of National Universities of Korea: Dynamic Forces, Key Features, and Challenges — 67
   Byung-Shik Rhee

5. Governance of the Incorporated Japanese National Universities — 85
   Jun Oba

6. Entrepreneurialism in Higher Education: A Comparison of University Governance Changes in Hong Kong and Singapore — 103
   William Yat-Wai Lo

7. University Governance Structure in Challenging Times: The Case of Malaysia's First APEX University (Universiti Sains Malaysia) — 125
   Morshidi Sirat and A. R. Ahmad

8. Shifting Governance Patterns in Taiwanese Higher Education: A Recentralized Future? — 139
   Sheng-Ju Chan

| 9 | Southeast Asian Higher Education in the Global Knowledge System: Governance, Privatization, and Infrastructure
Anthony Welch | 153 |
| 10 | Higher Education in India: Emerging Challenges and Evolving Strategies
Jandhyala B. G. Tilak | 171 |
| 11 | Governance and the Governance of Higher Education in Vietnam
Jonathan London | 193 |

Notes on Contributors — 215

Index — 219

Tables and Figures

Tables

3.1	Numbers of Regular HEIs, Their Enrollments, and Graduates	53
3.2	University Enrollments and Admission Rates in China, 1998–2007	57
4.1	Comparison of Key Differences between the Current System and Proposed NUC	76
5.1	Results of the Evaluation by NUC-EC for FY 2004–2007	94
9.1	National Innovation Indices, by Country, Region, and Level of Development	158
9.2	R&D Expenditure Levels, and as Percent of GDP, 2002	158
9.3	R&D Performance by Sector	159
9.4	Numbers and Types of HEIs in Southeast Asia, 2007	161
10.1	Growth of HEIs in India	175
10.2	Present Pattern of Growth of Higher Education in India	181
10.3	Proposals for Expansion of Higher Education in the Eleventh Five-Year Plan	185

Figures

1.1	The Transnational Heterarchy of the University of Nottingham and the University of Liverpool	19
4.1	Demographic Landscape	71
5.1	Governance Structure of NUCs	86
5.2	Factors Regarded as Important by the Presidents in the Selection of Executives	88
5.3	Participation of Students in Diverse Campus Activities in National Universities	92
5.4	Operational Grants and Total Revenues (External Resources Excluded) of NUCs	95

5.5	Evolution of the Authority of Collegial Bodies and Academic Units in National Universities	97
6.1	Numbers of Graduates of Full-time Accredited Self-financing Postsecondary Programs, 2002–2008	108
6.2	Numbers of Full-time Accredited Self-financing Postsecondary Programs, 2001/02–2008/09	108

Acronyms

AC	Administrative Council
ACE	Anglo-Chinese Education Management Ltd
ADB	Asian Development Bank
AICTE	All India Council for Technical Education
APEX	Accelerated Programme for Excellence
APSCHE	Andhra Pradesh State Council of Higher Education
ARW	Advanced Research Workshop
AURA	APEX University Research Agenda
BCI	Bar Council of India
BOD	Board of Director
BNU	Beijing Normal University
BOE	Board of Director
CEAS	Centre for East Asian Studies at University of Bristol
CEF	Continuing Education Fund
CEO	Chief Executive Officer
CERNET	Chinese Education and Research Network
CMOE	China Ministry of Education
CNUFM	Centre for National University Finance and Management
CPEC	California Post-Secondary Education Commission
CPI	Corruption Perceptions Index
CPV	Communist Party of Vietnam
EC	Education Commission
EDB	Education Bureau
EMB	Education and Manpower Bureau
ERC	Education and Research Council
FPT	Corporation for Financing and Promoting Technology
FY	Fiscal Year
GATS	General Agreement on Tariffs in Services
GCC	Global Commodity Chain
GDP	Gross Domestic Product
HDI	Human Development Index
HEI	Higher Education Institution
HEQAU	Higher Education Quality Assurance Unit
HK$	Hong Kong Dollar
HKCAA	Hong Kong Council for Academic Accreditation

HKIED	Hong Kong Institute of Education
HKU	University of Hong Kong
HKUST	Hong Kong University of Science and Technology
IGO	Inter-governmental Organization
IHEP	Institute for Higher Education Policy
IHT	International Herald Tribune
IMF	International Monetary Fund
INR	Indian Rupee
IPPTN	National Higher Education Research Institute
IPASS	Information Portal for Accredited Self-financing Post-secondary Programmes
IRAHE	Independent Regulatory Authority for Higher Education
IT	Information Technology
KEDI	Korean Educational Development Institute
KMOE	Korea Ministry of Education
KRW	South Korean Won
LDSS	Library and Documentation Support System
MBA	Master of Business Administration
MCI	Medical Council of India
MEFSS	Modern Equipment and Facilities Sharing System
MEST	Ministry of Education, Science and Technology
MEXT	Ministry of Education, Culture, Sports, Science and Technology
MGS	Matching Grant Scheme
MIT	Massachusetts Institute of Technology
MOET	Ministry of Education and Training
MOF	Ministry of Finance
MOHE	Ministry of Higher Education
MPI	Ministry of Planning and Investment
MTG	Mid-Term Goal
MTI	Ministry of Trade and Industry
MTP	Mid-Term Plan
NCNU	National Chi Nan University
NCTE	National Council for Teacher Education
NCUK	Northern Consortium United Kingdom
NET	National Eligibility Test
NGO	Nongovernmental organization
NSC	National Science Council
NT$	New Taiwan Dollar
NTU	Nanyang Technological University
NTU	National Taiwan University
NUC	National University Corporation
NUC-EC	National University Corporation Evaluation Committee
NUS	National University of Singapore
OECD	Organization for Economic Co-operation and Development
PHEI	Private Higher Education Institution
PPP	Purchasing Power Parity

PRC	The People's Republic of China
PS	Public Service
PSC	President Selection Committee
RIHE	Research Institute for Higher Education
RMB	Renminbi
QAC	Quality Assurance Council
QAFU	Quality Assurance Framework for Universities
RAE	Research Assessment Exercise
R&D	Research and Development
SD	Staff Development
SEAMEO	Southeast Asian Ministers of Education Organization
SEC	State Education Commission
SG$	Singapore Dollar
SMF	Singapore Manufacturing Federation
SMOE	Singapore Ministry of Education
SMU	Singapore Management University
SNU	Seoul National University
STEM	Science, Technology, Engineering and Mathematics
TSLN	Thinking Schools, Learning Nations
UC	University of California
UCCA	Universities and University Colleges Act
UCLA	University of California, Los Angeles
UGC	University Grants Commission
UGC	University Grants Committee
UK	United Kingdom
UNDP	United Nations Development Program
UNESCO	United Nations Educational, Scientific and Cultural Organization
UNICEF	United Nations Children's Fund
UNiM	University of Nottingham—Malaysia Campus
US	United States
UUCA	University and University Collages Act
WTO	World Trade Organization
WUN	Worldwide Universities Network
XJLU	Xi'an Jiaotong Liverpool University

Series Editors' Introduction

This book is part of Palgrave Macmillan's *International and Development Education Book Series*, which focuses on the complementary areas of comparative, international, and development education. Books in this series emphasize a number of topics ranging from key international education issues, trends, and development education initiatives. Local, national, regional, and global volumes (single authored and edited collections) constitute the breadth of the series and offer potential contributors a great deal of latitude based on interests and cutting-edge research. The series is supported by a strong network of international scholars and development professionals who serve on the International and Development Education Review Board and participate in the selection and review process for manuscript development.

This edited volume by Ka-Ho Mok tackles the increasingly critical higher education policy and development issue of governance, corporatization, and incorporatization. Mok, a prominent scholar in the field of higher education change and transformation, has assembled a leading group of scholars from the Asia Pacific Region to provide a region-wide analysis of the challenges that face higher education institutions in an era of privatization and neoliberal political policies. These issues, of course, are not restricted to Asia but are particularly significant there as this region of the world begins to take its place as a leader in higher educational reform. Here we see that market mechanisms have been strengthened and decision-making decentralized, public enterprises have been the focus of privatization efforts and the notion of a corporate identity for higher education has been introduced, closely coupled with sophisticated fund-raising and development strategies and bureaucracy. These are all new ways of speaking about higher education. The terms decentralization, accountability, assessment, strategic planning, privatization, autonomy, the service university, branding, corporatization, competitiveness and others, unthinkable back in the seventies when talking and writing about public higher education, now slip easily off the tongue. Recommendations being made in the Asia Pacific Region include finding alternative revenue streams through self-supporting degree programs, developing strategies for retaining the best faculty through innovative compensation plans, and restructuring the budget, governance, and planning process around three- to five- year strategic plans with annual budget management reviews based on performance in relation to the unit's strategic plan. Globalization, the knowledge economy, the IT revolution, the establishment of new privatized institutions (especially in China where a new privatization law has been put into effect), and the continued expansion of the demand for higher education have all contributed to new forms of university governance and management with an emphasis on efficiency, accountability, more involved stakeholders, strategic alliances, and competitiveness. This is true whether one is talking about governmental or nongovernmental higher education institutions.

The authors of this volume provide national case studies that cover China, Malaysia, Thailand, Japan, Hong Kong, Korea, Singapore, Taiwan, India, and Vietnam, with chapters that place these settings in a theoretical context of a paradigm shift for higher education governance. Implications for what has become known as the "global university" conclude the volume. This volume comes at a particularly timely point as countries such as the United States find their great and respected public higher education systems under siege as the state begins to accelerate what has been a gradual withdrawal of public support. The experiences of Asia will likely provide a useful guideline for those in Europe, North America, and elsewhere as these forces and factors play themselves out in the years to come. We are very pleased to offer this volume as part of our ongoing series on critical issues in international education.

John N. Hawkins
University of California, Los Angeles

W. James Jacob
University of Pittsburgh

Introduction

Paradigm Shift or Business as Usual: The Search for New Governance in Higher Education in Asia

Ka-Ho Mok

Introduction

Institutions of higher education in Asia, as in other parts of the world, have experienced intense pressure to perform well in order to be in a better position to compete on a global level and attain world-class status (Mok and Wei 2008). One way of achieving the goal is to secure a top position in the global university league tables. Since the launch of the first global university ranking exercise by the Shanghai Jiaotung University, universities in Asia have been particularly keen to improve their world-class status. As Salmi rightly points out, "these world-class universities are now more than just cultural and educational institutions—they are points of pride and comparison among nations that view their own status in relation to other nations" (2009, x). With the recent proliferation of ranking exercises, more systematic assessments for world-class universities have emerged (IHEP 2007). The principal goal of this introduction is to establish the theoretical context for the present volume by highlighting a few key issues related to the search for new governance in higher education among selected Asian societies. We also introduce the major arguments discussed in this book.

Globalization and University Governance

Despite the disagreements on and diverse interpretations of the effect of globalization on state governance, the dominant view is that globalization has not only weakened the power of the state but has also led to the end of the state (Zheng 2004). It is within this context that a growing number of modern states are rethinking their governance strategies to cope with rapid social and economic changes. In order to enhance global competitiveness, new forms of governance and new governance philosophies have emerged, which have in turn affected management of the public sector and the delivery of public services. A massive proliferation of tools and policy instruments, such as a dizzying array of loans, loan guarantees, grants, contracts, insurance, vouchers, and so forth has replaced government bureaucracies in terms of delivery of goods and services. Despite the fact that "governance" is a contested concept, political scientists and public administration scholars generally agree that postmodern societies require a shift in the state's function from a "rowing" to a "steering" role (Kooiman 1993a, 1993b; Pierre and Peters 2000; Salamon 2002).

Unlike the traditional form of public administration, which relies heavily on state bureaucracy for public service delivery, the "new" governance emphasizes the interpenetration of various domains (state, market, and civil society) and highlights the importance of "international interdependencies" (Greca 2002). Establishment of new governance is urgently needed, especially when provision of higher education is no longer monopolized by the state or the public sector. International and comparative research has clearly shown that higher education providers have multiplied and so the conventional public-private distinction is rendered inappropriate in describing higher education governance. With the rise of transnational higher education (particularly in Asia and other developing countries), the emergence of the global education market has challenged the traditional forms/modes of governance (Marginson 2007; Knight 2008; Chapter 1). Hence, modern governments are adapting to radical changes in their environments by turning to new forms of governance that are "more society-centered" and focused on "coordination and self-governance" (Peters 1995; Pierre 2000). In short, a new governance approach prefers redesigned agencies, favors networks over hierarchies, and promotes negotiation, persuasion, and collaboration (Rhodes 1997, 2000; Salamon 2002). Realizing that the centralized model, which asserts the control of the ministry of education, is less conductive to promoting good governance in higher education, some messy realities of "network governance" have evolved that move beyond government bureaucracy to "the judicious mixing of market, hierarchy and networks to achieve the best possible outcomes" (Jessop 2003, 15). This is particularly true for higher education provisions that offer programs or degrees or any other educational oppurtunities to students, financing, and management in the global education market across national borders, which is characterized by complex heterarchies and hybrid organizations (see Chapter 1). Therefore, decentralization and even privatization of services leads to the participation of both government and nongovernment actors in delivery of services. In addition, the role of government in managing the economy is more sharply delineated and circumscribed by new market-supporting instruments that are at arm's length from the government, in some cases relying on self-regulation (Gamble 2000; Jayasuriya 2001).

In the post–cold war era, the shaping of global social, economic, and political agendas has moved from United States to supranational organizations. But this shift has encountered its critics. A number of scholars suggest that the implementation of consensus between many countries, especially in developing or less-developed countries, has led to a situation where there is "global governance without global government." Similarly, the proposal to reduce state activity of the so-called Washington Consensus has been relentlessly attacked as an irresponsible act, particularly when many countries of the developing world conceive the reduction of state activity as an effort to cut back state capacity across the board (Fukuyama 2005). Before the present global economic crisis began in October 2008, the ideas and practices of neoliberalism and neoliberal institutionalism dominated, which aroused concerns about state capacity to manage an increasingly complex and global environment. Unlike the neoliberalist ideas that play up the role of the market at the expense of the state, the state capacity literature argues for "stateness" as the basis for effective governance. The call for bringing the state back in has become increasingly popular, particularly after the meltdown of the international financial markets in New York and London. Realizing that insufficient regulation and ineffective governance of the financial regimes is one of the major causes of the financial crisis, governments in the United States, United Kingdom, and Europe have recently tried to revamp their financial regulatory regimes.

Enhancing Global Competitiveness: Asian Responses

Fukuyama, who was well aware of the state's apparent inability to effectively govern complex economic, social, and political issues in the globalizing economy context, argues that "the state-building agenda, which was at least as important as the state-reducing one, was not given nearly as much thought or emphasis" (2005, 7). It is important to differentiate between state activities, that is, the different functions and goals taken on by governments, and the strength of state power, which refers to the ability of the state to plan and implement policies and political agendas. After witnessing the decline in state capacity to manage the contemporary world after a steady period of downsizing of state activities, a growing number of states revisited their approaches to governing the public sector. This book is set against the backdrop of this wider socioeconomic and sociopolitical context and examines major strategies adopted by selected Asian governments to transform one major public policy sector, that is, the university sector.

Against the global trend of searching for new governance, Asian states, similar to their Western counterparts, have launched public policy and public management reforms along the lines of ideas and practices of marketization, privatization, corporatization, and commercialization. In countries like Malaysia and South Korea, privatization has been a common theme in evolving patterns of the government-business relationship (Gouri et al. 1991; World Bank 1995). Intense pressure for broad change came to a head in the Asian financial crisis of 1997. A feature of these pressures is the presence of influential international agencies such as the International Monetary fund and the World Bank. Their preferred models of governance reflect many of the same tendencies noted earlier. Hence, it is not surprising that strategies, measures, and policy instruments in line with the global neoliberal orthodoxy of pro-competition have been introduced and adopted by Asian states to transform the management of the public sector (Cheung and Scott 2003; Mok and Welch 2003).

A central theme in this book is whether the neoliberal approach adopted by many Asian states to transform their higher education systems is still politically appropriate and managerially effective. In order to enhance the global competitiveness of their higher education systems, many Asian governments have initiated comprehensive reforms and adopted new governance measures to enhance their universities and gain a better position in the global ranking exercises. Incorporation and corporatization have been identified as important strategies to restructure and re-engineer university governance around the world. Contributors in this volume have been encouraged to critically examine how the quest for "world-class" university status (as a global movement) has affected the way their universities are governed. More specifically, authors in this focus on how Asian states and even the California state government have responded to the growing challenges of globalization by adopting more pro-competition policy instruments to reform or restructure their higher education systems in coping with ever-growing globalization challenges. We examine the extent to which restructuring of higher education governance along the lines of incorporation, privatization, and corporatization has really transformed the values and practices of those who work in the higher education subsector. The authors offer critical reflections on the governance change taking place in the Asian university systems.

About the Book[1]

The Search for New Governance of Higher Education in Asia opens with a contribution by Stephen Ball, "Global education, Heterarchies, and Hybrid Organizations." Witnessing the growing trend of rapid development of transnational education across different parts of the world, Ball argues that the conventional method of understanding higher education governance in terms of hierarchy is inappropriate. With a growing number of organizations running educational programs across national borders, Ball believes a better analysis of the complexity of university governance should critically examine heterarchical relationships instead of analyzing bureaucratic and administrative structures and relationships with a system of organization replete with overlap, multiplicity, mixed ascendancy, and/or divergent-but-coexistent patterns of relation. Well aware of the transnationalization of policy, Ball highlights the importance of university governance analysis to be focused on the entrepreneurial activities taking place in the university sector. Ball also suggests critical examination of the manner in which hybrid organizations are becoming increasingly significant in the governance and management of universities.

Countries in the Asia/Pacific region, including the United States, struggle to resolve challenges to higher education while faced with redefinitions of "public and private higher education sectors." The meanings and values imputed to the terms *public* and *private* have changed significantly in the past century. They have acquired new meaning and currency as notions of market competitiveness ("liberalization") have penetrated these societies, whether they are historically state capitalist, socialist, developmental or developed states. In Chapter 2, John Hawkins briefly looks at trends in higher education reform in California and provides commentary on parallel trends in Asia. California, of course, is not Asia. It is, however, a complex and large state with a diverse higher educational sector, not unlike other states with comprehensive "tier one" research universities. This reality, along with the history of the California Master Plan for Higher Education, has been of great interest to many Asian nations and therefore, according to Hawkins, such juxtaposition is of interest to scholars and practitioners of HEIs.

At the end of 1988, the Chinese central government decided to increase the number of students admitted to higher education in China. While the move was influenced by a combination of domestic and external forces, it was a decision fundamentally based on economic consideration. In Chapter 3, Rui Yang reflects on the university enrollment expansion policy in his examination of the rationale for and the contexts of China's new policies. Yang critically analyzes the measures and consequences of the implementation of the enrollment policy to illustrate the changing governance in mainland Chinese universities, particularly highlighting some major policy implications for the enrollment policy adopted in mainland China.

Education reform is a growing trend and the incorporation of public institutions of higher education is one such reform. Eventually, all of Korea's national universities will be incorporated. The legislature passed a law on March 7, 2007, that requires a new national university to be established as a corporation. Meanwhile, the Ministry of Education and Human Resources Development is finalizing the general law of the incorporation of national universities. In Chapter 4, Byung-Shik Rhee examines the driving forces and key features of the incorporation of national universities in Korea. The Korean model of incorporation follows global trends and shares key features with other countries, especially Japan. The Korean model of incorporation follows global trends and shares key features with other countries, especially Japan, but its unique historical development can enrich the discussion of the general trend of incorporation. In particular, the chapter focuses on how the dynamic interactions among global, national, and local forces influence the shape and adoption of incorporation. The emerging patterns and future challenges associated with the incorporation of national universities in Korea are also discussed.

Similar to South Korea, Japanese national universities were incorporated in April 2004, and subsequently their operations became more independent from the government. Their managerial structure was realigned, with the president placed at the center of the decision-making process and the external participants added, to be more responsive to the changing needs of society. Jun Oba explores the impacts of the reform on Japanese national universities in Chapter 5, focusing on how they handle increased autonomy in terms of financial and human resource management, evaluation, and related matters. Oba analyzes the challenges to come for national universities and argues for change in conditions and policies so they are better able to serve the society.

University entrepreneurialism has been adopted to promote quality education in both Hong Kong and Singapore. In Chapter 6 Will Lo critically reviews the rationale for corporatizing the university sector in light of the role of the state in the two cities' changing higher education governance. He focuses on the current trends of corporatization and examines how the entrepreneurial culture has changed university governance in Hong Kong and Singapore and the implications of these changes for the vision of promoting each city as a regional hub of higher education shared by two governments.

In many developing countries, including Malaysia, the national government has chosen to steer higher education policy in a direction that is in the "national interest." This notion of national interest is best exemplified by the changing relationship between the state, HEIs, and the market. Since the late 1960s, gradual but steady erosion of university autonomy has occurred as the state gained dominance. Malaysia's recently launched National Higher Education Strategic Plan 2020 and National Higher Education Action Plan 2007–2010, which operationalized the strategic plan, promise greater autonomy for the universities. Are these a reality or just the fantasies of the uninformed? Increased autonomy for universities is becoming increasingly untenable as the national government is preoccupied with issues relating to perceived political instability in the country after the 2008 general election. Morshidi Sirat and Abdul Razak Ahmad attempt to unravel these developments in Chapter 7. They examine the implications of current trends for the state-university relationship. Sirat and Ahmad argued that state centrism is still strong but the wave of neoliberalism is approaching Malaysia's shore. In the context of future developments in international higher education, both authors believe that painful decisions must be made in Malaysia.

In Chapter 8, Sheng-Ju Chan discusses the transformation of governance models of Taiwanese universities since the 1980s, focusing on the themes of institutional autonomy and market competitiveness. In the 1980s, the governance of universities in Taiwan was highly centralized through the Ministry of Education, which had control over universities' bureaucratic structure, student enrollment, course curriculum and funding, and so forth. But from the 1980s to the 1990s, along with political reform and democratization, Taiwanese universities embarked on a path of deregulation, institutional autonomy, and academic freedom. However, in the twenty-first century, universities in Taiwan have to confront fierce competition resulting from an oversupply of education services and rising demand for higher accountability. As the Taiwanese government increasingly regards universities as the engine of economic growth and national competitiveness, the state is tightening its control over university governance.

Using Manuel Castell's four principal functions of universities, in Chapter 9 Anthony Welch examines several key dilemmas relating to governance of higher education in Southeast Asia (especially Indonesia, Malaysia, the Philippines, Thailand, and Vietnam). While these five nations value universities highly and aspire to wider access to higher education for all citizens, none can provide public higher education to everyone who seeks it. Hence, private higher education is growing apace, intensifying problems in sectoral governance systems that are, in several cases, already stretched to capacity. Transnational developments are further complicating domestic regulatory demands. Issues of finance, devolution, and transparency are particularly assessed as key challenges to Southeast Asian higher education.

The introduction of neoliberal economic policies in India in the 1990s led to a significant change in public policy toward higher education. The immediate changes with long-term implications include reduction in public expenditure on higher education (as part of overall reduction in fiscal deficit); increased cost recovery through students fees, student loans, and other measures; nonrecruitment of faculty and other staff (as a part of overall policy of downsizing of the public sector); increased emphasis on private higher education; and initiating of measures for internationalization of higher education. As a result, there has been unbridled growth of private higher education, increased levels of out-migration of students and scholars, advancements in of some areas of study and recession of others, and so forth. In short, there has been overall neglect of higher education in India. The situation is also characterized by absence of clear long-term higher education polices. Chapter 10 is placed in this policy context to examine the emerging challenges and evolving strategies involved in coping with the rapid expansion of higher education in India. Jandhyala B.G. Tilak critically examines some of the most recent reform proposals issued by the Indian government. The author analyzes their conceptual soundness and feasibility, the desirability of some of the programs, and compatibility of proposals with the overall goals of inclusive growth in India.

The last chapter, by Jonathan London, seeks to clarify the dynamics of higher education governance reform in Vietnam in the context of that country's globalization. The major objective of the chapter is not policy recommendations but a discussion of the Vietnamese experience in light of recent international scholarship on higher education. The chapter attempts to examine the meaning of the term of *governance* in the context of Vietnam's transitional economy. With a historical overview of Vietnam's higher education reforms, the chapter focuses on how the Vietnamese government has responded to the global trend of university governance change by introducing reforms to the higher education subsector in the country.

Paradigm Shift or Business as Usual: Critical Reflections

The contributors to this volume examine how far the restructuring of higher education governance along the lines of incorporation, privatization, and corporatization has transformed the values and practices of those who work in the higher education sector. Despite the popularity of management reforms and restructuring exercises that reflect neoliberalism and management worldwide, whether these reforms have actually transformed the heart of the public sector (i.e., the core values held by people who serve in the public sector) is still subject to debate. Although restructuring of higher education in terms of corporatization has occurred in countries like Japan, Malaysia, and Thailand, the authors in this volume have observed that academics in these Asian societies have not genuinely felt liberalized and autonomous. Instead, many academics in these Asian economies have found their academic freedom reduced, especially when they are put under tremendous pressure via accountability and quality assurance. Even worse, the same process of transformation has widened the gap between the rich and the poor and the growing disparities between developed and developing economies have intensified, especially when the assessments of academic standards and university performance are predominantly dominated by the Anglo-Saxon paradigm.

In addition, some of the contributors to this volume go beyond describing the policy origins, key features, and recent developments of the university governance changes in their countries. They also point out the tensions between the state, the university administration, and the academic community when incorporation of HEIs becomes reality in these Asian societies. With democratization in Taiwan and South Korea, academics have become increasingly bold and some have spoken out against the governments' reform agendas. Nonetheless, rather than capitulating, the governments in Taiwan and South Korea have simply re-launched their university restructuring projects with modified policy objectives and strategies (see, for instance, Chapters 4 and Chapter 8). Using financial resources as incentives to appeal to university presidents and academics, Asian governments have tried to justify the university governance changes as part of the quest for world-class universities. Also noted is the reduction of states capacity to manage governance changes in some cases. Unlike the formation of regulation model of the government in Western economies such as the United States and the United Kingdom, the emergence of regulatory states in Asia has suggested that state capacity may have been strengthened rather than weakened. Re-engineering exercises in public management have actually reduced state burdens in the funding and provision of public services. The same processes have enhanced the state's ability to steer the development of the public sector in a more strategic and effective manner. Hence, we should distinguish between different aspects of state capacity when reflecting upon whether the modern states' ability to manage governance changes has in fact been reduced, as suggested by Fukuyama (2005).

The examination of major changes in higher education governance commonly experienced by selected Asian societies calls attention to a few policy implications:

- The quest for world-class university and the stratification of universities
- The increase in private funding sources and intensifying inequality in education
- The tension between internationalization and preservation of local and regional uniqueness
- The massification of higher education and assurance of academic quality
- The corporatization of universities and the impact on academic freedom
- The marketization of higher education and the potential threat to less market-driven disciplines

International research on higher education clearly suggests that privatization has caused the following consequences: (1) inequality between the affluent and the economically weak; (2) geographical inequalities between rural and urban areas, as it is metropolitan and urban areas that attract the private sector, leaving rural areas far behind; (3) imbalances between various disciplines of study in universities; and (4) imbalances in manpower production, creating mismatches between demand and supply. The World Bank published a report entitled *The Challenge of Establishing World-Class Universities*, which identified the widening gap between the rich and the poor, especially in regard to countries such as China and Malaysia where have made attempts to concentrate national resources to only a select few universities to make them globally competitive (Salmi 2009). Hence, tension between enhancing national/global competitiveness and promoting social equality through the provision of higher education is intensified.

As a result of globalization and privatization, many Asian states are caught in a dilemma of treating higher education as a "public good" versus a "private good," and many governments have adopted policies that favor private higher education more out of compulsion than any strong conviction. Therefore, we can easily find competing messages regarding the nature of private higher education whether it favors "privatization but not commercialization," "private participation but not privatization," or "not private participation but public-private partnership" (Tilak 2006, 120). Similarly, other comparative studies have indicated that the growth of private higher education to meet pressing demands have focused predominantly on teaching, hence undertaking few or even no research activities in Southeast Asia and other developing countries in Eastern Europe and South America. As Teixeira and Amaral (2001, 359) argued, private higher education "is characterized mostly by its low-risk behavior, and a concentration on low-cost and/or safer initiatives." By adopting a "lax approach" in running private higher education in Southeast Asia, institutions can choose whether to operate as a corporation or as a foundation. Some of these institutions seize the opportunity to make quick profits, which inevitably leads to lower academic quality, especially when government regulation is weak as is the case in some Asian countries (Gonzalez 1999).

Conclusion: Paradigm Shift or Business as Usual?

This book highlights the challenges that universities and academics have confronted. The adoption of pro-competition policy instruments and adherence to market-oriented ideologies and practices has raised social concerns with regard to quality assurance, accountability, academic freedom, and student learning. With comparative perspectives and critical analysis, we hope that this book creates an awareness of the social consequences of restructuring exercises guided by neoliberalist and managerialist doctrines and practices. Most important of all, we hope to provoke deeper reflections among Asian scholars to be cautious about the potential problems of policy copying rather than policy learning from the West. The global trend of reforming governance without proper contextualization during the process of policy transfer should be avoided. More importantly, policy makers must ask whether practices and ideas that follow these trends really enrich students' learning, enhance university governance, and empower academics. When higher education governance is driven by corporatization and marketization, we must continue to ask "Does it matter?" "Has higher education been improved?" and "What are the social consequences of reform?" In the present climate, which reflects the post-global financial crisis of October 2008, we must be sensitive to the role of the state in public management and governance. Therefore, attention must be paid to whether proposed changes to governance really lead to paradigm shift or retain "business as usual." We must narrow the gap between rhetoric and reality.

Note

1. Some of the chapters presented in this volume are revised versions of articles in the *Asia Pacific Journal of Education*, Vol. 27, no. 3.

References

Cheung, Anthony Bing-Leung, and Ian Scott, eds. 2003. *Governance and Public Sector Reform in Asia*. London: RoutledgeCurzon.
Fukuyama, Francis. 2005. "The Imperative of State-Building." *Journal of Democracy* 15 (2): 17–31.
Gamble, Andrew. 2000. "Economic Governance." In *Debating Governance: Authority, Steering and Democracy*, ed. Jon Pierre. Oxford: Oxford University Press.
Gonzalez, Andrew. 1999. "Private Higher Education in the Philippines: Private Domination in a Developing Country." In *Private Prometheus, Private Higher Education and Development in the 21st Century*, ed. P. Altbach. London: Greenwood Press.
Gouri, Geeta, T. L. Sankar, Y. V. Reddy, and K. Shams. 1991. "Imperatives and Perspectives." In *Privatization and Public Enterprise: The Asia-Pacific Experience*, ed. G. Gouri. New Delhi: Oxford & IBH Pub. Co.
Greca, Rainer. 2002. *Governance: Old and New Problems in the Interaction of State, Market and Civil Society*. Unpublished manuscript.
Institute for Higher Education Policy (IHEP), ed. 2007. *College and University Ranking Systems: Global Perspectives and American Challenges*. Washington, DC: IHEP.
Jayasuriya, Kanishka. 2001. "Globalization and the Changing Architecture of the State." *Journal of European Public Policy* 8 (1): 101–123.
Jessop, Bob. 2003. "Policies, Governance and Innovation for Rural Area." Paper presented at the International Seminar, November 21–23. Prague: Center for Social and Economic Strategies (CESES). http://www.ceses.cuni.cz.
Knight, Jane. 2008. "The Race to develop Regional Education Hubs." Paper presented at the International Symposium on *Positioning University in the Globalized World: Changing Governance and Coping Strategies in Asia*, Hong Kong, December 10–11.
Kooiman, Jan. 1993a. "Social-Political Governance: Introduction." In *Modern Governance: New Government-society Interactions*, ed. J. Kooiman. London: Sage.
———. 1993b. "Findings, Speculations and Recommendations." In *Modern Governance: New Government-society Interactions*, ed. J. Kooiman. London: Sage.
Marginson, Simon. 2007. "The Public/Private Divide in Higher Education: A Global Revision." *Higher Education* 53 (3): 307–333.

Mok, Ka-Ho, and Anthony Welch, eds. 2003. *Globalization and Educational Re-structuring in the Asia Pacific Region*. Basingstoke, UK: Palgrave Macmillan.

Mok, Ka-Ho, and Ian Wei. 2008. "Contested Concepts, Similar Practices: The Quest for the Global University." *Higher Education Policy* 21 (4): 429–438.

Peters, B. Guy. 1995. *The Future of Governing*. Lawrence, KS: University Press of Kansas.

Pierre, Jon, ed. 2000. *Debating Governance: Authority, Steering and Democracy*. Oxford: Oxford University Press.

Pierre, Jon, and B. Guy Peters, eds. 2000. *Governance, Politics and the State*. Basingstoke, UK: Palgrave Macmillan.

Rhodes, Rod A. W. 1997. *Understanding Governance: Policy Networks, Governance, Reflexivity and Accountability*. Philadelphia: Open University Press.

———. 2000. "Governance and Public Administration." In *Debating Governance*, ed. J. Pierre. Oxford: Oxford University Press.

Salamon, Lester M., ed. 2002. *The Tools of Government: A Guide to the New Governance*. New York: Oxford University Press.

Salmi, Jamil, 2009. *The Challenge of Establishing World-Class Universities*, Washington, DC: The World Bank.

Teixeira, Pedro, and Alberto Amaral. 2001. "Private Higher Education and Diversity: An Exploratory Survey." *Higher Education Quarterly* 55 (4): 359–395.

Tilak, Jandhyala, 2006. "Private Higher Education: Philanthropy to Profits." *Higher Education in the World 2006: The Financing Universities*. Basingstoke, UK: Palgrave Macmillan.

Williams, Ross, and Nina Van Dyke. 2007. "Measuring the International Standing of Universities with an Application to Australian Universities." *Higher Education* 53 (6): 819–841.

World Bank. 1995. *Higher Education: The Lessons of Experience*. Washington, DC: The World Bank.

Zheng, Yongnian. 2004. *Globalization and State Transformation in China*. New York: Cambridge University Press.

Chapter 1

Global Education, Heterarchies, and Hybrid Organizations
Stephen J. Ball

Introduction

My intention in this chapter is to be provocative and exploratory rather than definitive. I want to identify and explore a set of global trends within the forms and modalities of the state and the relationships of these trends to changes in the delivery of educational services and concomitantly in the values and ecologies of educational service organizations (both state and private). I will also use the chapter as an opportunity to discuss and develop the concept of heterarchy.

To some extent I want to draw upon and elaborate some of the points made in a recent article by Mok (2007) on new educational governance in East Asia both to develop some of the arguments he makes and give them a slightly different inflection. In doing this I want to move beyond the more abstract accounts of new forms of governance—although Mok's account is certainly not entirely abstract—to indicate some of the messy realities of "network governance." I also want to reiterate and reinforce Jessop's point that the "methods" and relations of heterarchy do not totally displace other forms of policy formation and policy action but rather take their place in "the judicious mixing of market, hierarchy, and networks to achieve the best possible outcomes" (Jessop 2002, 242). This mixing is evident in a number of ways and at a number of levels. The result is impurity and leakages of various sorts between capital, the state, and in the examples here, academe.

I also want, by giving some examples, to use the concept of hybridity in a number of different ways—to refer to state strategies, to a new iteration of "public sector organizations," to relationships between the public and the private sector, and to new public service values. Reflected by and embedded in these developments, as "trendy 'global practices'" (Mok 2007, 2) is an uneven convergence of and export and *transnationalization* of state modalities and higher education policies. As Bessusi (2006, 12) notes, "Governing through the negotiated interactions of a multiplicity of actors from public, semi-public, and private sectors has become a recognized form of making and implementing public policies in western states."

All these issues have been addressed and explored within a set of very extensive and diverse literatures. Mainly developed in western Europe, these seek to conceptualize of set of changes in the form and modalities of the state that in simple terms are referred to as the shift from *government to governance*, or more precisely, to use terms that offer somewhat greater possibilities of precision and leverage, a shift from *hierarchy* to *heterarchy*.

Government to Governance

The shift from government to governance is evident in the government of unitary states (and increasingly regions) in the deployment and "growth" of policy heterarchies. This would mean the installation of a new form of "experimental" and "strategic" governance based upon network relations within and across new policy communities and designed to generate new governing capacity and enhance political legitimacy and increase flexibility and adaptability, especially in relation to the needs of "soft capitalism" (Thrift 2005). These new policy networks bring new kinds of actors into the policy process, and they validate new policy discourses. These policy networks give space within policy for the articulation and validation of new kinds of narratives about what counts as a "good" education. In particular the network members enact, embody, and disseminate narratives of enterprise and enterprising solutions to social and educational problems. Mok (2007, 7) gives the example of the "Public service (PS) 21 Office" and the promotion of entrepreneurship in Singapore. Heterarchies enable new forms of policy influence and enactment and enable new kinds of actors to colonize the spaces opened up by the critique of existing state organizations, actions, and actors . Through heterarchies network governance involves the state in "catalyzing of all sectors—public, private, and voluntary—into action to solve their community's problems". In general terms this is the move toward a "polycentric state" and "a shift in the centre of gravity around which policy cycles move". It is important to note, however, governance networks, or heterarchies, do not tell us everything we need to know about policy and the policy process.

However, I am not suggesting that deploying such changes involves a giving up by the state of its capacity to steer policy. It is just that new modes of steering are required. This is not a "hollowing out" of the state; rather it is a new modality of state power, agency, and social action and indeed a new form of state. It is the achievement of political ends by different means, namely, "governing through governance" (Bache 2003, 301) or "meta-governance" (Jessop 2002, 242). In this the state becomes a contractor, performance-monitor, benchmarker, and target setter, engaged in the management of "the complexity, plurality and tangled hierarchies found in prevailing modes of coordination" (Jessop 2002, 243).

Within all of this then the form and modalities of the state are changing. States are "re-inventing themselves" (Mok 2007, 2) to successfully handle the challenges of globalization, though the extent to which such "re-invention" is undertaken varies from setting to setting, as Green (2007) points out in his discussion of the move away from state developmentalism in Southeast Asia. In certain settings the loss of state capacity for control of the economy or public services may be a crucial factor in "re-invention."

Introducing Heterarchies

Central to the shifts adumbrated above is what Jessop (2002, 199) calls "destatization" a complex "redrawing [of] the public-private divide, reallocating tasks, and rearticulating the relationship between organizations and tasks across this divide." This redrawing and reallocation involves varied tasks: the creation of executive agencies (and Boards, Councils and Trusts); the establishing of private-public partnerships (of many different kinds); contracting-out state services to private providers (see Burch 2006); the use of think tanks, consultants, and knowledge companies for policy research and evaluation; philanthropic activity, and sponsorship to fund educational programs and innovations; the involvement of the voluntary sector (charities, nongovernmental organizations [NGOs], Trusts and Foundations, etc.) in service provision; the "incorporation" of public sector organizations; and the use of social entrepreneurs to address intractable and "wicked" social problems—sometimes in complex combinations. In other words, tasks and services previously undertaken by the state and public sector organizations are now being carried out by various "others" in various kinds of relationships among themselves and to the state as well as the remaining more traditional organizations of the public sector. In many cases, however, the working methods of these public sector organizations have also been fundamentally reworked typically by the deployment of market forms (competition, choice, and performance-related funding) and the adoption of more business-like behaviors and attitudes especially when these organizations seek alternative sources of income when public funding is reduced.. Thus, new voices and interests are represented inside the policy process and new nodes of power and influence are constructed or invigorated in the policy field (Ball 2009a). There is thus an increased reliance on subsidiarity and "regulated self-regulation" or what Stoker (2004, 166) calls "constrained discretion," that is, *deconcentration* rather than *devolution*. In this changed environment, the already fuzzy divides between the public/state, the private, and the third sectors become even more drastically blurred. These experimental and evolutionary but nonetheless highly significant "moves" involve the so-called modernization of public services and state apparatuses, and the reform of the overall institutional architecture of the state and its scales of operation—what Castells (2000, 372) calls "reprogramming." In England the move from hierarchies to heterarchies at the school level has been in part a strategic means of public sector reform and, among other things, a tactic in the flexibilization of professional labor. (see Ball 2009b).

Heterarchical relationships replace bureaucratic and administrative structures and relationships with a system of organization replete with overlap, multiplicity, mixed ascendancy, and/or divergent-but-coexistent patterns of relation. Heterarchy is an organizational form somewhere between hierarchy and network that draws upon diverse horizontal and vertical links that permit different elements of the policy process to cooperate (and/or compete). For example, Mathews (2002, 633), in discussing the research and development consortia in Taiwan, describes the "bringing together of firms and public sector research institutions, with the added organizational input of trade associations and catalytic financial assistance from government."

Heterarchies have many of the characteristics of "assemblages" of and for policy and governance, inasmuch as they are heterogeneous elements placed in diverse relations to one another. They are sets of "functions," and cofunctioning, symbiotic elements that are though unalike are converging here. They are temporary, compared with what they replace, and operate differently according to local circumstances, and may be relatively loose and opportunistic. They are made up of processes (exchanges) and relationships rather than constituting a structure. They are, to an extent, self-organizing, and, to an extent imaginative and experimental, and, to an extent, polyvalent and often involve considerable stumbling and blundering. They may thus be "more likely to give bad decisions a second chance to be rectified" (Thrift 2005, 25), but bad decisions may equally lead to the demise of elements or sections of a heterarchy. Various forms of power flow through the relationships and elements of heterarchies and are dispersed. New forms of power, authority, and subjectivity are brought to bear through them in shaping governable domains and governable persons. New linkage devices and lead organizations are being created in place of and alongside existing ones, excluding or circumventing but not always obliterating more traditional sites and voices.

There are now various manifestations of policy heterarchies in education in many different settings, working on and changing the policy process and policy relations. Each of these combines elements of destatization and involves new players, stakeholders, and interests in state education, education planning and decision making, and education policy conversations (see Ball 2009a).

The changes I am describing here are situated in relation to a broader set of social and political movements in the techniques and modalities of government that have in part the aim and effect of producing new kinds of "active" and responsible, entrepreneurial citizens and workers; indeed there is an explosion in modes of governing of this sort. However, this is only a partial description of contemporary government. While I shall be focusing on the strategies and technologies that are involved in what is sometimes called "creative government," I do not in anyway want to suggest that older, more direct methods of government and governing have been totally displaced. *It is new kinds of mixes, different blends of steering and rowing that are enacted*. Moreover, various kinds of sovereignty and violence are very much still with us. Indeed, "there is a contemporary proliferation of the techniques of arrest, incarceration, punishment, expulsion, disqualification and more broadly coercion." (Dean 2008, 108). These are what Jessop (2002, 201) calls "countertrends in the state," drawing on Poulantzas' notion of "conservation-dissolution" effects. Such effects "exist insofar as past forms and functions of the state are conserved and/or dissolved as the state is transformed" (Jessop 2002, 201). Thus, alongside the use of new techniques of governing that rely upon the "conduct of conduct," existing methods based upon the sovereign and bio-political powers of life and death remain firmly in place. Dean (2008, 101) sums up these "moves" as the changing mix of modalities of governing and the shift of emphasis from sovereignty to governmentality, in the form of a "thought experiment."

The point is that we should not expect or look for consistency between sovereign forms of government and governmentality nor should we be surprised by failures of government, as the mixes involved are sometimes unstable. The particular form of hybridity of government in any setting requires empirical mapping.

Heterarchies are examples of what Kickert et al. (1997) refer to as "loosely-coupled weakly-tied multi-organizational sets." They are a policy device, a way of trying things out, getting things done, changing things, and avoiding established public sector lobbies and interests, an attempt to "routinize innovation," and incubate creative possibilities (Thrift 2005, 7). They can serve to "short-circuit" or displace existing policy blockages. Some potential or previous participants in policy are specifically excluded—trades unions, professional associations, and civil servants, for example. The state has always been a site of struggle in which resources and "voice" have always been differentially distributed across genders, ethnicities, and classes. Therefore, challenges from outside the shared basis of discourse "may be easily deflected or incorporated" (Newman 2001, 172).

Heterarchies also work to disperse and respatialize policy, creating new sites of influence, decision making, and policy action. That is, the "territory of influence" (Mackenzie and Lucio 2005) over policy is expanded and at the same time the spaces of policy are diversified and dissociated. As a result, as these new sites within the contexts of influence and text production (Ball 2002) proliferate, there is a concomitant increase in the opacity of policymaking and the potential for "democratic deficit" (Skelcher 1998). Many heterarchies are in part defined by commercial interests in certain policy outcomes, and some of the relationships within them are specifically contractual and financial, but they also encompass social commitments by volunteers and philanthropists. Sometimes the lines between business and philanthropy and profit motive and public service values are blurred and as we shall see below this blurring can work both ways. According to Shamir (2008, 2),

> commercial enterprises increasingly perform tasks that were once considered to reside within the civic domain of moral entrepreneurship and the political domain of the caring welfare state, dispensing social goods other than profits to constituencies other than their shareholders.

The public sector generally is worked on and re-worked by these new policy actors, from the outside in and the inside out, in particular through the dissemination of the values and practices of entrepreneurship and the transposition of the "international discourse of managerialism" (Thrift 2005, 33) and its metaphors, and attempts to *embody* those metaphors in the public sector workforce. New values and modes of action are thus installed and legitimated and new forms of moral authority established; the role of certain old ones are diminished or derided.

Heterarchies are indicative of a new "architecture of regulation" based on interlocking relationships between disparate sites in and beyond the state and display many of the characteristics of what Richards and Smith (2002, 28–36) call a "postmodern state," which is dependent, flexible, reflexive and diffuse but centrally steered. Policy is being "done" in a multiplicity of new sites "tied together on the basis of alliance and the pursuit of economic and social outcomes" (MacKenzie and Lucio 2005, 500), though the strength of such alliances should not be overstated. Relations here are complex but clearly asymmetric. There is an important shift of *emphasis* involved (a new mix), but it is not an absolute break or rupture; bureaucracies continue to be the vehicle for a great deal of state activity and the state does not hesitate to regulate or intervene, when it is able, or when its interests or objectives are not being served. Though the process of governance through heterarchies is becoming increasingly significant, it will always remain contingent on circumstances.

In this new environment, public sector organizations are positioned sometimes as clients, sometimes as contractors, sometimes as partners, and sometimes as competitors of private sector organizations—the relationships between the two kinds of organizations are hybridized. In practice a great deal of the work done by the new "public service businesses" (see Ball 2007) is not done by taking services out of public sector control but rather through collaborations of various kinds with the public sector, although some are more meaningfully collaborative than others and not all rest on shared objectives or a balance of influence. Partnerships also open up various kinds of flows between the sectors, of people, information, and ideas, language, methods, values, and culture: "states have a key role in promoting innovative capacities, technical competence and technology transfer...often involving extensive collaboration" (Jessop 2002, 121). Partnerships are a further aspect of the blurring between sectors.

I want to pursue some aspects of the foregoing discussion by outlining one particular transnational heterarchy that highlights new state forms and modalities and strategies and various partnerships, hybridities, and flows of ideas, information, and innovation.

The Transnational Entrepreneurial University

The particular heterarchy discussed here as represented in figure 1.1 is both partial and very schematic. Indeed it could be configured in a number of different ways. It selects and highlights a set of relationships that serve to illustrate some more general processes as well as moves and relationships. It identifies a limited set of actors and forms of relationships within a complex and fast-changing field of relationships; some of the elements such as the nature of heterarchies are out of date as I write. Not all of elements and relationships can be fully explained in this text within the limits of space available.

The transnational relationships that are depicted involve the United Kingdom, the United States, and a number of Southeast Asian states, mainly mainland China

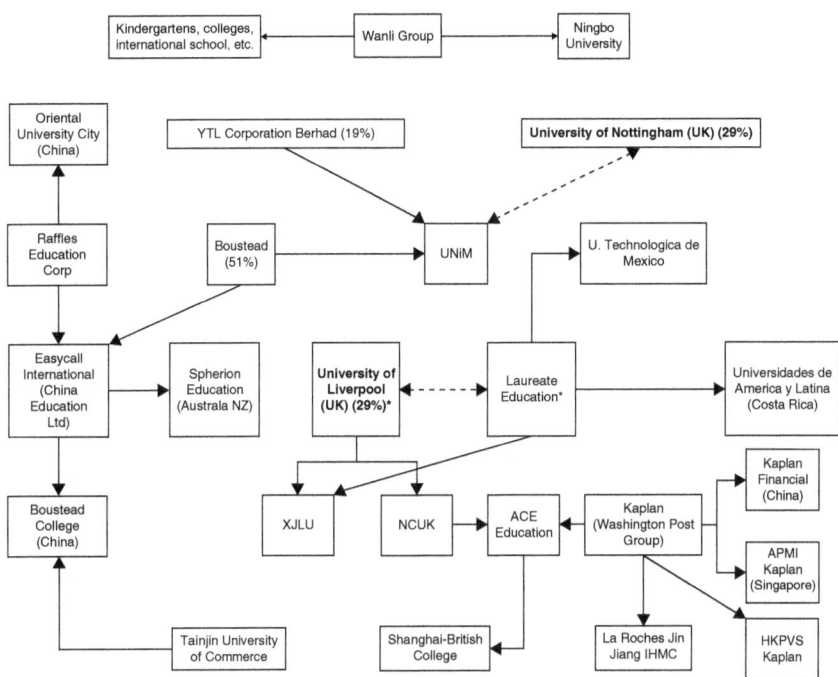

Figure 1.1 The Transnational Heterarchy of the University of Nottingham and the University of Liverpool

and Malaysia, but also Hong Kong, and Singapore. The network linkages "begin" from the involvements of two U.K. public sector universities in setting up offshore campuses in partnership with local and other international actors.

In 2000 the University of Nottingham opened a campus in Malaysia (UNiM). UNiM has 2,700 students from 50 different countries and Nottingham's U.K., Malaysia, and Chinese campuses now enroll over 30,000 students. The majority shareholder of UNiM is the Boustead Group, an engineering services and geospatial technology company. It is reported that Nottingham has spent UK£5.3 million in its Malaysia campus, and that it owns a 29.1 percent share (UNiM reports vary) (*Times Higher Education Supplement* 2007). It is not clear how Nottingham funded its investment in UNiM. The other partner is YTL Corporation Berhad, which owns and manages utilities and "infrastructural assets" and owns 19 percent of UNiM. UNiM awards University of Nottingham degrees. In effect, perhaps, Nottingham is licensing its trademark but the vice-chancellor at the time Sir Colin Campbell was adamant that a "[f]ranchise arrangement is too great a risk to reputation" and that "[e]xams, marking and quality assurance are consistent" (Shepherd 2007). The university describes its overseas strategy as "exporting excellence" (University of Nottingham 2005). It won the Queens Award for Enterprise in 2006 and 2007.

This was not Boustead's only educational investment. An associate company of the Boustead group, Easycall International (China Education Ltd.) owns Boustead

College in China, a joint enterprise with Tianjin University of Commerce. In 2004 Easycall purchased Spherion Education, a New Zealand company that runs 13 training institutes in Australia and New Zealand. Easycall has since been bought by the Raffles Education Corp., a Singapore-based company, which owns Oriental University City (China) and which has grown from its founding in 1990 to operate three universities and 26 colleges across ten countries in the Asia-Pacific region: Singapore, China, India, Indonesia, Vietnam, Malaysia, Thailand, Mongolia, Australia, and New Zealand.

Nottingham University also has strong market relations with China and the number of Chinese students at Nottingham in the United Kingdom is well over 1,000. Nottingham is also involved in a joint-venture university in China. Nottingham owns a 37.5 percent share in the Ningbo University campus, a joint venture with the state-owned Wanli Education Group. The Wanli Education Group is a state-owned independent provider that runs a full range of educational services, from kindergartens to the Chinese equivalent of a university college. It is described as being at the cutting edge of educational reform. Since its establishment in 1993, the Wanli Education Group has invested nearly US$60 million and the group is responsible for nine institutions including an international school, a vocational college, and a night school. The creation of opportunities for Chinese students to study abroad and the provision of wider access at home are key elements of the group's strategy.

Wanli provided the infrastructure for Ningbo, worth UK£14 million. Douglas Tallack, professor of American studies and pro vice-chancellor of Nottingham, has explained that about 30 percent of the "total investment" has come from Nottingham and that this figure includes notional values given to contributions in the form of nonmonetary intellectual property rights. In terms of hard cash, the university has made a "modest investment" as it is said. Some of the University library stock has been moved to the China campus. The license to operate the University of Nottingham-Ningbo is valid until 2055 (China Ministry of Education [CMOE] 2007).

Nottingham University's Ningbo campus now has 2,850 students studying for degrees equivalent to those in the UK. Nottingham says its aim is to build research and industry links with China and to improve student mobility between the countries. (*Times Higher Education Supplement* 2007)

In 2007, Liverpool University also launched a joint-venture university in China—the Xi'an Jiaotong Liverpool University (XJLU) near Shanghai. Liverpool has a 30 percent stake in this joint venture but the financial backing for Liverpool's stake comes from Laureate Education, a U.S-based private higher education company which owns 51 universities around the world and which had an income of US$160 million in 2005. The company provided the UK£1 million bond necessary for the University of Liverpool to operate in China. XJLU is a freestanding institution, that awards its own degrees and "[t]he purpose of this ambitious project was to boost Liverpool's global brand," according to the higher education think tank Agora (Fazackerley and Worthington 2007, 26). The University of Liverpool is not directly responsible for quality or standards. XJLU is run by a board, whose members include the U.S. company Laureate, the Suzhou Industrial Park, and the Chinese partner university. Laureate also owns and runs the Les Roches Jin Jiang

International Hotel Management College and Sichuan Tianyi University in China. XJLU is listed on their Web site as one of their universities. They recently purchased two U.S. universities, two in Costa Rica, and one in Mexico.

Laureate also provides the platform for Liverpool's online degrees (this was begun as a partnership with the Dutch corporation K. I. Telearning in 1999 and Laureate bought *K. I. Telearning* in 2004). In 2007 Liverpool announced another agreement with Laureate that will allow Laureate students to study on Liverpool summer school programs; it also established dual degrees with students taking parts of their degree in each university system, in addition to joint curriculum design projects in health sciences, information technology, and the humanities. Liverpool may also set up onsite courses at Laureate Campuses.

Liverpool is also involved in a number of projects with Kaplan. Kaplan is a subsidiary of the Washington Post Company (owned by News International) and has 70 campuses in the United States in 20 states, (as well as a variety of other higher education services) and campuses also in China, Hong Kong, and Singapore. In 2007 Kaplan's revenue was in excess of US$2 billion. In 1987, 11 U.K. universities banded together to form the Northern Consortium United Kingdom (NCUK) (there are now 22 partners including five Irish universities) that provides overseas transition centers for students wanting to study in the United Kingdom (including students from China, Ireland, Japan, Kenya, Nigeria, South Korea, Sri Lanka, United Arab Emirates, and Vietnam). The local partner in China is ACE Education and in 2006 NCUK and ACE opened the Shanghai-British College; in April 2007 Kaplan took a minority interest in ACE, and in November 2007 became the majority owner of Kaplan ACE. Liverpool and Kaplan have also established an international college located on the campus of the University of Liverpool. The aim is to prepare international students for entry into the university's undergraduate and graduate degree programs. Such colleges are already in partnership with the University of Sheffield, University of Glasgow, and Nottingham Trent University.

Discussion

Viewed in terms of the developments outlined above, U.K. public universities are now "hybrid organizational forms in which public and private interests are combined" (Clarke and Newman 1997, 111). There are many other universities from the United Kingdom and elsewhere involved in overseas "for-profit" ventures of the kind described above. The international market in higher education is lucrative and expanding. Jane Kelsey (2006, 1) also writes about what she terms "an unsustainable hybrid form of a modern/neoliberal university" which is, she says, an "integral yet incongruous part" of "a parasitic international education industry." She also argues that "University/business collaboration deepens the influence of corporate priorities and preferences and compress critical space" (Kelsey 2006, 9). Nottingham and Liverpool are no longer in any sense national public universities; they are transnational, corporate, and profit-oriented, and are positioned on the boundaries between academia and business—they are hybrids. Thrift (2005, 23) argues that there are "an increasing number of symmetries between academia and business." These universities are involved in complex "border-crossing" relationships with the private sector, state agencies, international consortia, and other national states. Partnerships, linkages, and networks "join up" state organizations with commercial ones and create discursive capillaries through which the sensibilities and dispositions of enterprise flow and the ontology of neoliberalism is generalized. Complex relationships, built upon contract rather than collegiality and aimed at profit generation rather than knowledge production or public services, enfold public universities into the arms of commerce. Complex and sometimes opaque financial relationships are involved as well, as in the case of Liverpool, Laureate, and Kaplan, which share knowledge, development costs, and facilities. In many national settings, the idea of a public university as a distinct and coherent social category has been dissolved, although Santos (2009, 65) goes on to say that the global crisis of the public university is "significantly different at the core, the periphery, and the semi-periphery of the world system." We may even want to think about some such organizations in some settings as what Wedel (2001, 152) calls "flex organizations." The "flex organizations" Wedel focuses on are efficient in canalizing resources through their "impressively adaptable, chameleon-like, multipurpose character;" and "they afford maximum flexibility and influence to those who use them, while burdening them with only minimal accountability" (Wedel 2001, 3). The "transactors" who work these flex organizations are, Wedel says, "to play the boundaries between national and international, public and private, formal and informal, market and bureaucratic, state and non-state, even legal and illegal" (Wedel 2001, 67). Some of the new players in the transnational higher education market have no previous experience in education and are moving away from their core business interests.

In such a tangled and complex situation it is no longer possible to talk sensibly about "private" and "public sector," state and market, and public and private goods. As Shamir (2008, 1) notes,

> Local, national and transnational authorities—state and non-state alike—increasingly follow the logic of "economic sustainability" and operate in a corporate-like form. Both state and non-state institutions in fields such as health, education, security and welfare are transfigured to act as if embedded in a competitive environment where the laws of economics reign.

There are both opportunities and dangers here for the "competition state." These institutional forms of higher education may provide quick and cheap means to upskill the local workforce in response to the supposed requirements of the knowledge economy, as well as satisfying the increased demand for access to higher education, especially those which offer forms of certification with international currency, and thus potential entry into the global labor market. In 2007 there were more than 27 million Chinese students in various higher education programs, and the higher education participation rate was 23 percent (CMOE 2008). States such as China have allowed the entry of foreign providers for exactly these reasons. Approximately 500 foreign campuses are up and running in China, but the government has now suspended further recognition of overseas providers. Other states such as Singapore have encouraged "elite" overseas providers to set up shop as a means of attracting overseas students from other parts of Southeast Asia and beyond and in an effort to reinvent themselves as a "global classrooms" and a regional hubs for higher education. By 2003 there were 14 elite transnational campuses in Singapore including the Massachusetts Institute of Technology, INSEAD of France, the University of Chicago's Graduate School of Business, and the Indian Institute of Technology. These offshore enterprises may, however, also be seen as part of a new educational colonialism. Business schools in particular have been key centers for the articulation and flow of new, Western, and particularly U.S. management ideas and metaphors in Southeast Asia. Worldwide it has been estimated that such schools generate more than US$4 billion per annum (Crainer and Dearlove 1998).

However, there are also fragilities involved in the proliferation of these ventures (e.g., market failure); a number of overseas campuses have not garnered the expected revenues and therefore have been closed; there are clearly problems of quality assurance at the bottom end of the market in particular. On the other hand, as indicated above, there is a very active international market in universities—a very real knowledge economy within which brands and infrastructure are bought and sold.

Conclusion

Heterarchies, national and transnational, are made up of a variety of types of relationships, and concomitant blurrings and hybridities. Organizations act for profit and for public interest in what might previously have been unpredictable ways as the public sector takes on the profit motive and private sector organizations and actors take on responsibility for the delivery of welfare and for addressing intractable social problems through philanthropic activity and as public service businesses, or as social entrepreneurs, or charity bankers.

Public sector actors move in and out of the private sector, and there is a reverse flow to some extent, as private sector actors take up roles in advocacy groups, charities and trusts, not-for-profit organizations, and government agencies. As actors move, discourse flows with them, as do values, with a tendency toward *the enterprise* as the generic form for all these organizations, and economism as the prevailing logic. These many "points" and sites, roles and responsibilities, constitute a grid of power "above, across, as well as within, state boundaries" (Cerny 1997, 253) through which the discourse and ontology of neoliberalism flows and becomes distributed, embedded, and naturalized. Through multiple and diverse engagements the particular social and commercial relations enacted through such sensibilities are increasingly insinuated into more aspects of the education policy and the practices of educational organization and control.

This is a new terrain of governance—complex and sometimes convoluted—which involves problems of coordination (and accountability and transparency), especially when dealing with multinational businesses, but which can bring to the state benefits in terms of flexibilities, and forms of flexibilization and substitution that are not normally possible in administrative systems. Four sorts of related changes are going on here. One is in forms of government, another in the form and nature of the participants in processes of governance, a third in the prevailing discourses within governance, and a fourth in the governing and production of new kinds of "willing" subjects. These together constitute in the language of political science "network governance"—that is, "webs of stable and ongoing relationships which mobilize dispersed resources towards the solution of policy problems" (Pal 1997). Although, as already noted above, and as Pal (1997, 5) goes on to say, "This new situation does not completely overturn conventional policy instruments, of course, but they will have to be placed within the context of new assumptions—a new regime." Increasingly, policymaking occurs "in spaces parallel to and across state institutions and their jurisdictional boundaries" (Skelcher et al. 2004, 3), and in the process, parts of *the state and some of its activities are privatized* (Ball 2009a).

The state is normally vigorous within these governance processes, although internationally this clearly varies from nation to nation. Mok (2007), following Fukayama, draws attention to the important difference between the scope and capacity of state to govern. There is no "institutional void" here (Hajer 2003), but rather the increasing use of reflexive de-centered guidance strategies such as contracting and performance management. While steering may become more complicated across the "tangled web" of policy networks, with the development of an increased reliance on "self-administered" policy communities, the "core executive" retains a substantial authoritative and coordinating presence over policy (Marinetto 2003). In some respects and certainly in education, this "core executive" has achieved an enhancement of "capacity to project its influence and secure its objectives by mobilizing knowledge and power resources from influential non-governmental partners or stakeholders" (Jessop 2002, 199). Nonetheless, certainly in the example above, it is not easy to identify a single point of control. In such a diverse network of complex relationships, the network has "a life of its own." This is pointed up by the various buy-outs, consolidations, and mergers that involve change of ownership and of scale; political changes and financial cycles will also have their effects; national boundaries are only of relative significance here. There is no simple local-global dualism that can be evoked here but rather a set of "connections" that cut across scales and territories. What is important are various attempts to manage the vocabularies, procedures, and rules through which the activities of the network are conducted—particularly in this case vocabularies like "hi-skills" and "the knowledge economy" on the one hand and those of "quality" and "quality assurance" with their procedures and technologies on the other. Governments, international agencies and institutions, and businesses struggle over the meaning, implementation, and enforcement of these newly acquired vocabularies and procedures. (see Vidovich et al. 2007). These struggles cut across academic, financial, and political agendas and interests.

Finally, I want to point to the way in which heterachies and the network form are both the medium for and the message of public sector reform. As Lingard and Rizvi (2009, 338) put it, "these processes are located within a global architecture of political relations that not only involves national governments, but also IGOs, transnational corporations, and NGOs. Policies are developed, enacted, and evaluated in various global networks from where their authority is now partly derived."

The discourses and practices of governance move through and are embedded within transnational policy networks of various kinds. Transnationalization involves the "import" and "export" of policy ideas, models, sensibilities, and practices through political and advocacy networks (Keck and Sikkink 1998) and commercial networks—the former may involve multilateral or regional organizations, think tanks, and NGOs and development banks, the latter involve private and hybrid educational providers and rest upon various forms of "cooperation" and partnership. National state authorities relate to and engage with transnationalization through a hybrid set of policy relationships (contract, private-public partnerships, cofunding, investment and development strategies), and establish their own hybrid agencies as well as encouraging hybridity in state organizations via incorporation and marketization and the dissemination of entrepreneurial values. I have in mind here a policy and services version of global commodity chains (GCC) as "cross-national forms of economic organisation" (Gereffi 1996, 428), which nonetheless acknowledges the continuing importance of national institutional differences. According to Gereffi, the GCC provides an appropriate organizational field for studying economic globalization. As Gereffi (1994, 2) explains,

> A GCC consists of sets of inter-organisational networks clustered around one commodity or product, linking households, enterprises, and states to one another within the world-economy. These networks are situationally specific, socially constructed, and locally integrated, underscoring the social embeddedness of economic organization.

In relation to higher education, GCCs link national skills and knowledge strategies to national and international higher education businesses and the aspirations of families for the access of their children to the global labor market. Such chains through access colleges and shared degrees also facilitate the movement of students between locations. Providers have different access to markets and resources within international higher education, and the value addition at each stage of production varies. However, as yet we have little understanding of the economics of this field and have barely begun to make sense of its structures of governance.

References

Bache, Ian. 2003. "Governing Through Governance: Education Policy Control under New Labour." *Political Studies* 51 (2): 300–314.
Ball, Stephen J. 2002. "Textos, discursos y trayectorías de la política: la teoría estratégica." *Páginas* 2: 19–33.
———. 2007. *Education Plc: Understanding Private Sector Participation in Public Sector Education*. New York: Routledge.
———. 2009a. "Privatising Education, Privatising Education Policy, Privatisating Educational Research: Network Governance and the 'Competition State.'" *Journal of Education Policy* 42 (1): 83–99.
———. 2009b. "Academies in Context: Politics, Business and Philanthropy and Heterarchical Governance." *Management in Education* 23 (3): 100–103.

Bessusi, Elizabeth. 2006. "Mapping European Research Networks." *Working Papers Series No. 103*. London: University College London.
Burch, Patricia E. 2006. "The New Educational Privatization: Educational Contracting and High Stakes Accountability." *Teachers College Record* 108 (12): 2582–2610.
Castells, Manuel. 2000. *The Rise of the Network Society*. 2nd ed. Malden, MA: Blackwell Publishers.
Cerny, Philip G. 1997. "Paradoxes of the Competition State: The Dynamics of Political Globalisation." *Government and Opposition* 32 (2): 251–274.
China Ministry of Education (CMOE). 2007. "Ningbo nuodinghan daxue zhongwai hezuo banxue jigou xinxibiao [The University of Nottingham-Ningbo: The Chinese and Foreign Co-Operative Institute Information Form]," September 5. Beijing: CMOE. http://www.moe.gov.cn.
———. 2008. "2007 nian quanguo jiaoyu shiye fazhan tongji gongbao [2007 National Education Development Statistics Bulletin]," April. Beijing: CMOE. http://www.moe.gov.cn.
Crainer, Stuart, and Des Dearlove. 1998. *Gravy Training: Inside the Shadowy World of Business Schools*. London: Capstone.
Clarke, John, and Janet Newman. 1997. *The Managerial State: Power, Politics and the Ideology in Remaking the Social Welfare*. London: Sage.
Dalton, Russell. J., Steve Recchia, and Robert Rohrschneider. 2003. "The Environmental Movement and the Modes of Political Action." *Comparative Political Studies,* 36 (7): 743–771.
Dean, Mitchell. 2008. *Governing Societies: Political Perspectives on Domestic and International Rule*. Maidenhead, UK: Open University Press.
Fazackerley, Anna, and Philip Worthington. 2007. "British Universities in China: The Reality Beyond the Rhetoric." *Agora Discussion Paper*. Devon, PA: Agora. http://www.agora.org.
Gereffi, Gary. 1994. "The Organisation of Buyer-driven Global Commodity Chains: How US Retailers Shape Overseas Production." In *Commodity Chains and Global Capitalism*, ed. G. Gereffi and R. P. Korzeniewicz. Westport, CN: Praeger.
Gereffi, Gary. 1996. "Global Commodity Chains: New Forms of Coordination and Control among Nations and Firms in International Industries." *Competition and Change* 1 (4): 427–439.
Green, Andy. 2007. "Globalization and the Changing Nature of the State in East Asia." *Globalisation, Societies and Education* 5 (1): 23–38.
Hajer, Maarten. 2003. "Policy without Polity? Policy Analysis and the Institutional Void." *Policy Sciences* 36 (2): 175–195.
Jessop, Bob. 1998. "The Narrative of Enterprise and the Enterprise of Narrative: Place Marketing and the Entrepreneurial City." In *The Entrepreneurial City: Geographies of Politics, Regime and Representation*, ed. T. Hall and P. Hubbard. Chichester: John Wiley & Sons.
Jessop, Bob. 2002. *The Future of the Capitalist State*. Malden, MA: Polity Press.
Keck, Margaret. E., and Kathryn Sikkink. 1998. *Activists Beyond Borders: Advocacy Networks in International Politics*. Ithaca: Cornell University Press.
Kelsey, Jane. 2006. "Taking Minds to Market." Paper presented at the Fourth Conference on Knowledge and Politics, University of Bergen, Norway, May 2006. http://www.knowpol.uib.no/portal/.
Kickert, Walter J. M., Erik-Hans Klijn, and Johannes Franciscus Maria Koppenjan. 1997. "Managing Networks in the Public Sector: Findings and Reflections." In *Managing Complex Networks: Strategies for the Public Sector*, ed. W. J. M. Kickert, E. H. Klijn, and J. F. M. Koppenjan. London: Sage.

Lingard, Robert, and Fazal Rizvi. 2009. *Globalizing Education Policy.* New York: Routledge.
Mackenzie, Robert, and Miguel Martinez Lucio. 2005. "The Realities of Regulatory Change: Beyond the Fetish of Deregulation." *Sociology* 39 (3): 499–517.
Marinetto, Mike. 2003. "Governing Beyond the Centre: A Critique of the Anglo-Governance School." *Political Studies* 51 (3): 592–608.
Marsh, David, and R. A. W. Rhodes, eds. 1992. *Policy Networks in British Government.* Oxford: Clarendon Press.
Mathews, John. A. 2002. "The Origins and Dynamics of Taiwan's R&D Consortia." *Research Policy* 31 (4): 633–651.
Mok, Ka-Ho. 2007. "Globalization, New Education Governance and State Capacity in East Asia." *Globalisation, Societies and Education* 5 (1): 1–21.
Newman, Janet. 2001. *Modernizing Governance: New Labour, Policy and Society.* London: Sage.
Novoa Santos, Roberto. 2009. "The University in the Twenty-First Century: Toward a Democratic and Emancipatory University." In *International Handbook of Sociology of Education*, ed. M. Apple, S. J. Ball, and L. A. Gandin. London: Routledge.
Osborne, David, and Ted Gaebler. 1992. *Re-inventing Government: How the Entrepreneurial Spirit is Transforming the Public Sector.* Reading, MA: Addison-Wesley Pub. Co.
Pal, Leslie A. 1997. *Beyond Policy Analysis: Public Issue Management in Turbulent Times.* Scarborough, UK: International Thomson Publishing.
Rhodes, R. A. W. 1995. "The New Governance: Governing without Government." *State of Britain ESRC/RSA Seminar Series.* Swindon, UK: ESRC.
———. 1997. *Understanding Governance: Policy Networks, Governance, Reflexivity and Accountability.* Buckingham, England; Philadelphia: Open University Press.
Richards, David, and Martin J. Smith. 2002. *Governance and Public Policy in the United Kingdom.* Oxford: Oxford University Press.
Shamir, Ronen. 2008. "The Age of Responsibilitization: On Market-embedded Morality." *Economy and Society* 37 (1): 1–19.
Shepherd, Jessica. 2007. "The Long Arm of the British University. Does a UK University Need a Campus on the Other Side of the World? A Battle of Words by Two Vice-chancellors." *The Guardian*, September 4. http://www.guardian.co.uk.
Skelcher, Chris. 1998. *The Appointed State: Quasi-Governmental Organizations and Democracy.* Buckingham, England; Philadelphia: Open University Press.
Skelcher, Chris et al. 2004. *Effective Partnership and Good Governance: Lessons for Policy and Practice*, (Imprint unknown).
Stoker, Gerry. 2004. *Transforming Local Governance: From Thatcherism to New Labour.* Basingstoke, UK: Palgrave Macmillan.
Thrift, Nigel. 2005. *Knowing Capitalism.* London: Sage.
Times Higher Education Supplement. 2007. "Nottingham University: Reaping 'A Phenomenal Return on a £40 Million Investment,'" September 21. London: *Times Higher Education Supplement.* http://www.timeshighereducation.co.uk.
University of Nottingham. 2005. *Annual Review for 2005: Broadening Horizons.* Nottingham: University of Nottingham. http://communications.nottingham.ac.uk.
Vidovich, Lesley, Rui Yang, and Jan Currie. 2007. "Changing Accountabilities in Higher Education as China 'Opens Up' to Globalization." *Globalisation, Societies and Education* 5 (1): 89–107.
Wedel, Jane. R. 2001. *Collision and Collusion: The Strange Case of Western Aid to Eastern Europe.* New York: Palgrave Macmillan.

Chapter 2

Higher Education Transformation: Some Trends in California and Asia

John N. Hawkins

Introduction

The social transformations rippling throughout education systems worldwide impact both basic and higher education. In general, higher education is being asked to provide graduates with skills and abilities commensurate with the workforce demands of rapidly changing economies. Frequently articulated critiques of higher education argue that its institutions have been elitist, dominated by faculties resistant to change, lacking in social relevance, and—as institutions—absorbing an increasing (and perhaps unwarranted) amount of societal resources. Where higher education has largely been a state function, conservative bureaucracies are viewed as impediments to necessary development and change. Virtually everywhere, voices are raised to demand necessary reforms yet, in spite of these apparently common challenges, it remains true that policy-related education issues are framed by and "spoken through" the particularities of distinct cultures and histories. For those of us seeking to understand and document appeals for higher education reform, the task is always to appreciate the distinctiveness of local/national articulations of these issues while also recognizing the structural commonalities that link global higher education issues. As one of my colleagues recently stated, "[A]ll globalization is local."

In many cases, issues of higher education reform appear in the context of aligning limited capacity with expanding social needs, while creating or retaining quality. In developing countries, capacity issues reflect the struggle to create and sustain a set of higher education institutions (HEIs) suitable to meeting the needs of rapid population growth, the demands of increased global interdependence, and the realities of emerging knowledge societies. In India, China, and Indonesia, to take but three examples, institutions of considerable age and distinction are being challenged to meet these internal demands while demonstrating their "competitiveness" by exhibiting "world class" attributes—a not very disguised code for developing competitive international research capacities and attracting the best students. Behind this "first tier," institutions of lesser status are expanding rapidly and new institutions including community colleges, technical institutions, and providers of on-line education are coming into existence. In any organization, rapid expansion of capacity begets dual quality concerns: "raising" the quality of older, traditional institutions to make them more globally competitive, and developing new institutions within acceptable quality guidelines.

An additional complicating factor is the shifting target posed by "quality" as its meanings and practical implications shift in response to changing social and economic situations. In Japan and Korea, to take two other examples, creating effective higher education institutional responses to rapidly changing social and economic conditions is viewed as a particular challenge, given the very strong developmental role government has played in creating the "modern university." The capacity/quality nexus in those societies with large numbers of university graduates condenses around providing enforceable norms of retraining for existing graduates and refocusing "output" for the university system as a whole. Japan, in particular, has a distinguished history of first-rate HEIs, which nevertheless, today are being challenged to dramatically change in light of twenty-first century imperatives.

Underlying this capacity/quality/reform tableau is the thorny issue of equity. Rapid, increased global interdependence has resulted in corresponding accelerations of economic and social inequality, massive population migrations (especially from rural areas to burgeoning cities), major changes in social and economic status, and pressures on prevailing cultural norms. Governments, particularly, are concerned with issues of growing inequality and the social, political, and (perhaps) economic instabilities to which it is conducive. Increasingly both governments and intergovernmental organizations are looking to education as an answer to these iconic effects of global integration.

Higher education is often seen as the capstone solution: an institutional response that will produce alignment among a complex set of social goals, from the creation of new intellectual capital, to the production of effective workforces, to the diffusion of effective "ways of being" in this world of escalating change. Higher education "reform" is shaped, of course, by the distinctive cultures and styles of national policy processes: policy may be policy, but how societies go about it can be radically different.

Almost every country in the Asia-Pacific Region, including the United States, struggling to overcome these challenges to higher education is faced with redefinitions of "public and private higher education sectors." The meanings and values imputed to "public and private" have changed significantly over the past century; these terms have acquired new meanings and currency as notions of market competitiveness ("liberalization") have penetrated these societies, be they historically capitalist, socialist, developing, or developed states.

Lodged somewhere within this distinction has been the notion of education (including higher education) as a public good—the idea that the state, through its institutions (whatever their shape and form), has both the need and obligation to create and support higher education for the benefit of larger public purposes. This notion itself, taking many specific forms, is derived from a variety of meanings that have been assigned historically to conceptions of the public good and public goods. It is proposed that the dynamics of increased global interdependence are working through societies in ways that problematize the prevailing distinctions between "public" and "private" in higher education, the "goods" associated with public and private sectors, what these distinctions mean in concept and practice, and how these ideas are being worked through in the policy processes of various countries.

In this chapter I want to briefly look at some trends in higher education reform in California, and then provide a few comments on parallel trends in Asia. California, of course, is not Asia. It is still a complex and large state with a diverse higher education subsector, not unlike other states with comprehensive "tier one" research universities. This reality, along with the history of the California Master Plan for Higher Education, has been of great interest to many Asian nations and therefore, I think, such juxtaposition is of interest to scholars and educationists in HEIs. Furthermore, California is a Pacific state with an economy, which even in recession, is larger than that of many countries in the Asian region. Its trade, cultural, and educational links to the Asian region are substantial and migration to and out of the region continues to grow and flourish. Higher education reforms and trends that occur in California are often later experienced in Asia or at the very least, of great interest to educational policy makers in the region. This can be seen in the early experience of neoliberalism in California and its later appearance in many Asian countries. It can also be seen in the heightened interest in the continuing reforms and changes in the California Master Plan (discussed in more detail later).

Here we focus on only four trends that it is argued affect both California and several Asian nations: higher education governance and management, higher education finance reforms, the changing research mission, and trends related to faculty and student concerns. While these trends do not constitute the entirety of higher education, they are central to the mission of the academy, and what is and has been happening in California can be interestingly discussed in the context of the Asia-Pacific Region.

Some Current Trends in Higher Education in California

Since the mid-1980s, the University of California (UC) has been in a state of transition as the overall budgetary picture in the state of California has been less than positive. A series of events including the end of the cold war, the decline of aerospace in California, the bursting of the tech bubble, and a consequent decline in state revenues have all contributed to a rethinking of the role of the state in supporting public higher education. Neoliberal thinking on the part of various governors beginning with Ronald Reagan as well as members of the business community and the Board of Regents has led to a new approach to governing, financing, and staffing public higher education. In this section, only a few examples are given of the changes that have already taken place and are still taking place in the University of California in this new era characterized by both globalization and localization.

Higher Education Governance and Management

At the central state government level, namely, the governor's office, a major new initiative is proposing further centralizing the overall coordination of the UC system. Specifically, the governor's office has proposed the dismantling of the state's independent planning and coordination agency, the California Post-Secondary Education Commission (CPEC), creating a new position of Secretary of Higher Education, and placing the responsibilities in the governor's office. In February 2004 the governor established the California Performance Review Commission to investigate ways to increase efficiencies throughout state government including the higher education subsector. While the governor's office has since temporarily abandoned the proposal to do away with CPEC, on the recommendation of the Review Commission as well as conservative elements in the legislature, the proposal has been put forward to reduce the autonomy of the University of California by limiting the authority of the Board of Regents. Every chancellor of every UC campus has opposed this proposal and the debate continues as of this writing.

In addition to the CPEC proposal, and the assault on the autonomy of the UC system, other suggested reforms focused on further blurring the distinctions between the different higher education subsectors as outlined in the Master Plan (extending the authority to grant four-year degrees to some Community Colleges, increasing nonresident tuition, extending the awarding of doctorates to the California State University subsector, and so on). The Master Plan itself, now 50 years old, has been the topic of debate as its relevance in light of the corrosive fiscal crisis facing California called into question (Keller 2009).

Those who have opposed CPEC, however, have proposed that if it remains, it should be reformed so that it

- is assigned a stronger role in the state budget;
- preserves its independence;
- strengthens the Commission's role as a data clearinghouse;
- assigns responsibility for accountability measures;
- clearly delegates responsibility for a statewide plan; and
- calls for coordination, integrate planning, including that for student aid.

As the Master Plan is reviewed, a new, empowered commission should be able to provide the kind of accountability that the public is demanding and the governor's office seeks (Warren 2005; CPEC 2009).

In addition to overall governance issues such as the reform of CPEC and the Master Plan, the University of California has entered into a different kind of relationship with the state of California and more specifically the governor's office (Fox 2005). For four decades, the California Master Plan has guided the UC system and assured access, quality, and affordability for the citizens of California, in addition to welcoming students from across the nation and the world. The basic structure remains fundamentally unchanged, that is, semi-autonomous campuses, reporting to the president's office, which in turn reports to the Board of Regents and is accountable to the state in a variety of ways. But what has changed is the nature of the relationship between the president's office and by extension the individual campuses and the governor's office. This has been expressed with the term, the Higher Education Compact.

In the context of persistent budget cuts (to be discussed below), the governor's office proposed entering into a compact with the UC system whereby the state commits to a long-term resource plan for the UC system so that a predictable financial plan is available to the president's office and the chancellors of the various campuses. In exchange for this long-term stability, the University of California (and California State University) further commits to focusing its resources to address long-term accountability goals for enrollment, student fees, financial aid, and program quality as well as serving certain specific human resource needs of the state. From the governor's perspective, there would be the following commitments:

- basic budget support and increases for the core budget and salaries;
- core academic support needs critical to maintaining the quality of the academic program;
- funding for enrollment growth;
- implementation of a more stable student fee policy for undergraduates with any increases based on the rise in California per capita personal income;
- increasing graduate student fees by 20 percent and in the future aligning graduate fees on such variables as average cost of instruction, average fees at other public comparison institutions, total cost of attendance, market factors, and the state's need in particular disciplines;
- professional school fees being aligned to similar factors, and any revenue from such increases will remain with the University and not be used to offset reductions in state support;
- capital outlay: state will provide funding for debt service to support general obligation bonds for each campus;
- one time funds: state will permit one time funding of high priority infrastructure needs; and
- with joint agreement between the state and the UC system, funding of specific initiatives.

For its part, the UC system will meet various productivity measures and accountability measures in such areas as the following:

- Enrollment levels should match the resources provided and maintain the commitment to enroll the top 12.5 percent of graduating high school students.

- UC will ensure that appropriate services and courses are provided and course articulation possible for qualifying community college students.
- UC will maintain progress toward "time to degree."
- UC will contribute to the state's need for K-12 teachers in science and mathematics and help improve the quality of K-12 instruction.
- UC will help to increase public service to meet community needs and educate students and citizens to perform community service that is of a high priority for the state.
- UC will maintain and improve the quality of instruction to serve the needs of the state's economic recovery while at the same time limiting administrative growth within UC.
- Student and institutional outcomes will be improved and measured by various accountability measures through timely and reliable data collection; UC will provide a comprehensive single report to the governor, the secretary of education, the fiscal committees of the Legislative Analysts Office, and the Department of Finance on an annual basis in such areas as efficiency in graduating students, utilization of system-wide resources, student-level information, and capital outlay among others.

(*Higher Education Compact* 2006)

At the individual campus level, each campus is required to develop strategic plans from the deans up. The plans go into a campus-wide planning document that is used by the president's office to provide the data required by the compact. The effect of the compact on the individual campuses varies but in general it can be said that campuses have lost some autonomy as they restructure programs (such as graduate schools of education now being required to do more in teacher preparation, long a domain of the California State University system, and in focusing the curriculum on mathematics and science teaching) to meet newly defined state needs. The overall effect has been increased centralization in the service of state economic needs, power shifting to the governor's office, and increased accountability for each campus. On the other hand, the governor's office is requiring increased public service to the community from the UC system, thus promoting commodification and public good at the same time. All of this is now up for discussion as California finds itself in the midst of the greatest financial crisis in its history.

Higher Education Finance Reforms

Fiscal problems affecting higher education in California are not unlike those facing other states (and some nations in the Asia-Pacific Region) and are rooted in two structural factors: an eroding tax base and an explosion in health care costs. For the past four decades, the percentage of the state budget for higher education has been declining. In California, the budget crisis was particularly severe due to the decline of the aerospace industry in the 1990s, the bursting of the Internet bubble in the spring of 2000, and various problems associated with energy provision. The result has been a reduction in state appropriations of 15 percent over the past four years

(2000–2004) while enrollments increased by 19 percent. This is in addition to previous cuts in the 1980s and 1990s. Data have consistently shown a direct positive correlation between years of schooling, employment, and income in California, all factors reinforcing the public good; yet public investment in higher education has been falling (Kissler and Switkes 2005). The current fiscal crisis will result in a further US$800 million drawdown in core support for the UC system (Keller 2009).

Although the effects of the current drawdown of state support for higher education are severe, there has been a long-term decline in the University of California's share of the state General Fund, from 7 percent to 3.5 percent over the past 35 years. It will now drop to 2.5 percent (Keller 2009). Taxes have been cut and spending priorities have favored prisons and health care over education. Once support has been withdrawn, it has not been restored even in times of economic recovery. There is a general belief that such losses to the UC system can be made up with fee/tuition increases and in fact, these tools have been used to offset cuts to the general fund. Yet, the increases in fees have not been sufficient to cover the increasing costs of educating a student in the UC system. It costed about US$9,000 to educate a UC student in 1985–1986 and over twice as much (after adjusting for inflation) in 2009. Since 1990, the state's contribution to the cost of education for each UC student has fallen 34 percent, from US$15,830 to US$10,370 in constant inflation-adjusted dollars (UC Newsroom 2007). There is now a funding gap of about US$3,000 per student and this has resulted in larger class sizes, less time with faculty outside the classroom, limited library resources, and more obsolete equipment. Students pay more for their education and get less.

When the cuts came, the UC Board of Regents and the president's office focused first on cutting administration, state-supported research, and public service programs. The public good mission of the university was clearly affected by the last two categories of reductions. Innovative methods were used to cope with the scope of the reductions, namely, utilizing technology, and economies of scale within the large UC system in such areas as library access and support (for example, the California Digital Library). Streamlining business operations also occurred through such programs as the Strategic Procurement Initiative, Information Technology Procurement, and Debt Restructuring. Individual campuses engaged in various forms of privatization, commercialization, and cost-center restructuring (Called Resource Center Management at the University of California, Los Angeles).

Nevertheless, the system overall has suffered in such areas as faculty recruitment and retention, the substitution of non tenure-track faculty for ladder rank positions, higher student/faculty ratios and larger class sizes, a general reduction in the quality of the educational experience for students, and less and less opportunities for lower-income students. Now that salary reductions are being implemented for faculty and staff, recruitment and retention will be even more difficult. While the system has been creative and innovative in avoiding the worst-case scenario of the reduction in state support, the longer-term effects of continued budget shortfalls would clearly reduce the degree to which the UC system can continue to promote the public good of the state of California.

The Changing Research Mission

Certainly, the research mission of the U.S. university is still held in high regard and not in danger anytime soon of being unduly affected by neoliberal or privatization policies. However, that does not mean that there are not some serious challenges to the research mission of large public universities such as those in the University of California. Some are arguing that the leadership position held by the University of California and other large public universities is beginning to falter. Fewer students are entering especially in the so-called Science, Technology, Engineering, and Mathematics" (STEM) fields, and therefore, the production of future generations of researchers and scientists is being threatened. For example, in China, ten times the number of graduates in engineering compared to the United States, were produced in 2007 (Chambers 2007). If you combine India and China, approximately one million engineering students graduate in a given year compared with 170,000 in Europe and the United States combined (Chambers 2007). While there are questions about these data and the quality of the engineers being produced in China and India, the challenges facing the United States in these fields is apparent. China represents the most competitive challenge for United States's STEM research as they have carved out creative limited partnerships with foreign providers while at the same time building first-rate native institutions. Their stated goal is to create 20 Massachusetts Institutes of Technology (MITs), a daunting task but one they are diligently pursuing. Finally, technology-based corporations such as IBM and Nokia have developed new research and development centers in major Chinese cities and in select locations in India. All this presents challenges to the research mission of the University of California, which has acknowledged being behind in this regard (Douglass, 2006).

As John Douglass (2006, 7) of the University of California Center for the Study of Higher Education reports,

> There is increasing evidence that the quality of these (China and India's) academic programs, and the clusters of research expertise that entices international companies, is growing and becoming increasingly competitive with the US institutions and research centers. This has lead critics of shrinking state and federal funding for higher education in the US to argue that the nation is on the brink of losing its long dominance in basic science. For example, of the articles in the world's top physics journal published in 1983, scholars in American universities authored 61 percent; in 2003, that proportion dropped to 29 percent.

Budget cuts, increased competition for resources, pressure to do more applied research as opposed to the research of discovery, the rise of new high technology industries and research clusters outside the university, all have shifted the research terrain at least with respect to the STEM fields.

In the social sciences, humanities, and other professions, research efforts that traditionally have been focused on furthering the public good are also in decline. Community-based research is the term most often used to describe research that intentionally and directly supports the public good (Ward 2005). When cost cutting resulted in various forms of university restructuring, professional schools associated with these missions were the first to go. Schools of public health, library science, social welfare, urban planning, and so on were either eliminated or merged in several instances at the University of California.

The research mission of the University of California remains strong and viable. But subtle shifts have occurred in how it is supported, its capacity to remain competitive in the world market (thus affecting its ability to serve the public good of the state and the nation), and the reward structure to conduct community-based research.

Faculty, Students, and Higher Education Reform

Students have felt the effects of the withdrawal of the state from promoting higher education as a public good more than most stakeholders in the system. "State support for public higher education on a per-student basis has dropped steadily... as a result, the United States has witnessed an unraveling of the successful higher-education financing partnership among government, institutions, and families that has served our nation so well over the last century," reports David Ward (2004, 1), president of the American Council for Education. It has already been noted that fees and tuition at the University of California have had several increases in the space of just a few years (2002–2009). About two-thirds of the students graduating now have student loans with an average debt of close to US$30,000, an increase of 70 percent in nine years. In terms of access and equity issues this means that the large public universities like UC are finding it increasingly difficult to recruit and retain the best students from low socioeconomic status groups and from minority populations.

A prolonged period of no pay increase has meant that UC faculty are now lagging behind their counterparts in several important respects. The UC system now has a much more difficult time of recruiting and retaining the best faculty; it is faced with an erosion of its faculty as there is heavy recruitment by competing institutions, often private ones. When department chairs were asked to identify the impediments to and strengths of UC recruitment and retention several key issues were mentioned:

- Location: This is both an asset and a deficit; California remains a desired location because of climate, industry, professional networks among others but the high cost of housing and living in general counteracts this to some degree.
- Academic support: High academic national rankings remains a primary strength in recruitment, as does the impression of collegial faculty and graduate and undergraduate students. However, there is concern that the persistent funding problems of the UC system may limit the university's ability to attract quality graduate students.
- Salaries, financial support, and campus facilities: Competing with peer institutions and industry for salary is the most frequently cited reason for difficulty in recruiting and retaining high quality faculty. The official salary "scale" is

noncompetitive and thus faculty are increasingly hired "off-scale," which creates shortfalls in other areas as well as morale problems with faculty who were not hired in that manner. For the STEM fields deteriorating campus facilities and laboratories are another frequently mentioned impediment to recruitment and retention.
- Family issues, spousal/domestic partner problems: The second most frequently mentioned set of problems with recruitment and retention involves spousal/domestic partner employment and quality of family life.
- The history of funding cuts in the UC system continues to plague faculty welfare and threats to the pension plan by the current governor only add to the decline in morale. The university is attempting to reinvent itself and address these student and faculty issues but the distance to be traveled remains great. Private interests seem to have subordinated those of the public good and it remains to be seen if the new compact will have the desired effect.

Parallel Developments in Asia

In Asia, many similar stresses and strains are beginning to occur in higher education. A variety of forces and factors have impacted higher education change and reform in East Asia, especially in Hong Kong, Singapore, Taiwan, South Korea, China, and even in Japan. While the changes are not precisely similar to those facing higher education in the United States, and in California in particular, they reflect similar neoliberal impulses and challenge the public good mission of the academy. Globalization, the knowledge economy, the information and technology revolution, the establishment of new privatized institutions (including in China where a new privatization law has been put into effect), and the continued expansion of the demand for higher education have all contributed to new forms of university governance and management with an emphasis on efficiency, accountability, more involved stakeholders, strategic alliances, and competitiveness. This is true whether one is talking about governmental or nongovernmental HEIs. As several scholars have reported, these trends have swept through the East Asia region and have several features in common (Hawkins 2001; Cheng 2002; Mok and Currie 2002). These features have all played a role in blurring the distinctions between public and private HEIs, and affecting the public good mission of higher education.

For example, many of the nations in the region realize that they must respond to the growing demand for more higher education with increasingly limited resources and in an increasingly competitive environment. Varying governance strategies involving decentralization, privatization, marketization, and commodification, have been adopted and this has demanded new and different ways of looking at university governance largely because of declining state capacity. The World Bank, among other agencies, has recognized the evolving role of the state as it becomes much more of a guiding than a controlling force. In most Asian nations, state officials are experimenting with new approaches to providing a regulatory environment, providing appropriate financial incentives, making rules for new private institutions, and developing formulas to link resources with institutional performance rather than the macro- and micromanagement of state level ministries that has characterized past state involvement. Furthermore, the idea that tertiary education was a luxury reserved only for wealthy countries has given way to the notion that nations must develop the right mix of basic, secondary, and tertiary institutions as a "third way" between central planning and chaotic expansion as well as an articulated approach toward public and private HEIs (Mok 2000; Salmi 2002). At a recent Institute on Education for 2020 held annually at the East West Center in Hawaii to bring together leaders in higher education in the Asia-Pacific Region, there was considerable interest among the participants from Asia in the new revision of the California Master Plan that takes into account the linkages between precollegiate and both public and private tertiary education.

Another common feature is a general change of philosophy regarding public management governance. Ideas such as "reinventing government" and "entrepreneurial government" have found their way into the lexicon of educational public policy officials in many East Asian nations. As public policy reform has occurred so has the notion of accountability so that we hear more about quality control, value for money, audit society, performance society, the evaluative state and so on. These are all policy shifts that further reduce the gap between public and private higher education as well as governmental and nongovernmental higher education. In China, for example, sophisticated data envelopment analysis has been applied to assess the research performance of Chinese HEIs. Data such as these are being utilized by Chinese educational officials to determine core funding and other resource allocations all of which will have implications for governmental and nongovernmental higher education (Ng and Li 2000).

A third common feature is the rise of the knowledge economy and its implications for the changing university. Education and research are no longer the sole purview of the formal higher education system but spill over into industry, nonformal enterprises of various sorts, nongovernmental HEIs, and individuals. Lifelong learning is increasingly taking its place alongside the formal public university structure as a sort of parallel private university; how this will play out in the future in settings in Asia may well give us part of the answer to the question about the future of the university as we know it. The Open University of Hong Kong and the National Open University of Taiwan are two such examples of the appeal of open and distance learning in Asia, which also have private characteristics, in many respects, similar to the growing extension programs in the University of California system (Sherritt 1999).

A final feature is the massification of higher education and the renewed emphasis on quality control. In Hong Kong, about 30 percent of the eligible cohort (18–21) is admitted to higher education. In Singapore it is closer to 66 percent (Singapore Ministry of Education 2008) and roughly 85 percent in both Taiwan and South Korea (Directorate General 2007; Korea Ministry of Education 2008), and about 15 percent in urban China (Mok 2001; Department of Planning 2003). The rapid increase in numbers has raised several questions about the quality of the high education being offered especially in newer private institutions, which in turn has led to a variety of accountability measures in all countries in the region.

Some Cross-National General Features

Given these trends, what are some of the features that will characterize the future of higher education, public and private, in Asia and other parts of the world?

The challenges are daunting: access, expansion, privatization, distance education, technology, decentralization, globalization, and so on. Higher education in Asia and the Pacific is faced with maintaining its core, and to some extent, conservative values (autonomy, elite status, liberal arts curriculum, commitment to research, teaching without intellectual restrictions, conviction that ideas are important) while at the same time adapting to the new circumstances of globalization. Several features of this challenge deserve to be watched closely; they also raise some interesting questions for future research:

- *Differentiation and Expanded Access*: Most countries in Asia are seeking to expand access to higher education (massification). Most wealthy and middle-income countries now educate more than 30 percent of the relevant age group in postsecondary education; many developing nations in Asia have doubled access as well (OECD 2008). This trend is continuing, challenging the more traditional research university as other models, both public and private as well as hybrid institutions of postsecondary education are emerging. How will traditional universities respond to policies focused on expanding access? What are some of the new postsecondary models that are emerging?
- *The Globalization of Research*: Research has always been at the core of the mission of most universities despite what we say about teaching. Universities are the central source for basic research and increasingly this research is conducted with multinational partners. Knowledge is becoming progressively more global yet many universities continue to view research as nation-specific. Education is becoming an internationally traded commodity; this is a real revolution. Education is no longer considered the production of a skill set to allow the student to become an effective participant in society but rather a skill set to be purchased and used in the marketplace or a product to be bought and sold by corporations. In some parts of Asia, there is concern that universities have transmogrified themselves into businesses. There is further concern that globalization results in the loss of skills necessary for an understanding of culture, values, civil society, and intellectual independence. Further complicating matters are new policies that include education as one of the twelve sectors covered by the *General Agreement on Tariffs in Services* (GATS). GATS and the World Trade Organization (WTO) policies designed to "open the doors" for international university partnerships have produced a backlash in some parts of Asia where countries such as Malaysia and Singapore are regulating which foreign universities may do business in their countries while China is very cautiously looking at such arrangements. Some view the GATS policies as a new kind of neocolonialism, a new era of power and influence, where multinational corporations, media conglomerates, and a few major universities are the new neocolonialists who view education as a source of commercial gain (Knight 2002;

Altbach 2002). In Singapore the recent University of Pennsylvania Wharton Business School venture has been critiqued as being solely focused on the market and making money, rather than academic collaboration and intellectual exchange (Salmi 2002). What adjustments will need to be made in faculties on the reward structure for promotion and retention, funding for research, copyright, and patent regulations as knowledge becomes more global? What are the implications for public/private partnerships?

- *Social Mobility*: Higher education has often been viewed as a principal means for social mobility and improvement in societies. As universities adapt to global pressures what will be the impact on issues of access and equity, especially for groups such as minorities and women who have traditionally had less access to higher education in many countries? Here, the expansion of nongovernmental institutions, and the merger of public and private features of higher education, will undoubtedly play an important role.

- *Decentralization*: In most nations in the Asia-Pacific Region the control and administration of higher education has been highly centralized, usually in a ministry of education of some sort. To respond to the need for rapid change, to become more nimble in decision making, and respond to opportunities more quickly, many national higher educational systems are experimenting with various forms of administrative decentralization. This movement has presented HEIs with a range of challenges, from the need to develop new management and leadership skills, to structural changes in the organization of HEIs. What are some of the models that are being tested in the Asia-Pacific region? What can nations learn from one another as decentralization proceeds? Does the California mix of central planning (the Master Plan) and decentralization (the semi-autonomous, three-tier system of research universities, state universities, and community colleges) have any relevance for higher education transformation in the Asia-Pacific region?

- *Differentiated Funding*: One of the most significant features of decentralization, and one that therefore deserves a separate section, is the issue of funding for higher education. For the past several decades most nations in the region have developed national systems of higher education, funded almost entirely by the state sector. Even the so-called private universities have often received substantial and important allocations from the state. Economic and other considerations no longer allow this luxury and one feature of decentralization has been the downloading of the financial burden to the university level. Presidents and chancellors are scrambling to seek new sources of funding from the introduction of tuition (or the dramatic increase in existing tuition, often accompanied by student unrest) to the development of alumni associations and other support groups for fund-raising purposes, to seeking funds from philanthropic foundations, developing industrial and corporate linkages, consulting fees, patents, and other income. What are some of the new models of differentiated funding and what can nations learn from one another in this critical area? Can nongovernmental HEIs teach the governmental HEIs how to do this effectively?

- *Internationalization*: As universities respond to the new global challenges, the internationalization of their student bodies, faculty, curriculum, and so on will only increase. More than two million students are already studying outside the borders of their home countries. There is a rapidly growing international labor market for researchers, faculty, and graduates. Knowledge production and dissemination are international in scope and widely available through new media and technology. In the European Union, there is a movement toward common degree structures (harmonization) and mutual recognition of academic qualifications, course credits, and so on. What are the implications for the universities of the Asia-Pacific region? Already we are beginning to see the beginnings of educational regional organizations in the region (Hawkins 2005).

Educational policy makers interviewed in Asia recognized that there are both national and institutional rationales for internationalization. At the national level, it is acknowledged that there remains a strong need for human resource development that is prepared for the knowledge economy and that strategic alliances have shifted from cultural collaboration to economic needs. At the institutional level, universities are concerned with their international profile and reputation, brand name and brand recognition; these were concerns that in the past were primarily of the private HEIs. Internationalization may also provide new knowledge and skills for increasing income, for student and staff development and for achieving scientific, economic, and technological objectives. What about the language of instruction and research—will English become the new Latin of the twenty-first century? What will happen to national languages? Or, in the case of East and Southeast Asia, will Chinese become the regional language for trade, commerce, and maybe education? This is particularly critical in view of the expansion of the Internet and other new media.

- *The Politics of Education*: With the expansion of the Internet, e-mail, cross-national research and student exchange, and the new managerialism, what will be the implications for academic freedom and freedom of inquiry? Some academics are already questioning whether the faculty can maintain academic autonomy amidst these very formidable challenges (Altbach 2002). Others are concerned about the role of the Internet on student achievement and the possible negative influences on study hours and social development (Chou and Hsiao 2000).
- *Virtual Education*: Probably the biggest challenge to conventional higher education is virtual education, now a US$300 billion market. It is on the move and Jones University (now serving students in 38 countries) and University of Phoenix in the United States (offering a proliferation of "overseas validated courses") are just the beginning. Today more than 80 percent of all American colleges and universities offer some educational programs online (University of California, Los Angeles; Carnegie Mellon; MIT; Duke; Harvard; and Stanford, to name a few) (Neal 2008). John Chambers, chief executive officer of Cisco, noted, "[S]chools and countries that ignore (virtual education) will suffer the same fate as big department stores that thought that e-commerce was over-rated" (Wilms and Zell 2002). This is a major private higher education initiative that is spreading worldwide. In Asia the concern is that only a handful of distance education providers will dominate the market and these will be principally from the West. Currently, seven out of ten of the largest distance-learning corporations are in

developing nations. Local academic institutions find it hard to compete and multinational corporations cream off the most lucrative markets. Educational officials in many parts of Asia find that they are no longer able to control the basic elements of the curriculum, language of instruction, pedagogical philosophies, and other key elements of the educational delivery system at the tertiary level. Supporters of this trend, however, argue that an increase in distance learning opportunities will help satisfy the demand for increased access to higher education. Their view is that most Asian countries are in a financial bind anyway, so why not allow higher education alternatives? Nevertheless, a number of issues continue to nag higher educational policy makers in Asia: regulation (licensing, accreditation), transferability of credits, quality assurance, professional mobility, culture and acculturation, and the risk of "trade creep" whereby educational policy issues are increasingly framed in terms of trade and economic benefit (Knight 2002). In any case, this movement will provide a challenge for domestic nongovernmental and governmental HEIs.

Conclusion

This discussion of higher education transformation in California, the United States, and Asia has touched on several sensitive topics including the relationship between higher education and the public good versus commodification, privatization, centralization versus decentralization, as well as others. In California and elsewhere in the Unites States, this has raised questions of whether historic conceptions of the "public good" can be sustained within the policy frame it has created. Neoliberalism with its focus on the market privileges economic values and relationships at the expense of other social values. Concern over this reductionism is exemplified by the National Forum on Education for the Public Good, organized and supported by the W. K. Kellogg Foundation, and designed to counterbalance pressures to transform higher education's social role to make it function as an industry. As Kezar (2005, 23) has noted,

> Traditionally, higher education's public role has included educating citizens for democratic engagement, supporting local and regional communities, preserving knowledge and making it available to the community, working in concert with other social institutions such as government or health care in order to foster their missions, advancing knowledge through research, developing the arts and humanities, broadening access to ensure a diverse democracy, developing the intellectual talents of students, and creating leaders for various areas of the public sector. The values undergirding this social mission include equality, service, truth, justice, community, academic freedom, and autonomy.

As for California and the University of California (as well as many other HEIs in the United States), decades of reduction in state financial support have indeed taken a toll on both the teaching and research mission of the university. The system remains a substantial force in higher education but there has been a discernable shift in its public good mission, as the system has privatized in subtle and not so subtle ways. Proposals to further centralize the system under the governor's office or the state legislature represent a real setback to the tradition of faculty governance and independent coordination. Counterproposals have been put forth which would strengthen the independent coordinating body of CPEC while at the same time linking it closer to the governor's office. It remains to be seen how this particular reform will be implemented.

The new compact brings financial stability to the UC system while at the same time demanding more accountability and specifying in ways not seen before, how the UC will contribute to state needs as defined by the governor's office. This represents a new direction for the UC system and one that further centralizes the mission at the same time that the system is being asked to be more entrepreneurial and risk-taking. But the current economic crisis has seen that initiative tabled as well. New campus management strategies have been experimented with (e.g., the Resource Center Management at the University of California, Los Angeles), and in general, daily operations have been more privatized and commercialized.

The research mission remains strong but targeted weaknesses exist in the science and technology areas. The pipeline issue is critical as fewer U.S. students study in these areas or have the abilities and motivation to move forward to the university level where they can become the next generation of researchers. Thus, the state and nation as a whole are diminished in this regard. Other fields have also been commercialized as the ability to obtain extramural funding increasingly drives the disciplines.

Finally, the effects on faculty and students have been obvious. For the former, difficulty in recruiting and retaining has been the most challenging and though a number of innovative measures have been taken, this remains a difficult area for the future. For students, the biggest challenge is financial, as "fees" have been raised consecutively for the past several years. This has affected the public good aspect of public universities by making them more elitist than was envisioned in the original charters. The new compact also addresses this issue and proposes some short-term solutions.

In Asia, the historical trajectory of higher education may be different from that in the United States and California in particular, but the challenges are quite similar. The notion of higher education as a public good, especially for the large public research universities, is also being challenged in the Asian region as, in most cases, the state withdraws from maintaining the levels of financial support it has provided in the past. Political economic systems as diverse as Japan and China have begun to privatize their higher education systems or, in the case of Japan, "incorporate" them. These moves have not been met with general approval, at least among the faculty. In personal conversations with faculties at such prestigious institutions as Peking University and Tokyo University, faculties have referred to such privatization policies as disastrous. Their American colleagues have shared these sentiments as well.

Many of the trends outlined in the section of this chapter on Asia (decentralization, globalization, internationalization, virtual education) have contributed to the current status of higher education in Asia and in some cases can be credited with major advances in HEIs in that region. As Douglass (2006) notes above, the research mission of higher education in the United States has faltered in some respects while that of the best universities in Asia has been moving forward. Targeted research investments in the Asian region are beginning to pay off in new science and technology developments and knowledge advancement. So in the midst of concern over privatization, the research communities in some parts of Asia are being encouraged by renewed state and private investment interest.

Accountability measures are another area where some similarity exists between the two regions. Much as the compact has defined a new way of justifying continued state support for higher education in the University of California, new accountability procedures in Asian higher education, as Bilgalke and Neubaurer (2009) have pointed out, are beginning to define higher education-state relations in Asia; what some are calling "centralized de-centralization." These new relationships between HEIs and the state have had implications for faculty recruitment and retention, an area that remains problematic for both the Asian region and the United States and California (as the private sector competes with the academy for the best minds). For students, who have shouldered much of the financial burden of decentralization and privatization, higher education reform has made institutional choice difficult. The increase in cost has raised additional questions about the public good mission of higher education.

Educators in both regions are struggling to come to terms with a new world of higher education, one that is influenced by neoliberal domestic policies, forces of globalization, and countervailing forces of localization. The particular mix of centralization and decentralization evolving in the state of California and other systems in the United States may be of interest to the formerly highly centralized systems of Asia as they seek to find their own path to decentralization. On the other hand, some of the national research investment strategies in higher education in the Asian region have been yielding positive results in science and technology, providing a challenge to HEIs in the United States. It will be worthwhile for scholars and practitioners in both Asia and the United States to remain engaged with each other and continue to share policies and practices as their respective HEIs seek to develop and grow in the increasingly global knowledge society in which we all live.

References

Altbach, Philip G. 2002. "Knowledge and Education as International Commodities." *International Higher Education* 28 (Summer): 2–5.
Bilgalke, Terance W., and Deane E. Neubauer. 2009. *Higher Education in Asia/Pacific: Quality and the Public Good.* New York: Palgrave Macmillan.
Chambers, John. 2007. "India, China Produce More Graduates, But What of the Quality of Their Degrees?" Framingham, MA: *Cisco Subnet Blog.* http://www.networkworld.com.
Cheng, Yin-Cheong. 2002. "Educational Reforms in the Asia-Pacific Region: Trends and Implications for Research." Paper presented at the Globalization and Educational Governance Change in East Asia Conference, Hong Kong, June 14.
Chou, Chien, and Ming-Chun Hsiao. 2000. "Internet Addiction, Usage, Gratification, and Pleasure Experience: The Taiwan College Student's Case." *Computers and Education* 35 (1): 65–80.

California Postsecondary Education Commission (CPEC). 2009. *CEPC Website: "Commission History."* Sacramento, CA: CPEC. http://www.cpec.ca.gov/.
Department of Planning, Ministry of Education, PRC. 2003. *Report of Education Statistics* 1 (26), February 27.
Directorate General of Budget, Accounting and Statistics, Executive Yuan, ROC. 2007. *Statistical Yearbook of the Republic of China 2007.* Taipei: Directorate General of Budget, Accounting and Statistics. http://eng.stat.gov.tw.
Douglass, John A. 2006. *The Waning of America's Higher Education Advantage: International Competitors Are No Longer Number Two and Have Big Plans in the Global Economy.* Research and Occasional Paper Series No. CSHE.9.06. Berkeley: Center for Studies in Higher Education, University of California, Berkeley.
Fox, Warren H. 2005. *How Best to Coordinate California Higher Education: Comments on the Governor's Proposed Reforms.* Research and Occasional Paper Series No. CSHE.4.05. Berkeley: Center for Studies in Higher Education, University of California, Berkeley.
Hawkins, John N. 2001. "Recent Higher Education Reform in China." In *The Transformation of Higher Education: A Comparative Perspective*, ed. S. Aroni. Paris: ESTP Press.
———. 2005. "Educational Partnerships With and Within Asia." In *The Possibility of an East Asian Community: Rethinking the Sino-Japanese Relationship*, eds. T. Satow and E. Li. Tokyo: Ochanomizu Shobo.
Higher Education Compact. 2006. "Agreement between Governor Schwarzenegger, the University of California, and the California State University, 2005–06 through 2010–11." UC Internal Memo. Sacramento: State of California.
Kezar, Adrianna J. 2005. "Challenges for Higher Education in Serving the Public Good." In *Higher Education for the Public Good: Emerging Voices from a National Movement*, eds. A. J. Kezar, T. C. Chambers and J. C. Burkhart. San Francisco: Josey-Bass.
Keller, Josh. 2009. "California's 'Gold Standard' for Higher Education Falls upon Hard Times." *Chronicle of Higher Education* 55 (39), June 11. http://www.chronicle.com/.
Kissler, Gerald R., and Ellen Switkes. 2005. *The Effects of a Changing Financial Context on the University of California.* Research and Occasional Paper Series No. CSHE.16.05. Berkeley: Center for Studies in Higher Education, University of California, Berkeley.
Knight, Jane. 2002. "Trade Creep: Implications of GATS for Higher Education Policy." *International Higher Education* 28 (Summer): 5–7.
Ministry of Education, Science and Technology, Republic of Korea (MEST). 2008. "Higher Education Statistics." Seoul: MEST. http://english.mest.go.kr.
Mok, Ka-Ho. 2000. "Marketizing Higher Education in Post-Mao China." *International Journal of Educational Development* 20 (2): 109–126.
———. 2001. "Globalization, Marketization and Higher Education: Trends and Developments in East Asia." Paper presented at the International Conference on Marketization and Higher Education in Asia, Shanghai, April 7–8.
Mok, Ka-Ho, and Janice Currie. 2002. "Reflections on the Impact of Globalization on Educational Restructuring in Hong Kong." In *Globalization and Education: The Quest for Quality Education in Hong Kong*, eds. K. H. Mok and K. K. Chan. Hong Kong: Hong Kong University Press.
Neal R. 2008. "Earning a Degree Online." New York: CBS. http://www.cbs.com.
Ng, Ying-Chu, and Sung-Ko Li. (2000). "Measuring the Research Performance of Chinese Higher Education Institutions: An Application of Data Envelopment Analysis." *Education Economics* 8 (2): 136–156.
Organization for Economic Co-operation and Development (OECD). 2008. *OECD Fact Book 2008.* Paris: OECD Publishing.

Salmi, Jamil. 2002. "New Challenges for Tertiary Education: The World Bank Report." *International Higher Education* 28 (Summer): 7–9.

Sherritt, Caroline. 1999. "Hong Kong and Taiwan: Two Case Studies in Open and Distance Learning." *Asian Affairs Journal* 26 (1): 37–41.

Singapore Ministry of Education (SMOE). 2008. *Education Statistics Digest Factbook 2008*. Singapore: SMOE. http://www.moe.gov.sg.

UC Newsroom. 2007. "Regents Vote to Oppose Proposition 92." Oakland California: UC Board of Regents. http://www.universityofcalifornia.edu.

Ward, David. 2004. "That Old Familiar Feeling—With an Important Difference." *The Presidency*, Winter 1.

Ward, Kelly. 2005. "Rethinking Faculty Roles and Rewards for the Public Good." In *Higher Education for the Public Good: Emerging Voices from a National Movement*, eds. A. J. Kezar, T. C. Chambers and J. C. Burkhart. San Francisco: Josey-Bass.

Warren, Paul. 2005. *K-12 Master Plan, Starting the Process*. ERIC File no: ED438590.

Wilms, Wellford W., and Deone M. Zell. 2002. *Awakening the Academy: A Time for New Leadership*. Bolton, MA: Anker Publishing Company.

Chapter 3

Changing Governance in China's Higher Education: Some Analyses of the Recent University Enrollment Expansion Policy

Rui Yang

Introduction

Globalization, as a description of both putatively real processes and of certain kinds of discourses (Urry 1998, 8), has been taken as a salient feature of our times in significant modern and postmodern social theories. Its impacts on the university are substantial, inasmuch as they challenge the long tradition of higher education as a "public good" (Marginson 2006, 12). In a context of increasingly intensified globalization, higher education entrepreneurialism has become prevalent. It is therefore common for political and institutional commentary to cite "globalization" as justification for "rationalization" and "corporatization" (Kenway and Langmead 1998), and as a governing discourse to justify governmental policy options.

However, it is misleading to treat globalization as unilateral. Indeed, globalization processes are complex and often contradictory. While it accelerates changes in public administration or public management, it does not initiate them (Mok 2005). The nonunilateral, complex, overlapping, and unpredictable characteristics of globalization indicate that the distribution of power under its influence is fluid and changing. People who are influenced by globalization could have positive or negative impacts on its process, depending on their recognition of globalization "in what respects and on whose terms" (Burbules and Torres 2000, 17).

> China's universities today operate within a neoliberal discourse, with the main organizing concepts being consumer choices, personal investment (private good), and rising consumer demand with which governments cannot keep pace (Marginson 2002).[1] Using the university enrollment expansion policy in late 1998 as an example, this chapter attempts to illustrate how the Chinese government has adapted a variety of common trends and patterns in public policy and management to justify its political agendas. In the following sections, I analyze the contexts of the policymaking, examine the major measures employed to implement the policy, and discuss the consequences of this policy.

Previous Policy Arrangements along the Market Line

The university enrollment expansion policy resulted, to some extent, from previous related policies. Since China abandoned its planned system and adopted an open-door policy, Western ideas and theories have flooded into China. With the memory of rigid state-controlled options still fresh, the Chinese have been particularly keen on market ideologies, though on the latter there were hardly any comprehensive, systematic studies. Education policy, management, and governance are pressured to improve service delivery and governance (Kaufmann et al. 2005). Chinese universities have been pushed by the government to change their governance paradigm to adopt a doctrine of monetarism characterized by freedom and markets replacing Keynesianism (Apple 2000). Revitalizing the engagement of nonstate sectors in education including the market, the community, the third sector, and civil society become increasingly significant in China (Meyer and Boyd 2001). Commoditization of education institutions becomes an instrument of economic and social policy.

Chinese education reforms have since been aligned with those in the economic sector. In 1985, China launched its first comprehensive education reform policy *The Decision on the Reform of the Educational Structure* (hereafter The Decision). However, reformative actions had started as early as 1978. Over the past 25 years, great efforts have been made to introduce the role of the market in education. Building up close links between education and the market together with decentralization of finance and management in education reforms has been the most prominent orientation of the government.

The impact of the market was most evident in higher education, when universities and colleges started offering contract training in exchange for fees. Market-oriented experiments became part of the reform. As the market gained more significance, especially in the more developed coastal and urban areas, more substantial reform policies were introduced to make structural changes in education. *The Program for Education Reform and Development in China* (hereafter The Program) in 1993 reaffirmed The Decision's commitment for central government to refrain from direct control of education. Instead, the government was to act as a facilitator, and was thus increasingly reluctant to continue to subsidize students. Tuition and other fees started to become a reality.

It did not take very long before Chinese education institutions had to face the market on all fronts, with the potential employers as clients (Yang 2007). This is one aspect of China's market-oriented reforms, reflecting radicalism in a far-from-sophisticated market. China's education policies are made by economists to "meet the needs of a socialist economy" (Lao 2003, 5). In 1992, *The Decision on the Development of the Tertiary Industry* stated that education was part of the tertiary industry, and those who invested in it would own it and benefit from it. The central government raised the idea of education as a stimulus for economic growth. Private investment in education was encouraged and the first auction of a public school took place in Zhejiang, in the eastern part of mainland China. A basis for ownership transfer from public to private was provided and the commoditization of education gradually became legitimized.

Specifically, two policy developments have contributed directly to the commoditization of education in China. The first was the establishment of the higher education tuition fee policy. Commoditization started when China first embraced human capital theory to acknowledge the economic value of education. With the legitimate shift in the understanding of education from a public to a private good that could be purchased on the basis of the buyer's perceived need and financial capacity, China initiated the higher education tuition fee policy. Institutions of higher learning were first allowed to collect 100 RMB accommodation and 20 RMB tuition fees from students in 1989. In 1993, cost-sharing policy in higher education was written into the Program. Tuition fees increased dramatically from 4.34 percent of the cost of a course in 1992 to 12.12 percent in 1993 and 25 percent in 1998 (Zhang 1998, 246).

The second was the organization of educational production. The changed understanding of education has led to a growing exchange of education commodities, which has impacted the organization of educational provision. Since the 1980s, the organizational changes of Chinese education institutions have been in four forms: derivation, function differentiation, change of ownership, and new organizations.

Derivation is the emergence of a new entity within education institutions that is committed to market operation. This refers to the university-run companies during the early days of the reform, and the so-called *erji xueyuan* (the second-tier colleges), *duli xueyuan* (independent colleges), or *fenxiao* (branch campuses) nowadays. They are profit-making branches of public institutions, supported by government funding yet operating as private businesses.

Function differentiation means that the existing organization allows itself or part of it to have some additional functions without changing the overall structure, in particular the coexistence of one part operating on the state framework and the other on market principles. Such differentiation has been practiced in public education institutions for years, such as the university admission policy on accepting privately sponsored students with higher tuition fees and lower academic standards while maintaining national quotas.

Change of ownership of public education institutions into private operation causes dramatic school organizational culture changes after ownership transfer. Schools and teachers become employers and employees; schools and students turn into service and customers. Meanwhile, school decision making and management also change fundamentally, with most schools governed by a board of trustees.

New organizations that constitute the education industry, aiming at profit and operating as a business are, as a typical example of this, the chain schools belonging to big education companies.

Within this policy context, Chinese universities started to change their governance model along business lines. By the late 1990s, through implementing decentralization and marketization, China had initiated fundamental changes especially in the orientation, financing, and management of higher education. The market had entered into government-university relationships in China to form a "trinity" (Dong 2003). Such reforms were finance-driven (Carnoy 2000), subjecting education to the language and logic of neoliberal economics as part of a larger process of commoditization (Dale 2000).

The Formation of the Expansion Policy

The immediate context played a direct role in the formation of the higher education expansion policy (Taylor et al. 1997; Marinetto 1999). At the Fifteenth National Congress of the Chinese Communist Party in 1997, developing the country through science and education was identified as a national strategy of paramount importance for economic improvement and modernization of the nation. Also influenced by the World Bank's (1999) research finding that showed major challenges to China's higher education subsector due to its fast-growing economy in the previous two decades, with increasing pressure from the growing market economy, the Chinese government realized that its higher education had been problematic and its supply insufficient (Yang 2009).

Until 1999 Chinese higher education expanded gradually. From 1978 to 1996, tertiary student enrollments increased from 0.86 million to 0.97 million. After the implementation of the fee-charging system nationwide, the enrollments in regular higher education institutions (HEIs) increased to 1.04 million in 1997 and 1.1 million in 1998. On December 24, 1998, the State Council promulgated the "Education Development Plan" for the twenty-first century, drafted jointly by the State Planning Commission and China's Ministry of Education (CMOE) to accelerate the pace of expansion to enroll 15 percent of each age cohort into higher education by 2010.

Since 1999, enrollments in HEIs have been continuously increasing, as shown by table 3.1 below. With the fast expansion, the 15 percent enrollment target was moved to 2005 in the Tenth National Five-Year Plan (2001–2005).

To some extent, the reason why the Chinese government decided to increase the enrollment in higher education by over 40 percent from 1999 remains unanswered. In fact, the government had decided to implement an average of 9 percent annual increase for the higher education subsector. The official explanation indicated that the decision was made in response to a growing demand for highly qualified manpower which, in the context of economic globalization, had become a decisive factor that could affect China's capacity to compete with other countries. The policy was

Table 3.1 Numbers of Regular HEIs, Their Enrollments, and Graduates

Year	Numbers of institutions	New students	Graduates	Total enrollments
1990	1,075	609,000	614,000	1,206,300
1995	1,054	926,000	805,000	2,906,000
1998	1,022	1,084,000	930,000	3,409,000
1999	1,071	1,597,000	848,000	4,134,000
2000	1,041	2,206,072	949,767	5,560,900
2001	1,225	2,682,800	1,036,300	7,190,700
2002	1,396	3,205,000	1,337,300	9,033,600
2003	1,552	3,821,700	1,877,500	11,085,600
2004	1,731	4,473,400	2,391,200	13,335,000
2005	1,792	5,044,600	3,068,000	15,617,800
2006	1,867	5,460,500	3,774,700	17,388,400
2007	1,908	5,659,200	4,477,900	18,849,000

Source: Figures from 1990 to 1999 were from *China Statistical Yearbook 2000*; figures of 2000, 2001, and 2002 are from http://www.edu.cn/20010827/208329.shtml; figures of 2003, 2004, 2005, 2006, and 2007 are from http://www.edu.cn/jiao_yu_fa_zhan_498/.

claimed to be "a natural outcome of the growing market economy" and a "logical follow-up" to the implementation of the "user-pays" system (Xi 1999, 21).

The policymaking was an economic consideration. It had become politically correct in China to advocate market-driven reforms in education since 1998. Market ideologies had been underlying China's policymaking and implementation for about a decade. China's mainstream economists stressed educational development as an effective way to stimulate consumption and investment. To them, education was an ideal stimulus for China's economic growth in the twenty-first century. Considering that China has the world's largest population and the rising demand for quality labor, the mainstream economists in China believed that the potential of the Chinese education market was huge. Therefore, user-pays education should be encouraged to stimulate economic growth (Lao 2003). Again this is little surprising considering the dominant open and reform discourse in China during the past decades has been to link its higher education system and institutions more firmly to the market.

An immediate reason for the Chinese government to introduce the policy was the Asian Financial Crisis in 1998, which greatly affected China. From the late 1970s up to the first half of 1997, a reasonably high economic growth rate had been politically crucial for the regime. The financial crisis caused China's economy to slow down because of sluggish demand. Although the government took various measures to stimulate consumption and cut the interest rates seven times, bank savings remained extremely high. Investment decreased, exports reduced, and deflation continued (Li 1999). At the same time, China's urban unemployment rate was on the rise. The number of retrenched workers had been increasing every year since 1993. The situation would have become much worse if most of the three million senior secondary school graduates were not able to enter universities.

The government needed to find a trigger to stimulate domestic spending. Two economists, Hu Angang and Shi Zulin (2000), based in Tsinghua University, suggested that Chinese policy-makers treat the expansion of higher education as a priority in the government's efforts to stimulate domestic consumption. In November 1998, Tang Min, the chief economist of the Asian Development Bank Mission in China, further advocated the use of education to stimulate the economy. They insisted that the expansion of university enrollments would have a positive and immediate impact on the economy and society: increased enrollments could earn much income through tuition fees, and thus contribute at least a 0.5 percent increase in Gross Domestic Product (GDP); enrolling more secondary-school graduates into higher education from 1999 to 2002 would leave five to six million job opportunities for unemployed workers (Bai 2006). Such recommendations fitted exactly with the Chinese government's wishes.

In order to implement the expansion policy, the government made a few corresponding decisions. One was to support and standardize the running of education institutions by nonstate sectors or through joint programs between Chinese institutions and their foreign partners. *The Law on the Promotion of Non-governmental Education* and *The Regulations of the People's Republic of China on Chinese-Foreign Cooperation in Running Schools* were issued. The first encouraged nonstate resources to undertake the provision of higher education. The other aimed to encourage people to go to university by abolishing the longstanding restrictions on marital status and age for undergraduate admission.

The university enrollment expansion policy was top-down, based almost exclusively on economic considerations. Some other factors were taken into account, including the strong willingness of Chinese parents to invest heavily on their children's education. Those considerations, however, demonstrated little respect for the great Confucian education tradition and even abused it.[2] The knowledge and practice of higher education development was almost completely ignored. It was a decision of a handful of political elites, based exclusively on the advice of selected economists. It showed that the government retained ultimate claim on legal jurisdiction of the Chinese state, even in the face of the increasing need to respond to external pressures generated by international forces.

Major Measures to Implement the Policy

While the formation of the expansion policy demonstrates how powerful the Chinese state capacity remains against a backdrop of revitalizing the role of the market and private sectors in educational service delivery (Knill and Lehmkuhl 2002), the implementation of the policy shows the diversification of policy instruments, and the changed relationship between the state and nonstate actors in education delivery and financing from "hierarchy" to "network" (Mok 2005, 299). Despite the fact that the two models of "command and control" and "negotiation and persuasion" are not always in harmony, indeed conflicting under many circumstances, they coexist in today's Chinese university governance. The measures taken by the Chinese government to implement the expansion policy were along the direction already set by previous reforms, which were further enhanced by the implementation of this policy.

The first measure taken was autonomy, which is at the heart of the university and has been seen as a necessity for universities to properly discharge their mission. According to Neave and van Vught (1994), there are two government steering models in higher education: the state-supervised and the state-controlled. The Chinese system belongs to the latter; it is characterized by the monopoly of provision, financing, and governance of higher education by the central government, which assumes responsibility for formulating higher education policies, allocating resources, exercising administrative controls, employing teaching and research staff, developing curriculum, compiling textbooks, recruiting students, and assigning jobs to university graduates. In tradition, with all key responsibilities and tasks taken over by the state, the incentives of universities and local governments in higher education were being stifled.

With the rapid expansion of higher education and the ever-increasing student numbers, calls for better governance modes became louder. Realizing that the state-controlled model would not help much in the implementation of the expansion policy, the Chinese government quickened its steps to introduce reforms in higher education governance. The role of provincial governments in higher education was substantially strengthened. Institutional autonomy was increased. Instead of direct governmental intervention in the everyday operation of universities, the government tended to manage universities through legislation, funding, planning, information provision, advice, and other necessary administrative means. Universities had more autonomy to formulate their recruitment plans, adjust student quotas among departments and programs, restructure and develop programs, reshape their internal structure, hire and fire teachers and staff, raise and use funds, and distribute bonuses and benefits to their employees. Within a university, faculties and departments could also enjoy greater autonomy and power in matters relating to teaching, research, personnel, and resource allocation.

The second was financing, which is directly related to and which resulted from the changing governance. China's investment in education had been gravely insufficient. In order to have a better financial situation, the state had been searching for "multiple channels" of education funding to replace sole reliance upon the government's support. The desired system of educational investment included, in addition to the central government budget, an increasing portion of resources from local taxation, tuitions, donations, fund-raising, and income from university-run enterprises. Funding from the central government was reduced, while grants, funds, and loans generated from nonstate sectors became increasingly important. By 2002, funding sources for HEIs comprised governments (49 percent), tuition fees (27 percent), social organizations and individuals (3 percent), donations and gifts (2 percent), and others (19 percent) (Wang 2006).

Tuitions and fees were a growing source of income, representing nearly 50 percent of a student's direct education expenditure. For private universities, tuition fees accounted for more than 90 percent of their revenue. Tuition fees were up year by year, and so was its percentage of the total revenue. In 1997, the revenue from tuitions and fees were about 71.1 billion RMB, which is about 16 percent of the total revenue from all sources. In 2002, the revenue from tuitions and fees has jumped to 426.5 billion RMB, so that its percentage of the total revenue from all sources has increased to 27 percent (Wang 2006).

Another striking feature of financing in the new governance mode in Chinese higher education is revenue-generating activities. Financial constraints were the main difficulty confronting Chinese universities. Unwilling and unable to provide the entire funding to universities, the Chinese government's policies encouraged universities to earn money by themselves. As a result, to sustain themselves, Chinese universities engaged in different revenue-generating activities including offering commissioned courses, running adult classes and evening courses to attract more students, charging consultant fees, linking with business and industry to attract grants and funds, transferring technology, and commercializing research findings. One prominent way for universities to generate revenue is to run a business. The profit collected from such business was a major part of the revenue source listed above as "others." Many universities set up their own business to raise income (Mok 2001). Although the number of businesses has decreased from 5,444 in 1999 to 4,839 in 2003, the income earned by those businesses has increased from 379 billion RMB to 826 billion RMB. In the same period, the overall profit has increased from 31 billion RMB to 43 billion RMB, and the profit collected by HEIs has increased from 16 billion RMB to 18 billion RMB (Wang 2006).

The third was in curriculum development. With the introduction of macromanagement through legislation, funding allocation, planning, information services, and policy guidance, Chinese universities were required to provide education geared toward meeting societal needs. Universities were required to establish new courses to accommodate emerging societal demand for higher education, while existing programs were reconstructed on the basis of the market needs. Many universities broadened their previously overspecialized curricula to make their graduates more employable and to suit employers' demands. Most courses and programs became evidently market-driven, with a central emphasis on practical and applied values. Programs that failed to attract students were phased out.

By adopting the policy of decentralization and making use of market forces in the educational arena, without being fully committed to the underpinning ideologies of different governance modes, the Chinese government was driven by pragmatic considerations of enhancing the efficiency and effectiveness of higher education in the face of financial stringency. The adoption of these measures reflected an attempt to make use of market forces and new initiatives from the nonstate sectors to mobilize more educational resources. China tried to utilize both market-based and regulatory interventions (Clark 1983; Coaldrake 2000).

Social Consequences of the Policy

The social effects of any policy need to be analyzed with both the desired and the unintended consequences in mind. In terms of university enrollments, the goal of the expansion policy has been achieved. The total number of students enrolled in regular HEIs has increased substantially from 3,408,700 in 1998 to 15,617,800 and

18,849,000 respectively in 2005 and 2007. China's national overall enrollment rate of 21 percent of the age cohort has made it the world's largest higher education system, marking a transition from elite to mass higher education (Trow 1974; Pretorius and Xue 2003).

As Zhou Ji, China's minister of education, claimed at the 32nd UNESCO General Conference, "China was possibly one of the countries that had undergone the most dramatic changes since 1998" (Xinhua News Agency 2003). The policy has provided Chinese citizens with more chances to participate in higher education. The percentages of secondary school graduates receiving higher education rose from 43.05 percent in 1998 to 83.52 percent in 2002, while in 1981 only 2.4 percent of them could be admitted, as shown in table 3.2.

The other major task, however, has not been well fulfilled. Indeed, it has left some serious problems in China's labor market. The most direct and negative consequence is the rise of graduate unemployment at both undergraduate and postgraduate levels. The problem loomed large in 2003 when the 1999 cohort began to enter the job market with a total of 750,000 graduates failing to find a job upon graduation. The number soared to 1.2 million in 2005 (Xinhua News Agency 2007). In 2007, 20 percent of the five million graduates were unemployed throughout the year after graduation (Zhao and Sheng 2008, 3–4). Up to one-third of the 5.6 million university graduates in 2008 are still looking for work, and 2009 is expected to see another 6.1 million hit the labor market. Finding jobs for graduates has become a national priority. The central government recently ordered local governments and state enterprises to hire more graduates to maintain China's "general stability." On June 13, 2008, the Chinese Communist Party held a high-level meeting in Beijing to assess political and socioeconomic challenges facing the party and government in 2008. President Hu Jintao highlighted that creating jobs for university graduates remained one of the major concerns for 2008 (Ye 2008).

Although China's overall potential labor market demand for university graduates is great, many people still doubt whether the labor market can absorb such a sudden increase in supply. Indeed, soon after the expansion policy was made, some

Table 3.2 University Enrollments and Admission Rates in China, 1998–2007

	1998	1999	2000	2001	2002	2003	2004	2005	2006	2007
University enrollments (million)	1.0840	1.5970	2.2061	2.6828	3.2050	3.8217	4.4734	5.0446	5.4605	5.6592
Graduates form senior secondary schools (million)	2.5178	2.6291	3.0151	3.4046	3.8376	4.5812	5.4694	6.6157	7.2707	7.8831
Enrollment rate (%)	43.05	60.74	73.17	78.79	83.52	83.42	81.79	76.25	75.10	71.79

Source: Ministry of Education, China. 1998–2007. *Bulletin of Statistics on National Education Development*. http://www.edu.cn/jiao_yu_fa_zhan_498/.

scholars already anticipated that the job market would not expand as quickly as higher education and thus educated unemployment would become a problem. With the central focus on immediate economic growth, previous studies on higher education development and graduate employment in other countries that had long been available were not even considered. Many measures taken by the Chinese government to implement the policy were similar to the tips for planning higher education elaborated by Sanyal (1987), for example. In 1969, a study of the causes of graduate unemployment in India already pointed out that "poor countries can have too much education, and the manpower shortage of yesterday can become the manpower surplus of tomorrow" (Blaug et al. 1969, 1), and such surpluses were common in poor countries, particularly those with long histories of formal education. The Chinese government, however, chose to ignore these experiences.

As a result, there has been a mismatch between labor supply and demand. As noted by Johnson (2009), Robert Ubell, who heads a New York University program in China to train young Chinese employees of foreign companies, "Chinese graduates often have few practical skills. There is a misalignment between the university system and the needs of the economy." With the shortage of practical skills, it is not surprising that Chinese companies are picky and many refuse to hire some of the products of China's higher education system. Meanwhile, in many local labor markets, skilled workers are much more sought after than university graduates. In Guangdong, approximately 88 percent of the 2.35 million jobs offered in the second quarter of 2007 had specific educational requirements, with 60 percent for graduates from senior secondary schools or below, only 28 percent for university graduates (Lin 2007).

The misalignment goes beyond the way Chinese students are trained. The issue becomes more serious when one considers how the expansion was distributed among fields of study. Often, institutions tend to take in more students in less expensive programs because of the lower costs. This results in an oversupply in some fields and short supply in others. This has led to a considerable number of unemployed graduates. In 2001, only four among the hundreds of HEIs in China had job placement rates of 95 percent. They were all from institutions of engineering (Min 2001), echoing the general situation in developing countries where more emphasis has been placed on scientific and technological development in order to catch up with the developed countries. China's graduates from humanities and social sciences programs have increased considerably since 1999, accounting for about half of the total in 2006, but only 24.8 percent of jobs offered were for them (Xinhua News Agency 2008).

The mismatch reveals another far more serious issue of the ignorance of context in China's policy-borrowing. The desired transition from elite to mass higher education was based on the experience of the major developed countries. However, in those countries, the transition was built on sound foundations laid by their higher education systems and structures for decades (in some cases, centuries). For instance, HEIs in the United States already had the organizational and structural framework of a system of mass higher education by 1900, long before it had mass enrollment. Moreover, underpinning all this was the spirit of competition, institutional diversity, responsiveness to markets (especially to the market for students), and institutional autonomy by strong leadership, and a diversity of sources of support (Trow 2000). In contrast, China's higher education system prior to the 1999 expansion had not been prepared for large-scale expansion, with its lack of diversity in curricula at different levels and in different divisions of higher education. Consequently, Chinese graduates lacked the expertise and flexibility to respond to market demand.

There are a variety of other serious undesired consequences of the policy. First, there is a major concern about the decline in higher education quality. Quality inputs, especially quality faculty, could not be developed as rapidly as needed. During the expansion, a few specialized institutes offering two-year courses upgraded themselves into colleges, and some colleges enlarged their programs—in both cases without sufficient attention to quality. Although the CMOE had required that universities ensure their teaching quality after the enrollment expansion in 1999 when the policy was about to be implemented, to improve or even maintain teaching quality remained a serious challenge for nearly all HEIs because of the high demand for more investment in resources and time. The expansion was so fast and the pressures for HEIs to pay off their debts so intense that many of the providers turned into diploma mills, churning out poorly qualified students.

As tuition fees become an increasingly important financial resource for higher institutions, the expansion of enrollment is given priority over the creation of a good teaching and learning environment. Priorities are also given to the expansion of office buildings over laboratory and library facilities, to the creation of profitable programs over the improvement of academic programs, and to the creation of large, "comprehensive" universities through merger and acquisition over the restructuring and consolidating of merged institutions for a more efficient use of educational resources.

One indicator is student-teacher ratio, which has been used by the Chinese government to raise the efficiency of higher education resource utilization and boost staff salaries and welfare. Compared with the unprecedented growth of the student population, the increase in academic staff in regular higher learning institutions has been slow, rising from 404,000 in 1997 to more than 1 million in 2006. The ratio rose from 9.8:1 in 1997 to 16:1 in 2006 (Zhao and Sheng 2008, 6). The decline in quality has also been confirmed by public opinion surveys. In 2006, when asked whether China's higher education system had been successful, only 2.1 percent of 4,802 respondents responded positively, while 92.3 percent was negative. One main factor leading to such decline is insufficient qualified teaching staff. A recent survey amongst teachers in HEIs in Beijing found that the average class size for undergraduate, master's, and doctoral courses were 83, 35, and 19 respectively, and 52 percent of the surveyed teachers thought there were not enough teachers and their teaching load was too heavy (Wu and Zheng 2008).

The second issue is the rampant illegal fee collection in higher education, which is both profiteering and an abuse of public power. Justified as a way to achieve "cost recovery," university tuition fees were introduced as part of the targeted diversification of education funding. However, as fees surged, real diversification never materialized. Instead, tuition fees have become one of the two major revenue sources for public universities. Tuition at many Chinese universities had increased by 20 percent by 2000 (Min 2001). The rapid expansion of university enrollments accelerated this trend. Public universities charged 4,000 RMB in 1999, reached 5,000 RMB in 2001, while some private institutions and the for-profit independent colleges affiliated to public universities charged well above 10,000 RMB. In 2003, 40 billion RMB in fees was changed by HEIs, in contrast to the national expenditure of 70 billion RMB on higher education in total. China's higher education had become the most expansive in the world, relative to the average resident's income.[3]

While students are human resources in the eyes of the government, they are buyers to universities, which took the opportunities to deepen their pockets. This often led to illegal charges. The national government audited 18 institutions in 2003 and found that 868 million RMB was illegally gained, representing 14.5 percent of all their charges and a 32 percent increase over 2002 (Luo and Ye 2005). From 1999 to 2005, the average annual tuition fee paid by college students increased from 3,335 RMB to 5,365 RMB. In many independent colleges, which are primarily funded by tuition fees, the annual tuition fees could reach as high as 15,000 RMB. The minimum cost for an average student could be well above 10,000 RMB a year, which is a huge financial burden for most rural and many urban households (Zhao and Sheng 2008).

Third, with the introduction of tuition and miscellaneous fees comes the issue of access to higher education for poor rural and urban families. It is somewhat ironic to see such a loss of higher education opportunities in the movement toward massification. Availability of higher education does not mean accessibility for many poor youngsters if their families do not have the capacity to pay in the first place. Unequal access to higher education has contributed to a widening economic and social inequality. There are two dimensions of such inequality. First, as a direct result of the increase of higher education costs and the illegal charges, disparities in educational inequality are widening between social classes and urban/rural communities. Among the rural school-age children, 80 percent do not have the opportunity to compete for university entrance examination, and thus few rural students have the opportunity to receive higher education. Inequalities have been repeatedly confirmed by studies, especially since the 1990s.

The issue of university students from impoverished rural areas began to catch people's attention from 1997, because of the surging tuition and accommodation fees charged by universities. Rising fees have substantially increased the difficulties of poor rural families in sending their children to HEIs, especially to the prestigious universities. Zhang and Liu (2005) revealed an inverted pyramid shape of the disparities among different social strata: the more prestigious institutions had a lower percentage of rural students. They collected data from China's most prestigious Peking and Tsinghua universities, which have a concentration of the best of the nation's higher education resources and produce "the elite of the elite," to show striking urban-rural disparities. Among their undergraduate students, 17.8 percent were from rural areas, while the overall national population proportion from rural regions of the country was 70 percent.

It is extremely difficult even for those already enrolled to complete their university education. By the late 1990s, when student fees were considered relatively low, a student needed at least 10,000 to 10,500 RMB annually for a 10-month academic year. Such an amount was already astronomical for many rural families. According to a survey in Shandong province, only 8.01 percent students' families could cope with the entire amount on their own, 22.43 percent could only manage half of the amount, 43.68 percent could afford less than one third, and 10.2 percent students felt absolutely helpless to raise the amount (Yang 2007, 235).

According to a survey among graduates in regular HEIs carried out by Peking University, 41.6 percent of respondents believe that social networks provide the most efficient job-seeking channel (Li et al. 2008). Such social capital is precisely what poor working-class families lack, both in rural and urban areas. Consequently, affordability is increasingly an issue for low-income families, and education has become one of the three most singled out financial burdens, together with soaring housing and health care costs. There have been rising concerns that students from poor families may choose to work rather than study in anticipation of the prohibitively high cost in higher education. In this sense, the expansion policy has contributed to the exacerbation of the already large socioeconomic divide.

Another major dimension of China's inequality in higher education is geographical. There are great disparities in the distribution of higher education. China's national higher learning resources have always concentrated in a few major cities. The concentration has been further enhanced by the recent rapid expansion. At present, 26 percent of China's top-tier universities and 30 percent of the universities under the jurisdiction of the central government are located in Beijing where the gross higher education enrollment rate exceeds 50 percent, which is more than double the national average. At the other end of the spectrum, 42 percent of regular HEIs are located in medium or small-sized municipals outside provincial capitals. They are marginalized as they lack central and provincial government support and have limited financial capacity.

The fourth issue relates to university debts which have hurt China's higher learning institutions, the higher education system, and the nation very hard. In order to generate income, many universities have been resorting to developing "university towns," where there is a concentration of branch campuses of public universities operating as private businesses. In 2004, there were 249 university branch campuses established, with an intake of 680,000 students. Many of the "university towns" have financial irregularities. The Oriental University City in Langfang, Hebei, for example, owed a scandalous 2.2 billion RMB in debt (Yang 2006). With proportionate decreasing of government funding, Chinese universities tapped into alternative sources to finance their radical expansion. Apart from charging higher tuition fees, many universities turned to banks for relentless lending as both universities and banks believed that the government would come to their rescue should the university fall into a financial crisis. Bank loans are estimated to total 150–200 billion RMB in the past decade, substantially more than the government spending on higher education in any single year (Zhao and Sheng 2008). Hundreds of universities across China are crippled by debt. Some, such as Jilin University, have difficulty paying even the interests of bank loans (Cai and Zhang 2007).

University towns are strongly supported by local officials as one of the most easily seen achievements in their political career. They have overexpanded into "image projects." Together with some political intentions are serious issues of financial corruption, as they occupy a great deal of cultivated land acquired at low prices from the government on condition that they are used for educational purposes and large-scale construction work is needed in building them. Jiansu, for example, built three university towns in Nanjing with the capacity to host 600,000 students. Only 200,000 high school students sit for the national college entrance examination in Jiangsu every year, with 25 percent eventually going to universities in other provinces. The three university towns would be large enough to accommodate all Jiangsu students. The university town in Guangzhou covers an area of 43.3 square kilometers which required an investment of more than 30 billion RMB. Many of them are in debt crisis because of the much lower returns than what they had expected. A notorious example is the Eastern University Town in Zhengzhou (Zhao and Sheng 2008).

Although the unintended social consequences of the expansion policy have become increasingly evident and have affected the Chinese government, higher education providers, students, and their parents, it is necessary to reiterate that the policy was made hurriedly and partially in 1998 in the midst of the Asian financial crisis when the then Chinese Premier Zhu Rongji ordered universities to open their doors, with the assumption that a more skilled Chinese workforce would jump-start domestic consumption, helping to wean China's economy off exports. It is also important to note that even against a backdrop of such consequences, some of those who supported the policymaking still see the trend optimistically. For example, Hu Angang, one of the original proposers of the policy compares China's expansion with that in the United States after World War II when the GI Bill allowed returning soldiers to attend college, thus opening higher education to broad reaches of society and supporting the nation's long-term economic rise. He insists that the current problems in China will work themselves out in the long run. "China's expansion was correct. It was part of a new deal launched to spread education beyond the elites" (Johnson 2009, A1).

Conclusion

Market relevance is becoming a key orientating criterion for the selection of discourses, their relation to each other, their forms, and their research (Bernstein 1996). The impact of this movement is particularly damaging to education in countries with a substantial population of poor people, such as China. The rapid transition from free education to a fee-based system has taken a heavy toll on China's poor families, many of whom see education as their only way out of poverty. China's situation demonstrates how serious these issues are and their detrimental social effects, especially in developing (not accidentally, non-Western) countries, due to the strikingly different sociocultural traditions compared with developed nations and the lack of relevant infrastructure required for the commoditization of education to operate properly. Developing countries will benefit from the prevailing neoliberal form of globalization only if they possess what most of them manifestly lack: sound institutions. Without the necessary support of institutional infrastructure and sociocultural traditions, the commoditization of education affects them even more seriously. Poor people in these countries have been particularly affected by the combination of the lack of democracy and widespread corruption in the societies (Yang 2006).

Here, it is important to point out the Chinese government's inaction. The Chinese state has always been strong in education, even against a backdrop of decentralization and devolution (Yang 2004). For years, government expenditure on education has fluctuated between 2.0 to 3.5 percent of GDP (United Nations Development Program 2005), a far cry from what has been recommended by UNESCO, and lower than the 4.0 percent promised by the government in the program. The percentage reached a plateau around 2.0 percent during the 1990s, when commercialization of education was like a ranging fire, reflecting the government's tacit consent to it. As a result of the reallocation of educational resources based on a principle of financial capacity to pay fees, China's public education contributes to social divides, instead of promoting equity and equality. As policy can also be defined as what governments choose not to do (Hogwood and Gunn 1984), the state's inaction shows its role in promoting commoditization of education, in view of the dramatic current situation.

On a positive note, by adopting decentralization and making use of market forces in the educational arena, more social forces have been encouraged to provide educational services. Meanwhile, the initiatives and enthusiasm of universities and local governments have been enhanced, and the scale of higher education has expanded rapidly within a relatively short period. By utilizing both market-based and regulatory interventions, China is trying to get the mix of state, market, and civil society right. Without necessarily being fully committed to the ideologies underpinning new governance strategies, including decentralization and marketization, the Chinese government has been driven mainly by pragmatic considerations to make use of market forces and new initiatives from the nonstate sectors to mobilize more educational resources. In fact, since its open-door policy was introduced, China has been attempting to apply a capitalist form of governance into a socialist system (Bray and Li 1992). This is precisely where the dilemma lies. Chinese policy makers cannot hope that it will work for China simply by putting the different modes together, without being able to tell where one stops and where the other starts. The costs and benefits in China's practice show the need for a focus on the local policy context, instead of a policy agenda steered solely by the global trends or the West (Steiner-Khamsi 2005). Chinese policy makers and researchers need to critically negotiate the global/Western customs and traditions with their own ones.

Notes

1. In this chapter, "China" refers to mainland China for ease of expression. I recognize that, in constitutional terms, Hong Kong, Macao, and Taiwan are all parts of China.
2. Confucian traditions are particularly featured by the great value they attach to education. The purpose of Confucian education is to transmit and develop knowledge as well as to

deliver and apply values. Relatively, little emphasis is placed on material gains (de Bary 2007).
3. For example, in 1999, the average incomes of peasant and urban residents in the east region were 3,344.6 and 9,125.92 RMB, respectively, while in the West they were 1,604.1 and 4,472.91 RMB, respectively.

References

Apple, Michael W. 2000. "Between Neoliberalism and Neoconservatism: Education and Conservatism in a Global Context." In *Globalization and Education: Critical Perspectives*, eds. N. C. Burbules and C. A. Torres. New York: Routledge.
Bai, Limin. 2006. "Graduate Unemployment: Dilemmas and Challenges in China's Move to Mass Higher Education." *The China Quarterly* 185: 128–144.
Bernstein, Basil. 1996. *Pedagogy, Symbolic Control and Identity: Theory, Research, Critique*. London: Taylor & Francis.
Blaug, Mark, Richard Layard, and Maureen Woodhall, eds. 1969. *The Causes of Graduate Unemployment in India*. London: Allen Lane (Penguin).
Bray, Mark, and Shouxin Li. 1992. "Attempting a Capitalist Form of Financing in a Socialist System: Student Loans in the People's Republic of China." *Higher Education* 23 (4): 375–387.
Burbules, Nicholas C., and Carlos Alberto Torres, 2000. "Globalization and Education: An Introduction." In *Globalization and Education: Critical Perspectives*, eds. N. C. Burbules and C. A. Torres. New York: Routledge.
Cai, Yugao, and Xiaojing Zhang. 2007. "Expansion, Construction and Asthenic Fever: Keywords of the Universities with Huge Debts." *China View*, March 16. http://news.xinhuanet.com.
Carnoy, Martin. 2000. *Sustaining the New Economy in the Information Age: Reflections on Our Changing World*. University Park, PA: Pennsylvania State University Press.
China's Ministry of Education (CMOE). 1998–2007. *Bulletin of Statistics on National Education Development*. Beijing: CMOE. http://www.edu.cn.
Clark, Burton R. 1983. *The Higher Education System: Academic Organization in Cross-National Perspective*. Los Angeles: University of California Press.
Coaldrake, Peter. 2000. "Reflections on the Repositioning of the Government's Approach to Higher Education, or I'm Dreaming of a White Paper." *Journal of Higher Education Policy and Measurement* 22 (1): 10–21.
Dale, Roger. 2000. "Globalization: A New World for Comparative Education?" In *Discourse Formation in Comparative Education*, ed. J. Schriewer. New York: Peter Lang.
de Bary, Wm. Theodore. 2007. *Confucian Tradition and Global Education*. Hong Kong: The Chinese University of Hong Kong Press.
Dong, Yunchuan. 2003. "Trinity: The Relationship between the University, Government and Society." [In Chinese] *Fudan Education Forum* 1 (6): 6–9.
Hogwood, Brian W., and Lewis A. Gunn. 1984. *Policy Analysis for the Real World*. Oxford: Oxford University Press.
Hu, Angang, and Zulin Shi. 2000. "Quicken the Step to Reform the Higher Education in Our Country." In *China Education Policy Review 2000*, ed. Z. G. Yuan [in Chinese]. Beijing: Educational Science Publishing House.
Johnson, Ian. 2009. "China Faces a Grad Glut after Boom at Colleges." *The Wall Street Journal*, April 28, A1.

Kaufmann, Daniel, Aart Kraay, and Massimo Mastruzzi. 2005. *Governance Matters IV: Governance Indicators for 1996–2004*. Washington, DC: World Bank.
Kenway, Jane, and Diana Langmead. 1998. "Governmentality, the 'Now' University and the Future of Knowledge Work." *Australian Universities Review* 41 (2): 28–32.
Knill, Christoph, and Dirk Lehmkuhl. 2002. "Private Actors and the State: Internationalization and Changing Patterns of Governance." *Governance* 15 (1): 41–63.
Lao, Kaisheng. 2003. "Challenges to the Public-Welfare Nature of Education." [In Chinese.] *Educational Research* 24 (2): 3–9.
Li, Fengliang, W. John Morgan, and Xiaohao Ding. 2008. "The Expansion of Higher Education, Employment and Over-Education." *International Journal of Educational Development* 28 (6): 687–697.
Li, Yan. 1999. "Economy Remains Healthy." *Beijing Review* 42 (32): 17–19.
Lin, Li. 2007. "University Graduates Face Tough Test in Guangdong Job Market." *China Daily*, August 2. http://news.xinhuanet.com.
Luo, Yan, and Fugui Ye. 2005. "The Elimination of Educational Industry?" In *Report on China's Educational Development: 2005*, ed. D. P. Yang [in Chinese]. Beijing: Social Sciences Academic Press.
Marginson, Simon W. 2002. "Nation-Building Universities in a Global Environment: The Case of Australia." *Higher Education* 43 (3): 409–428.
———. 2006. "Dynamics of National and Global Competition in Higher Education." *Higher Education* 52 (1): 1–39.
Marinetto, Michael. 1999. *Studies of the Policy Process*. London: Prentice Hall.
Meyer, Heinz-Dieter, and William L. Boyd, eds. 2001. *Education between States, Markets and Civil Society: Comparative Perspectives*. New Jersey: Lawrence Erlbaum Associates.
Min, Weifang. 2001. "Current Trends in Higher Education Development in China." *International Higher Education* 22 (Winter): 22–24.
Mok, Ka-Ho. 2001. "From State Control to Governance: Decentralization and Higher Education in Guangdong, China." *International Review of Education* 47 (1): 123–149.
———. 2005. "Globalization and Governance: Educational Policy Instruments and Regulatory Arrangements." *International Review of Education*, 51 (4): 289–311.
Neave, Guy, and Frans van Vught. 1994. *Government and Higher Education Relationship across Three Continents: The Winds of Change*. Exeter, NH: BPC Wheaton Ltd.
Pretorius, Stephanus G., and Yanqing Xue. 2003. "The Transition from Elite to Mass Higher Education: A Chinese Perspective." *Prospects* 33 (1): 89–101.
Sanyal, Bikas C. 1987. *Higher Education and Employment: An International Comparative Analysis*. London, New York, and Philadelphia: Falmer Press.
Steiner-Khamsi, Gita. 2005. "Non-Travelling 'Best Practice' for a Travelling Population: The Case of Nomadic Education in Mongolia." *European Educational Research Journal* 4 (1): 22–35.
Taylor, Sandra, Fazal Rizvi, Bob Lingard, and Miriam Henry. 1997. *Educational Policy and the Politics of Change*. London: Routledge.
Trow, Martin. 1974. "Problems in the Transition from Elite to Mass Higher Education." In *Policies for Higher Education*, ed. OECD. Paris: OECD.
———. 2000. "From Mass Higher Education to Universal Access: The American Advantage." *Minerva* 37 (4): 303–328.
United Nations Development Program (UNDP). 2005. *China Human Development Report 2005: Development with Equity*. New York: UNDP.
Urry, John. 1998. "Contemporary Transformations of Time and Space. In *The Globalization of Higher Education*, ed. P. Scott. Buckingham[England]; Philadelphia PA. Open University Press/SRHE.

Wang, Yingjie. 2006. "Financing Restructuring of Higher Education in China." Paper presented at the Sino-Swiss Project on Policy Dialogue on Financing Higher Education and Sustaining the Quality, Geneva, April 3, 2006.
World Bank. 1999. *Higher Education Reform*. Washington, DC: World Bank. www.worldbank.org.cn/English/content.
Wu, Bin, and Yongnian Zheng. 2008. "Expansion of Higher Education in China: Challenges and Implications." *Briefing Series*, Issue 36, The China Policy Institute, University of Nottingham, February.
Xi, Mi. 1999. "Market Confronts Education Reform." *Beijing Review* 42 (44): 21–22.
Xinhua News Agency. 2003. "China Gives Strategic Priority to Education: Minister." Xinhua News Agency, October 2. Beijing: Xinhua News Agency. http://www.china.org.cn.
———. 2007. "Hard for University Graduate to Find Jobs." Xinhua News Agency, March 4. Beijing: Xinhua News Agency. http://news.xinhuanet.com.
———. 2008. "More Difficult for Graduates from Social Sciences and Humanities to Seek Employment." Xinhua News Agency, January 16. Beijing: Xinhua News Agency. http://news.xinhuanet.com.
Yang, Rui. 2004. "Toward Massification: Higher Education Development in the People's Republic of China since 1949." In *Higher Education: Handbook of Theory and Research*, ed. J. Smart. Dordrecht,.The Netherlands: Kluwer.
———. 2006. "The Commodification of Education and Its Effects on Developing Countries: A Focus on China." *Journal Für Entwicklungspolitik* XXII (4): 52–69.
———. 2007. "Urban-Rural Disparities in Educational Equality: China's Pressing Challenge in a Context of Economic Growth and Political Change." In *International Handbook of Urban Education*, ed. W. Pink. Dordrecht, The Netherlands: Springer.
———. 2009. "International Organizations and Asian Higher Education: The Case of China." In *International Organizations and Higher Education Policy: Thinking Globally, Acting Locally?*, ed. R. M. Bassett and A. Maldonado-Maldonado. New York: Routledge.
Ye, Pengfei. 2008. "China's National and Local Leaders Meet to Face a New Serious Challenge." [In Chinese.] *Lianhe Zaobao*, June 14. http://www.zaobao.com.
Zhang, Minxuan. 1998. "Changing Conceptions of Equity and Student Financial Support Policies." In *Higher Education in Post-Mao China*, eds. M. Agelasto, and B. Adamson. Hong Kong: Hong Kong University Press.
Zhang, Yulin, and Baojun Liu. 2005. "Professional Strata and Higher Education, Opportunities in China." [In Chinese.] *Journal of Beijing Normal University* 3: 71–75.
Zhao, Litao, and Sixin Sheng. 2008. "Fast and Furious: Problems of China's Higher Education Expansion." *East Asian Institute Background Brief No. 395*. National University of Singapore.

Chapter 4

Incorporation of National Universities of Korea: Dynamic Forces, Key Features, and Challenges

Byung-Shik Rhee

Introduction

Educational reform crosses national borders more frequently than it has in the past. As soon as higher education reform is initiated in one place, usually in an advanced country, a variation is soon discovered elsewhere in the world. Incorporation of national universities is one such reform. It began in the United Kingdom and migrated to other European countries, such as Germany, Austria, and France. Now we see it taking root in Asian countries, including Mainland China, Japan, Hong Kong, Singapore, and soon Korea. The changes that accompany incorporation have serious ramifications for public institutions of higher education. Corporate status forces institutions out of their government's administrative control and places them in a disadvantaged and uncomfortable position with regard to their former patron.

Many scholarly explanations have been provided for the underlying causes of this emerging trend. Globalization has been frequently cited as a distal but influential force. Some other potential drivers include financial constraints, shifting educational policy paradigms (Mok 2005), a misaligned national policy environment, system design and work processes (Richardson et al. 1999), and other "perennial issues" (McGuinness 1999). Three theoretical approaches—new public management, entrepreneurialism, and academic capitalism—are useful for understanding the recent changes in the governance of higher education (Sporn 2006). While these conceptions shed light on the external conditions or contexts for the incorporation of national universities, which is increasingly regarded as a viable policy option for public higher education reform, we have only begun to understand the interaction among global, national, and local forces that influence its adoption and shape (Mok and Lo 2002).

Despite surprising similarities in the rationale or rhetoric for the incorporation of national universities among the adoptive countries, there are considerable differences in their key features because governance structures are cultural configurations (Tierney 2004). For example, China has adopted a "supervisory model," whereas a "contract model" characterizes Japanese incorporation (Huang 2006). Governance models also vary depending on the traditional relationship among the higher education institutions (HEIs), the government, and the market in the respective countries. While shared governance is a dominant form of institutional governance in the United States, a corporate model is emerging in European countries. When examining the other specific aspects of incorporation, one can often find more differences than similarities.

This chapter investigates the dynamics of the global, national, and local forces that propel the incorporation of national universities in Korea and analyzes key features of incorporation. This is followed by a discussion of the hidden triggers, emerging patterns, and remaining issues and challenges. Three research questions guide this study: First, what factors at the global, national, and local levels drive the incorporation of national universities in Korea? Second, what are the main features of the incorporation of Korean national universities? Finally, how can this framework of incorporation be improved?

Background on Public Higher Education in Korea

Higher Education System

The history of modern higher education in Korea is relatively brief. The oldest private university celebrates its 125th anniversary in 2010. The national universities are even younger. The first public institution of higher education, Seoul National University (SNU), came into existence only about 60 years ago. The government has traditionally assumed strong leadership in higher education; but as society democratizes and globalizes, its influence has gradually eroded. However, the government remains influential in setting agendas for higher education.

Over the last few decades, Korean institutions of higher education have expanded substantially in size and in type. There are seven legally approved types of colleges and universities, which include universities (four to six years), junior colleges (two to three years), teachers' colleges, industrial universities, technical colleges, open (cyber) universities, and other college-level institutions offering mostly nondegree programs.[2] The Korean higher education system is also characterized by private institutions making up a large proportion of total HEIs: roughly 85 percent of HEIs are private.

Current Status of National Universities

Fifty-two national universities have been established by the Korean government. These institutions, except for SNU, were established in local provinces in the 1950s and 1970s to serve regional needs for higher education. National universities have been relatively well-funded compared to private HEIs, which rely mainly on tuition fees for their revenue (on average 70 percent of total revenue). The government is a primary source of revenue for national universities (about 60 percent). Students also contribute a sizable portion (about 30 percent). Substantial government support enables national universities to keep their tuition roughly 40 percent lower than their private counterparts.[3] These three factors—reliable revenue from the government, relatively low tuition, and the economy of scale[4]—have helped to maintain a teaching and learning environment attractive to university staff, as well as to students who are competent but economically disadvantaged. Financial advantage, however, is gained at the price of institutional autonomy. Since national universities are a part of the government, their structure and management are regulated by law. This restricts university leaders from running institutions at their discretion. Furthermore, the absence of a buffer organization between the government and educational institutions makes them susceptible to the decisions of the government, especially those of the KMOE.

Policy Context: Society, Government, and Higher Education Reforms

Societal Changes

In recent years, Korean higher education has seen significant changes in its external environment at the national and global levels. At the macro level, supranational organizations, such as the Organisation for Economic Co-operation and Development (OECD) and World Bank continue to have a powerful influence on higher education policies. After Korea joined the OECD in 1997, pressure on system transparency and regulatory reform has intensified. The OECD has reviewed the Korean government's policies in 26 areas, including public governance and management and education, for the past decade. Recently, the OECD completed three major reviews of national policies governing higher education (Duke et al. 2006; Grubb et al. 2006; OECD 2006). In those reviews, the OECD consistently recommended that an indirect or supervisory role for the government would be preferable in higher education, and that the government should devote more energy to developing a context or policies that nurture institutional autonomy and accountability.

A massive expansion of college enrollment is another distinct trend in Korean higher education. Current statistics show that three out of four high school graduates enroll in college, compared to one-third of high school graduates in college in 1980. The steep increase in college student enrollment should be accompanied by a comparable increase in public funding for higher education. In reality, however, the increase in funding was not as steep as that for primary and secondary education. For example, from 2000 to 2006, public funds for primary and secondary education increased at an average annual rate of 7.9 percent, compared to 6.7 percent for higher education. The sharp upward curve in college enrollment with only a slight increase in public funds for higher education would have enticed higher education institutions to increase tuition fees. Under such circumstances, where the government intervenes in higher education pricing and students protest against tuition increases, the quality of education has been gradually compromised, instead. There is abundant evidence that Korean higher education fails to live up to the public expectations for quality education, and even top-ranked institutions such as SNU fall behind world class universities in competing countries (International Institute for Management Development 2008; *Times Higher Education* 2008).

The demographic landscape is also worth noting. Korea's birth rate (1.19 percent in 2008), which is among the lowest in the world, coupled with the widening gap between the number of high school graduates and the college student enrollment capacity, will likely cause higher education to shift from a supply-oriented market to one driven by demand . Figure 4.1 shows that without downsizing or reaching out to the latent group of college students, HEIs are likely to offer more seats than needed and the gap between supply and demand will drastically widen in 2015.

The economic crisis in 1997 had a severe impact on Korean society. Many sectors were forced to restructure and undergo massive layoffs. Companies even changed their recruitment patterns; they preferred to hire experienced workers over recent college graduates to save on training and education costs. Society, HEIs as a social system, and students are all connected and interact (Dey and Hurtado 1999). The massive scale of changes in the private and public sectors fundamentally changed the public's view of higher education. College students witnessed layoffs and encountered difficulty in getting decent jobs. They started to flock to the fields of study that appeared to guarantee better jobs, such as business, law, and medicine, and to ask their institutions to offer more courses that would help them get a job. It has also affected students' college choices. Students who are more concerned with their employment after graduation prefer to go to the universities near the Seoul metropolitan area, where more job opportunities are available. Society apparently has become more cost-conscious, job-oriented, and wary of uncertainties.

Dynamics Within the Government

Deregulation in the public sector has been pursued since the early 1990s. Starting with the Presidential Committee on Administrative Reform in 1993, various ad hoc organizations were formed within the government, including the Regulatory Committee for Economic Administration (in March 1993 under the Economic Planning Bureau), the Business Activity Regulatory Deliberation Committee (in August 1993 within the Commerce, Industry, and Resource Department), and the Joint Council for Administrative Regulations (in May 1994 with members from both the private and public sectors). These committees initiated intensive regulatory

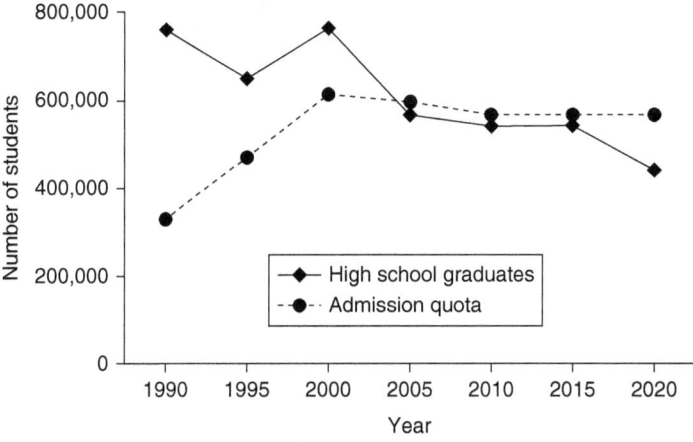

(a) Number of high school graduates and college enrollment capacities, 1990–2020

(b) Birth rates, 1970–2008

Figure 4.1 Demographic Landscape

Note: College enrollment capacity beyond 2010 was assumed to remain the same and the number of high school graduates between 2010 and 2020 was estimated based on the number of elementary and secondary students and their respective advancement rates in corresponding years.

Source: Ministry of Education and Human Resources Development (1990–2009); Korea National Statistics Office (1970–2008).

reforms in the public sector (Kim and Rhee 2002). Deregulation was pursued some time later in the education sector. KMOE, for example, dropped all of the administrative orders that they had issued themselves that were valid to the end of 1996. Beginning in 1997, all administrative orders that were not separately deliberated were abolished. As of 1999, all new regulations are submitted to the Educational Deregulation Committee for review before implementation. In addition, all central administrative bodies, including KMOE, register all regulations with the Regulatory Reform Committee. More recently, the Institutional Autonomy Promotion Committee was established in December 2003 as a subsidiary to the KMOE. This committee's role is to expedite regulatory reform in higher education.

As the higher education subsector expands, so does the government's role as regulator. The current higher education policies and programs being carried out by the government show that multiple central ministries are involved in the business of higher education. For example, KMOE and seven other agencies financially support research projects in science and technology, such as Brain Korea 21, World Class University, and Global Frontier Project. The projects for industry-university cooperation are sponsored not only by many central ministries including the Ministry of Commerce, Industry, and Energy, the Ministry of Science and Technology, and the Ministry of Information and Communication, but also intergovernmental organizations such as the Presidential Committee on Balanced National Development. It is evident that many higher education programs go beyond what KMOE traditionally leverages, such as labor market linkage, industry-academia cooperation, and technologically advanced research. The policies and programs dispersed across the ministries apparently require intergovernmental coordination for their implementation. Currently, the National Science and Technology Committee (NSTC), chaired by the president of Korea, evaluates and supervises projects in the field of science and technology that cost more than KRW10 billion. Beginning in 2001, the Human Resource Development Council (HRDC), chaired by the Minister of Education,[5] began overseeing all matters related to human resource development policies. Both the NSTC and the HRDC are limited in that they focus on their respective fields and are unable to cover all aspects of higher education.[6]

Recent Higher Education Reforms

The government continues to deal with issues that have arisen from the practices of the old days, which include quantitative expansion of higher education for access and concentration of resources for efficiency. The way the government has handled these newly emerging issues shows its inclination to ensure institutional accountability through market competition and financial incentives (Son 2002). The Roh administration (2004–2008) had set the diversification of higher education institutions and the development of local universities as top priorities. To this end, KMOE actively sought structural reforms of colleges and universities. In 2006, eight national colleges and universities that offered similar programs or were believed to have a synergistic effect when merged were consolidated into four universities. Altogether, about KRW80 billion was provided to support their restructuring. KMOE managed to carry out the structural reform of national universities with an approval of legislators and its financial partners, the Ministry of Planning and Budget and the Ministry of Finance and Economy. The cost to the government for restructuring national universities was estimated to be KRW250 billion for 2006 to 2009 (Rhee et al. 2006). The government expected the restructuring funds to help national universities develop specialty areas in alignment with the national strategic industries of the region as set out by the Roh administration.

Regional development was also among the top priorities of the Roh administration, which was evident in its tremendous effort to relocate the nation's capital even when it put the president at risk for impeachment. The government planned to relocate its agencies and research institutes to reinforce the link among industry, academy, government, and research institutes. Major competitive funding projects, such as Brain Korea 21 (first stage: 1999–2005 with KRW1.3 trillion; second stage: 2006–2012 with KRW2.03 trillion), New University for Regional Innovation (2004–2008 with KRW1.4 trillion) and industry-academy cooperation programs, were designed to strengthen the link between key stakeholders in research and development and serve regional economic needs.

The Roh administration, in collaboration with the opposing party, which had a majority in the National Assembly, had also initiated a controversial reform (effective July 1, 2006) relating to the governance of private schools. The reform targeted all private schools, including colleges and universities, and was intended to increase the external influence on school management through the school operation committee (university council for private HEIs) composed of teachers, parents, and outside parties. The increased influence of external members on school management is believed to make schools more accountable to society. The confrontation between the government and the owners of private HEIs, however, did not appear to be as serious as that between the government and the owners of primary and secondary schools. Nevertheless, private HEIs also faced increasing influence of external stakeholders and more diverse internal constituents. National universities were also likely to experience more pressure from external stakeholders since they were accountable to regional communities as well as to their old allies, the government agencies.

The Lee administration's higher education policy appears to remain consistent with those of its predecessors. Nevertheless, the market will play an increasing role in Korean higher education reform in the near future. The School Information Disclosure Act, which was passed in May 2008, required HEIs to make information on the educational conditions of school and institutional performance available to the public, such as student enrollment indices and employment rates. Furthermore, a newly enacted law requires that HEIs should carry out institutional self-evaluation every other year and release the results online starting in 2010. It stands to reason that college choice patterns and university behavior are expected to change substantially once the information is available to the general public.

Development of Incorporation

While the initial discussion of giving corporate status to the national universities started more than a decade ago (Educational Reform Committee 1987), it has received renewed attention in the last six years. The government is actively seeking a policy tool for reforming national universities. KMOE hinted about a plan to draft a bill on the incorporation of national universities in 2007, which ignited a heated debate. Besides the constituents of the national universities, political parties and nongovernmental organizations (NGOs) also joined the discussion. Proponents, including KMOE, government agencies, and the legislature, posited that the incorporation of national universities would strengthen institutional competitiveness, enhance efficiency, and help institutions to better serve local communities by the increased flexibility of institutional management. The opposition, mostly made up of faculty representatives, labor unions, and student organizations, was suspicious of the government's concealed intention. Among their counterarguments were the following: the government should be financially responsible for higher education; incorporation would lead to a widening institutional gap and basic disciplines, such as the humanities, would collapse; and, finally, tuition would likely increase.

From the early stages of discussion, university constituents appeared to prefer the British model, in which the management of public HEIs remains independent even though they are government agencies (Lee 2002). In contrast, KMOE's proposal drafted in early 2007 resembled the Japanese model, in which national universities are legally separated from the government (Yamamoto 2004). While the conflict between the two groups continues, the incorporation of national universities has moved forward. The National University Corporation (NUC) Ulsan University of Science and Technology was established by a majority vote at the National Assembly on March 6, 2007.

Three days after the bill was approved by the legislature, KMOE proposed a general law that would establish an NUC that would apply to all national universities. This proposal was refined further and presented to legislators for formal review in June 2007. Unfortunately, the proposed bill faced harsh opposition from faculty members at national universities and failed to go through the National Assembly.

While the enactment of the general law was bogged down in the legislature, individual universities including SNU and University of Incheon managed to reach a consensus on their own incorporation plan. After conducting a series of self-studies and a myriad of discussions, SNU was announced that they would be incorporated in 2011. The University of Incheon, a city university, goes one step ahead as their incorporation bill is under the legislators' review.

The process of incorporating national universities in Korea is slow, but it is moving forward. Despite several years of hard work, Korea has only one corporate national university and two others to be incorporated sometime in 2011. As the government intended from the beginning, national universities in Korea are being incorporated one by one. As a result, each national university to hold a corporate status comes to have its own incorporation proposal. Although it is true that the three national universities have their own incorporation plans, they share many things in common simply because they are grounded in KMOE's general law. In this regard, this chapter will use KMOE's proposed bill to identify the key features of the incorporation of Korean national universities.

Key Features of Incorporation

The KMOE continues to refine the general law that will be used to incorporate the existing national universities. In the meantime, an institutional version of the general law which was adapted to a newly established Ulsan National University of Science & Technology, was passed by the legislature and implemented on July 6, 2007. It provides a framework for governing the national universities. This law fundamentally changed the relationship between the government and national universities and the way they are governed, funded, and evaluated. The central tenets of the incorporation are to give more institutional autonomy to the national universities and make them directly responsible for their performance.

Once incorporated, national universities are legally separated from the government. The NUC has ownership of public properties and facilities, except for national treasures such as extremely rare old books. It can loan, use, and profit from these properties. The new 2007 also lifted many of the managerial restrictions imposed by earlier legislation. Currently, the alteration of academic structure and appointment, that is, the transfer and promotion of administrative staff that belong to the central government, are no longer at the university president's discretion. Under the new law, the NUC presidents are given greater authority and flexibility to manage their respective institutions. The changes to the structure of the institutions, however, are inevitably accompanied by changes to university staff, who are no longer public servants. Academic staff is regarded as similar to their counterparts in private HEIs (to ensure accountability, however, university employees are subject to the same punishment as public servants). Administrative workers have two options can either to stay in their current institutions as employees of the respective universities or transfer to other government organizations and maintain their status as public servants.

The NUC will have its own governing board to act as a buffer between the government and the institution. The board will deliberate and make decisions on important internal affairs. The board will include both internal and external members, such as government officials, businesspeople, and professionals. Governance structure in the approved bill is different from what is described in the more recent KMOE draft. The initial proposal of the passed bill included two subcommittees, the Education and Research Committee and the Financial Management Committee.[7] These were dropped during the review of the education subcommittee at the national assembly. The assembly records show that legislators demanded the removal of the two subcommittees because their roles would overlap with those of other internal organizations, such as the faculty senate or association, labor union, and student association (National Assembly 2007).

The process of selecting of individuals to head institutions will also change. Currently, faculty members select their president, typically from among their colleagues. This direct selection of the president results from the democratization of Korean society. Previously, it was a routine practice for the government to select and appoint an external person as president. These individuals often lacked commitment to the university. In the new system, the governing board will select a president from among two or three candidates recommended by a Presidential Search Committee. In the latter case, however, the president is still formally appointed by the president of Korea, which further complicates the nature of the NUC.

Another distinct feature of the Korean incorporation plan mimics the Japanese system—the contract-based approach to financial resource allocation (Oba 2005). Currently, a funding formula that takes into account the number of students and

Table 4.1 Comparison of Key Differences between the Current System and Proposed NUC

Area	Current national university	Proposed NUC
Governance		
Legal status	A government subsidiary organization for education and training within KMOE	A special corporation independent of the government
Structure	No governing board; faculty senate (or association) as advisory body on academic affairs; collective bargaining allowed for administrative staff	Individual governing boards
Management		
Leadership	The president has limited authority on institutional management; the minister of education has responsibility for national universities by law	The president has full authority on institutional management
Selection of president	Selected by academic staff and formally appointed by the president of Korea	Selected by the governing board among the candidates recommended by the Presidential Search Committee; appointment practice remains the same
Structure/ organization	Regulated by law	At the individual institution's discretion
Personnel	The minister of education is involved in personnel management; staff members are public servants	Personnel management at the president's discretion; staff status is mixed, but most are not public servants
Profit-making activities	Not allowed	Allowed to the extent that these activities do not interfere with core functions of the university, i.e., teaching and research
Performance		
Goal setting	Not required	The president sets up a four-year performance plan in consultation with the minister of education
Evaluation	Self-evaluation; no link to funding	The minister of education or a designated agency reviews the performance; performance results linked to funding
Finance		
Funding	Central government grants	Central and local government grants; external private support; long-term loan and school bonds issue
Budgeting	Itemized budgets; budgeting guidelines	Bloc grants; the president's full discretion on planning budgets
Accounting	Fragmented accounts	Consolidated corporate account
Auditing	Multiple government organization; no formal auditing required	Internal and external audits by professional accountants

university staff is used to calculate the amount of money allocated to the universities. The new system necessitates the development of a performance-based funding formula to estimate who gets how much based on how many of their specified goals are achieved. Along with the shift to the performance-funding system, the itemized funding system will be replaced by lump-sum budgets, as is common in OECD countries (OECD 2003). The president of the NUC will be required to indicate institutional performance goals every four years in consultation with the minister of education. He or she must also announce a university management plan that reflects these goals at the start of each academic year. The minister will review institutions' performance and the results will be made public. Furthermore, performance results will be linked to the government's administrative and financial support.

The current accounting system of national universities is fragmented.[8] It has been criticized for the lack of transparency and inefficiency because university funds are managed by separate national and institutional accounts, which often disguises improper uses. As shown in Table 4.1, the new system will consolidate the separate accounts into a corporate account. In addition to the president's full discretion on the university funds, the new law allows the NUC to diversify its funding sources. Unlike the current system, which restricts external funds, the local government and private sectors will be permitted to make financial contributions through the board members. In addition, profit-making activities will be allowed, as long as they do not interfere with the university's core functions of teaching and research. On the other hand, the president of the NUC will be responsible for submitting an annual budget plan of revenue and expenditure to the minister of education and making the revenue and expenditure of the NUC public. As in the Japanese model, to ensure accountability, every NUC will undergo internal and external audits by professional accountants. The current system allows multiple supervisory organizations, including the KMOE, the Board of Audit and Inspection, and the National Assembly, to audit the universities' accounts, but no formal requirement for auditing has been imposed.

Discussion

Dynamics of Driving Forces

Multiple dimensions of global, national, and local forces have introduced new elements and problems to the governance and management of Korea's national universities (Marginson 2004). The global trends of deregulation, decentralization, and marketization have influenced the process of incorporating national universities in Korea. These general trends, however, do not adequately explain why the Korean government has chosen the current form of incorporation. A close look at proximal factors and their interaction with global and national forces should help us to better understand the reasons underlying the adoption of the current model and its unique features.

As previously noted, Korea faces radical changes in demographics and social values as well as redundancy in educational provision, which is common in other advanced countries. What is unique to Korea is that existing regional disparities create a challenging environment for restructuring national universities. Restructuring at the institutional level is difficult to pursue under the current regulatory framework. Thus, the need for change is enormous; and the KMOE also must change. Internally, the ministry is perceived to be falling behind with regulatory reform in the public sector (OECD 2006). The increasing complexity of governing HEIs along with the difficulty of coordination may be another reason for making national universities independent from government. But a more proximal reason for reorganization stems from KMOE's frustration with trying to move the national agenda on higher education reform forward. The structural reform intended to restructure national universities has often stalled over the determination of competitive fields of study and resource allocation at the institutional level. KMOE has had difficulty in ridding the system of duplicate programs, even at the consolidated campuses (Rhee et al. 2006).

Emerging Patterns

The incorporation of Korea's national universities is still in progress. Some of the features mentioned in this chapter may change. The emerging patterns, however, are more likely to persist unless there are significant, unexpected changes in the underlying forces. The proposed framework for incorporation reveals prospective trends in the way Korean public higher education will be governed. One apparent trend is toward an entrepreneurial university. The drafted KMOE bill clearly shows the government's intention to move in this direction. Although all the pieces are not yet in place, the bill aims to create an environment where entrepreneurial universities can flourish (Clark 1998). National universities, once incorporated, are expected to be given considerable autonomy, capacity for self-management, and diversified funding sources, all of which are severely limited under the current system.

Another expected development is for the government to reinforce its influence on national universities more indirectly, as is common in OECD countries and some areas of the United States (Richardson et al. 1999; OECD 2003). While national universities with independent corporate status appear to have more procedural autonomy, the KMOE developed an alternative mechanism that maintains its influence on institutional governance and management: government officials serve on the institutional governing board, the KMOE requires consultative goal setting that involves the minister of education, and institutions must submit annual budget plans to the ministry for review. To ensure that institutions are held accountable to multiple constituents, the changes in governance allow outside persons and students participate in decision making or deliberation over important internal matters. This line of action by the government is epitomized by their attempt to establish a new agency, arguably independent, that manages information on institutional performance and carries out evaluations of the HEIs.

The government is likely to switch to a "steering role," as noted by Richardson and colleagues (1999). Building upon Clark's (1984) framework of higher education systems consisting of three components—state, market, and academic oligarchy—they proposed four roles that the government can play, that is, provider of resources, regulator, consumer advocate, and market oriented guide. In the Korean case, the government plays a steering role that "structures the market for higher education services to produce outcomes consistent with governmental priorities" (Richardson et al. 1999, 14; Rhee 2008).

Design Flaw or Conflicting View

The proposed framework of governance still lacks some key elements. Among these is a quality assurance system. The new system obviously requires that institutional performance should be evaluated annually so that funds can be distributed accordingly. The university evaluation system in Korea is fragmented and needs substantial improvement. To address these issues, the KMOE attempted to establish a new organization to take over the job of institutional evaluation, which the Korean Council for University Education has headed since 1994. But negotiations with legislators have reached an impasse. The lawmakers perceived the new organization as the KMOE's attempt to increase its control over HEIs. The university evaluation law proposed by the ministry, which contains the establishment of the university evaluation institute, did not even make it to the general meeting of National Assembly for a vote. This is a somewhat delicate issue relating to the role of government. The legislators favor the increasing role of the market as opposed to the government in higher education. This is evident in their efforts to enact the School Information Disclosure Act and University Self-Evaluation Act. Unless this issue of who should evaluate institutional performance is addressed in a timely manner, the incorporation of national universities is likely to come to a halt or to be faulty.

The institutional governance structure also needs further refinement. Given the shared governance tradition in which academic staff plays an exclusive role in institutional management, the KMOE's proposal on the internal governance structure of the NUC has a radical element: it allows students, administrative staff, and even outsiders to partake in institutional financial management. This challenge to the traditional form of shared governance, however, was not successful. Legislators were concerned that the new committees might overlap existing organizations, such as faculty associations and unions. However, given that the revised Private School Law requires the establishment of a new university senate, consisting of diverse internal and external stakeholders, the structural flexibility allowed in the NUC seems ironic. If no further revisions are made, the internal governance structure of the NUC will resemble the traditional shared governance model.

Cultural Elements to Be Considered

As ambiguity and uncertainty rise in an organization, "sense-making" becomes more important (Weick 1995; Tierney 2004). What is missing in the discussion of the incorporation in Korea is serious talk about the mission of higher education, the role of national universities, and the government's expectations. Given its infancy and the complexity of influences shaping our higher education system, clear, agreed-upon ideas of the university have yet to be developed (Kim 1994). The past decade witnessed an expansion of the traditional university mission (i.e., teaching and knowledge creation) to encompass collaborative activities with industries and profit-making businesses Consequently HEIs in Korea face "the paradox of scope," that is, the blurring of traditional boundaries of the institution (Collis 2004). The discussion also lacks specificity as to what national universities are expected to do, and how their roles should be different from others in the system. The state of California provides a good example of clarifying the mission of the higher education system (Greenwood 2005). The consensus on the role of national universities, whether explicit or implicit, is particularly important during a financial retrenchment. Since research universities typically receive more research funds from the government and private sector, if national universities lack a clear role or mission, once incorporated they may be tempted to do more research at the expense of teaching, especially at the undergraduate level, as the resource-dependent theory would predict (Pfeffer and Salancik 1978).

Designing a sophisticated governance structure is just one element necessary for the effective performance of higher education. Meaning matters more in our discussion of incorporation. In following the current discourse on incorporation, however, we frequently encounter with deficiency inthe elements that are considered important, in the cultural perspective, for improving academic governance: trust, a common language, identity, and walking the talk. Because each of these elements is not yet sufficiently developed in our discourse on incorporation in Korea, the effective functioning of the new governance is less guaranteed.

Conclusion

This chapter suggests that the investigation of the complex interplay among global, national, and local forces helps us to better understand the reasons behind the incorporation of national universities and the timing of its adoption. More specifically, to fully understand this trend the dynamics between the government agencies, a broader range of higher education policies and their implementation, and the country-specific policy context should be reviewed. In Korea, global trends toward deregulation, decentralization, and marketization shape the framework of incorporation. More proximal and invisible forces—such as the increasing complexity of governing HEIs, pressures from within the government, and consistency with concurrent higher education reforms—may explain the reasons for the adoption of incorporation in Korea.

This also shows that the incorporation of Korean national universities follows general trends that can be observed in other parts of the world (OECD 2003). The unique features of the Korean higher education system interact with the driving forces at the global, national, and local levels to shape the key features of incorporation. The Korean model is a hybrid; a mixture of the "supervised" and "contract-based" models.

The system can be improved in many ways and the cultural perspective may enlighten us on how to refine the governance system of higher education. University constituents in Korea will be better off when we know where we are heading and we align our roles in relation to others in the system and, finally, when stakeholders in Korean higher education community can trust each other on what we are doing. There challenges ahead for everyone working toward the goal of providing strong institutions of higher education in Korea.

Notes

1. The Korea Ministry of Education (KMOE) was renamed Ministry of Education and Human Resources Development (MEHRD) in January 2001 and Ministry of Education, Science and Technology (MEST) in February 2008. For the purposes of this chapter, I use the acronym KMOE to represent the Korean Ministry of Education, MEHRD, and MEST.
2. Among these types, university and junior college are dominant. About 43 percent of the HEIs are universities while 36 percent of them are junior colleges.
3. As of 2008, about 13 percent of national universities served 25 percent of the student population nationwide.
4. The title Minister of Education was used until it changed in January 2001 to Minister of Education and Human Resources Development, and then again in February 2008 to Minister of Education, Science and Technology. Minister of Education is used throughout this chapter for consistency purposes.
5. The higher education programs spread out across the ministries and government agencies during the Roh government are mostly handled by the newly consolidated ministry, the Ministry of Education, Science and Technology.
6. This was borrowed from the Japanese model (National Assembly 2007, 69).
7. National universities are funded through three different accounts. Roughly 60 percent of the total funding comes through the National General Account, which is controlled in terms of line items such as personnel costs and capital expenditure. Another 30 percent of the funding is channeled through the institution-based account, which is called the School Supporting Associations Account; each university has discretional power over this account. In addition, by law, all universities that collaborate with industry in research and development have to set up another separate account, the Industry-Academy Cooperation Foundation Account.

References

Clark, Burton R. 1984. *The Higher Education System: Academic Organization in Cross National Perspective.* Los Angeles: University of California Press.

Clark, Burton R. 1998. *Creating Entrepreneurial Universities: Organizational Pathways of Transformation.* New York: Pergamon.
Collis, David J. 2004. "The Paradox of Scope: A Challenge to the Governance of Higher Education." In *Competing Conceptions of Academic Governance: Negotiating the Perfect Storm,* ed. W. G. Tierney (pp. 33–76). Baltimore: The Johns Hopkins University Press.
Dey, Eric L., and Sylvia Hurtado. 1999. "Students, Colleges, and Society: Considering the Interconnections." In *American Higher Education in the Twenty-first Century: Social, Political, and Economic Challenges,* eds. P. G. Altbach, R. O. Berdahl, and P. J. Gumport (pp. 298–322). Baltimore: Johns Hopkins University Press.
Duke, Chris, Henry Etzkowitz, Fumi Kitagawa, and Byung-Shik Rhee. 2006. *Supporting the Contribution of Higher Education Institutions to Regional Development, Peer Review Report: Busan, Republic of Korea.* Paris: Organisation for Economic Co-operation and Development (OECD). http://www.oecd.org.
Educational Reform Committee. 1987. *5.31 Educational Reforms for New Educational System: 4th Report.* Seoul: Educational Reform Committee.
Greenwood, M. R. C. 2005. "Master Plan for Higher Education." Paper presented at the Assembly Higher Education Committee, Sacramento, California, USA, February 2005.
Grubb, W. Norton, Richard Sweet, Michael Gallagher, and Ossi Tuomi. 2006. *Thematic Review of Tertiary Education: Country Note.* Paris: OECD. http://www.oecd.org.
Huang, Futao. 2006. "Incorporation and University Governance: A Comparative Perspective from China and Japan." *Higher Education Management and Policy* 18 (2): 1–15.
International Institute for Management Development. 2008. *World Competitiveness Yearbook.* Lausanne: International Institute for Management Development.
Kim, Ok-Hwan. 1994. *The Idea of University.* Seoul: Educational Science Publication.
Kim, Young-Chul, and Byung-Shik Rhee. 2002. *International Trends of Regulatory Reform in Education* (Research Report RR 2002–16). Seoul: Korean Educational Development Institute (KEDI).
Korea National Statistics Office. *Birth Rates, 1970–2008.* Korean Statistical Information System. Seoul: Korea National Statistics Office. http://kosis.nos.go.kr.
Lee, Se-Woo. 2002. "Directions of Japanese Higher Education Reform: Governance Reorganization of Japanese Universities." Paper presented at the Annual Meeting of Korean Association for Public Administration, Seoul, South Korea, May 2002.
Marginson, Simon. 2004. "Going Global: Governance Implications of Cross-border Traffic in Higher Education." In *Competing Conceptions of Academic Governance: Negotiating the Perfect Storm,* ed. W. G. Tierney (pp. 1–32). Baltimore: Johns Hopkins University Press.
McGuinness, Aims C. Jr. 1999. "The States and Higher Education." In *American Higher Education in the Twenty-first Century: Social, Political, and Economic Challenges,* eds. P. G. Altbach, R. O. Berdahl, and P. J. Gumport (pp. 183–215). Baltimore: Johns Hopkins University Press.
Ministry of Education and Human Resources Development. *Educational Statistics Yearbook 1990–2009.* Seoul: Ministry of Education and Human Resources Development.
Mok, Ka-Ho, and Eric H. C. Lo. 2002. "Marketization and the Changing Governance in Higher Education: A Comparative Study." *Higher Education Management and Policy* 14 (1): 51–82.
Mok, Ka-Ho. 2005. "When Asian States Adopt Western Public Policy Instruments: Corporatization of Public Universities in Hong Kong and Singapore." Paper presented at the 4th International Convention of Asian scholars, Shanghai, China, August 2005.
National Assembly. 2007. *265th Meeting Records of Education Committee* (pp. 58–77). Seoul: National Assembly.

Oba, Jun. 2005. "The Incorporation of National Universities in Japan: Initial Reactions of the New National University Corporations." *Higher Education Management and Policy* 17 (2): 105–125.

Organisation for Economic Co-operation and Development (OECD). 2003. "Changing Patterns of Governance in Higher Education." *Education Policy Analysis* (pp. 59–78). Paris: OECD.

———. 2006. *OECD Review of Regulations in Tertiary Education in the Republic of Korea: Draft Examiners' Report (Report No. EDU/EC [2006] 18)*. Paris: OECD.

Pfeffer, Jeffrey, and Gerald R. Salancik. 1978. *The External Control of Organizations: A Resource Dependence Perspective*. New York: Harper & Row.

Rhee, Byung-Shik, Young-Chul Kim, Yong-Woo. Park, Sung-Oh Bae, Hee-Jae Cho, Tae-Jong Kim, Chun-Shik Woo, and Yun-Kyu Yoon. 2006. *Review of Restructuring Proposals of National Universities*. Seoul, South Korea: KEDI, Samsung Economic Research Institute, and Korean Development Institute.

Rhee, Byung-Shik. 2008. "Neoliberalism and Challenges of Korean Higher Education Policy." *The Journal of Politics of Education* 15 (2): 7–25.

Richardson, Richard, Kathy Reeves Bracco, Patrick M. Callan, and Joni E. Finney. 1999. *Designing State Higher Education Systems For A New Century*. Phoenix: Oryx Press.

Son, Heung-Sook. 2002. "The Neo-Liberal Governmentality in Higher Education." *Journal of Educational Research* 40 (4): 73–196.

Sporn, Barbara. 2006. "Governance and Administration: Organizational and Structural Trends." In *International Handbook of Higher Education*, eds. J. J. F. Forest, and P. G. Altbach (pp. 141–157). Dordrecht, The Netherlands: Springer.

Tierney, William G. 2004. "Improving Academic Governance: Utilizing a Cultural Framework to Improve Organizational Performance." In *Competing Conceptions of Academic Governance: Negotiating the Perfect Storm*, ed. W. G. Tierney (pp. 202–215). Baltimore: Johns Hopkins University Press.

Times Higher Education. 2008. "World University Rankings, 2008." London: *THE*. http://www.timeshighereducation.co.uk.

Weick, Karl E. 1995. *Sensemaking in Organizations*. Thousand Oaks, CA: Sage.

Yamamoto, Kiyoshi. 2004. "Corporatization of National Universities in Japan: Revolution for Governance or Rhetoric for Downsizing?" *Financial Accountability & Management* 20 (2): 153–181.

Chapter 5

Governance of the Incorporated Japanese National Universities
Jun Oba

Introduction

In recent years, numerous governments have proceeded with reforms to increase the efficiency and effectiveness of university systems. These reforms aimed generally at according greater freedom to institutions and, at the same time, rationalizing their governance by clarifying the responsibilities of the management in the institutional decision-making process (OECD 2003). The reform of national universities in Japan has also reflected such a global trend. This chapter examines the impact and challenges of the recent reform of Japanese national universities, focusing on their internal governance.

Incorporation of National Universities and Its Impact

Japanese national universities were, until March 2004, a part of the national government under the Ministry of Education, Culture, Sports, Science, and Technology (MEXT) and were directly operated by it, although they enjoyed limited academic freedom. In April 2004, by acquiring the status of national university corporations (NUCs), they became legal entities and became more autonomous in their management. The reform was carried out swiftly and without incident, although preparations for the incorporation had not been an easy task. Now after more than six years since the incorporation, remarkable changes as well as problems can be observed in diverse aspects of the NUCs' governance.[1]

The Central Administration

NUCs' decision-making system has fundamentally been altered from a collegial system to a regime centered on the university president, and participation of external persons in the university governance has been institutionalized. Being detached from the government's direct control, central authorities of the NUCs are required to strategically manage their institutions within the legal framework and given resources, which tend to decrease and be allocated on a competitive basis.

Structure of the Central Administration. Traditionally, national universities were managed predominantly based on the consensus of academic staff, although the scope of their autonomy was restricted under direct government control. Such collegial system protected by the government was long criticized for slowness in making decisions and little responsiveness to society. By virtue of incorporation, the decision-making system of national universities has been fundamentally altered—at least legally[2]—from a collegial system to a regime centered on the university president.

In each NUC, the president, the final decision maker, is now selected by a president selection committee, composed of external and internal members. The president is seconded by a board of directors (BODs), whose members are appointed by the president. The BOD receives recommendations from an administrative council (AC) concerning administrative affairs and an education and research council

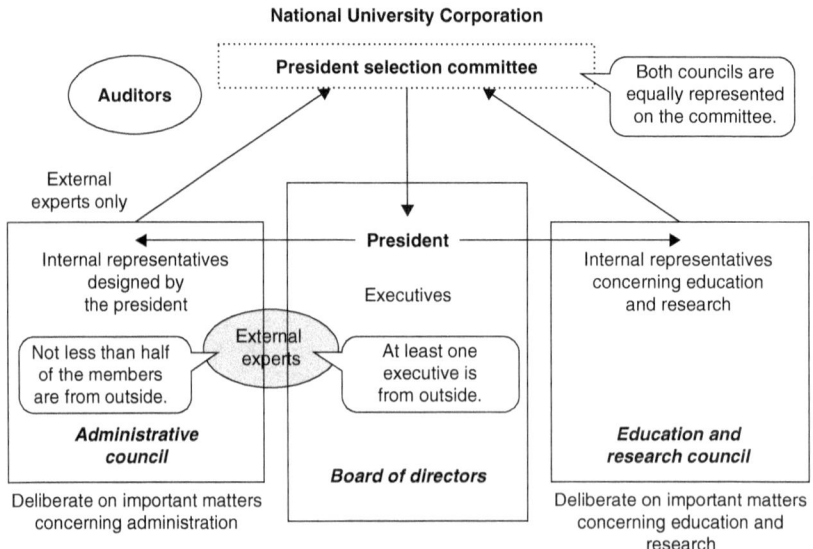

Figure 5.1 Governance Structure of NUCs
Source: Author.

(ERC) concerning academic affairs. In addition, there are two auditors, appointed by MEXT and entitled to check business operations of the NUCs (see figure 5.1).

Presidents and Boards of Directors. The reform notably extended the authority of the president and the BODs. To effectively centralize decision making by concentrating administrative powers in the presidents and BODs, national universities have reduced the number and frequency of various committee meetings. Before incorporation, a considerable number of committees had been set up to build consensus among academic staff members, which was a time-consuming process. For example, the Aichi University of Education reduced the number of committees from 36 to 24, as well as the number of committee members from over 400 to approximately 100.

Traditionally presidents had been elected by the academic staff members by vote and endorsed by the council before formal appointment by the minister of education, which was practically a formality. After incorporation, although the president must still be appointed formally by the minister, the selection is made by a president selection committee (PSC) set up in each NUC, which includes as many external members as internal representatives. In many universities, PSCs have made it a rule to take into consideration the vote by staff members, but the selection is not always dependent upon the ballot outcome. In some universities, while several presidents—known as reformers for their audacious managerial innovations—have been defeated at the polls (Sakimoto 2005), and the second-ranked candidates have been deliberately favored. Elsewhere, universities have either not employed or have abandoned the voting system entirely. However, presidents selected against voting results or without voting often lack legitimate authority. In some cases, first-ranked candidates have filed suits in courts to seek revocation of the appointments as presidents of the second-ranked candidates.

Each BOD is composed of the president and executives. Executives are selected and appointed by the president; the majority of them are recruited from the professoriate (Kaneko 2007). The maximum number of executives is defined by the *National University Corporation Law*; the average number of executives is 5.8 (CNUFM 2007). At least one of the executives should come from outside the university. According to a survey (CNUFM 2007), the factor regarded most important in potential executives is ability and experience as administrators (see figure 5.2). Presidents also attach much importance to expertise in the candidates' area of responsibility and the balance of power in the university. However, if responses in the categories "Strongly agree" and "Agree" are combined, the most important factor perceived to influence selection is the "policy and wish of the president." Relationship with academic units—most important in the precorporate collegial system—is no longer an influential selection criterion.

Participation of External Members. Every NUC has to include external persons as members of the BOD and of the AC, whereas the ERC is composed solely of internal members. The majority of these members are from the business community (34 percent for BOD and 35 percent for AC in 2004 (JANU 2004).

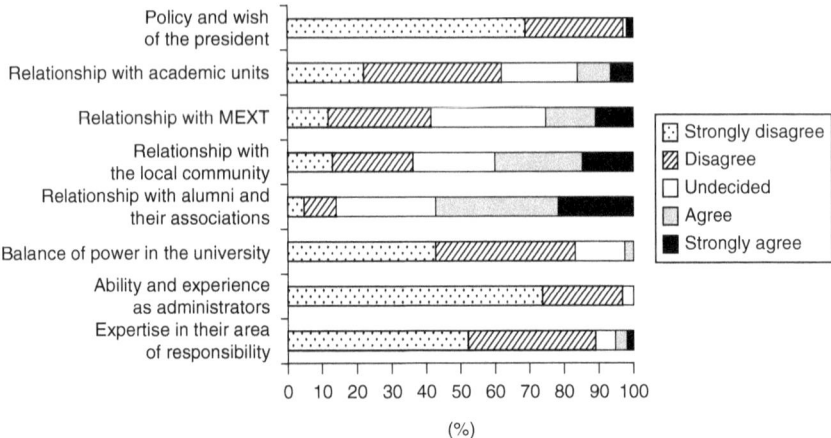

Figure 5.2 Factors Regarded as Important by the Presidents in the Selection of Executives
Source: CNUFM (2007).

External members on the BOD are expected to provide diverse expertise difficult to find in the university and to contribute to ensuring efficient management. In 2005, out of 403 executives (internal and external) in all NUCs, 80 were from the business community, but most of them (over 80 percent) are in part-time positions (Honma 2005). Some NUCs appointed foreigners as board members. A solid majority of the NUCs declare using their participation very effectively (59 percent) or relatively effectively (39 percent) (Honma et al. 2007). Miyagi University of Education, for example, invited the ex-superintendent of the prefectural board of education to join its BOD for his expertise in school education.

The extent of involvement of external members in university management through the AC varies. Some universities have expressed their intention to consult their AC in detail concerning their management, including their budget allocation. Others intend to consult them only for general directions. The president of Kyoto University, for example, was reported to have said that the council should discuss matters only from a broad perspective (Yokoyama 2004). According to a survey (Yokoyama 2005), in fiscal year (FY) 2004, the majority of the external members (60.1 percent) felt that their opinions had been sufficiently reflected in the decisions of the AC; but nearly a quarter of them (24.3 percent) thought that their opinions had little impact, and 9.4 percent of them found only a small number of important matters in the discussion. In comparison with the same survey carried out the previous year, fewer members found the council performing a core role in university management (62 percent against 66 percent), and orienting reform of the university (53 percent against 60 percent). Further, more members feared that the council might become merely a formality before decisions are taken by the BOD (40 percent against 35 percent). The surveys reveal a certain measure of disappointment among the external members.

Finance and Human Resource Management

Financial Management. Given greater autonomy over financial management, and in the context of an annual reduction of operational grant (block grant from MEXT, see below), NUCs have taken various measures to use their resources efficiently. Many universities have focused their reforms on managerial efficiency in allocation and utilization of existing resources. Shiga University of Medical Science, for example, carried out a detailed cost analysis and applied cost improvement measures to certain areas to enhance the financial situation of the university. Yokohama National University set up a financial analysis office to conduct longitudinal and comparative analysis to improve its financial basis. All the universities have adopted annual budgeting policies and have set aside a budget at the disposal of the presidents. In 2004, the Tokyo Institute of Technology dedicated about 650 million yen out of their budget to the discretion of the president, and spent it selectively on activities such as development of education research infrastructure, improvement of student services, research funding for young academic staff members, and other activities. Tohoku University deducted 5 percent of the total academic staff salary and channeled it to a centrally managed personnel budget, and founded a "University Professor System" designed to attract Nobel Prize-class scholars with a special salary.

Efforts to Acquire Competitive Funds and Promotion of Income-Generating Activities. Academic staff members are increasingly encouraged to acquire external research grants and other types of competitive funds. Niigata University, for example, defined numerical targets concerning acquisition of Grants-in-Aid for Scientific Research in its action plan. Ryukyu University deducted 1 percent from the research infrastructure funds of the faculties, for which the collective application ratio was under 70 percent as incentive funds for applicants, to encourage grant applications.

On the other hand, almost all universities reduced the amount of research funds that were distributed uniformly among all academic staff members, in favor of funds at the disposal of the president or competitive funds. These funds have been utilized for projects proposed by academic staff members or selected by the university authority, distributed to research-intensive units, and so on. Okayama University, for example, developed an Okayama University Priority Projects program with a view to setting up new scientific research projects that are not limited to one faculty, and to developing creative international research centers (e.g., an On-campus Center of Excellence). Some universities have decided to penalize academic staff that do not apply for Grants-in-Aid for Scientific Research (*Kakenhi*)[3] (Kojima 2009).

Elsewhere, external sources of revenue have been vigorously sought by national universities. Income-generating activities include industry–government–academy cooperation and various entrepreneurial activities. Most universities have set up or enhanced offices for technology licensing and other collaborative activities. The University of Tokyo was reported to very effectively manage its intellectual property from creation to licensing, conjointly with TOUDAI TLO Ltd. and the University of Tokyo Edge Capital Co. Ltd.,[4] within the office of intellectual property. However, these resources tend to concentrate on a small number of large universities in metropolitan areas (Kitagawa and Oba 2009).

Human Resource Management. NUCs have much more discretion over their human resource management. Before incorporation, the number of staff for each unit was fixed by the government by positions, and a university could not modify its staff quota nor establish new units or restructure existing units without authorization. The staff quota tended to be considered a vested right for each unit, which impeded efficient manpower policy at the campus level. In addition, permanent clerical staff could be recruited only from among successful candidates of the national public service examination. High-level secretarial officers were regularly relocated from one university to another by MEXT. This system came to an end at the time of the incorporation, when the appointing power was transferred from the minister of education to the president of a university.

NUCs have realigned their human resource management systems so that they may centralize staff management and strategically make use of given human resources. Gifu University, for example, passed from a staff quota management system to a "points system," allowing deans and other unit directors flexible staffing within the limit of points allocated to each component.[5] Many NUCs have made it a rule that the posts of retiring academic staff should be centrally managed, not automatically filled by researchers from the same area.

Although some high-level secretarial officers are being relocated under the initiative of MEXT, the recruitment of nonacademic staff comes under the auspices of NUCs. Some NUCs have begun recruiting experts in various areas as staff with either academic rank or administrative title. The larger universities have set up diverse units for supporting education and research activities. In 2004, the University of Tokyo, for example, recruited ten experts from the business community as associate managing directors or specially appointed experts. Among these experts is a patent attorney in the office of intellectual property.

On the other hand, increased autonomy emphasizes the need for staff development (SD), particularly in managerial roles. Most NUCs have realigned their SD programs and promotion schemes in that direction and revised their recruitment and evaluation systems. The University of Tokyo advertised a few director-level positions internally and appointed seven successful candidates to the positions in FY 2004.

Academic Structures

In 2004, 43 corporations out of 93 were reported to periodically review their education research structures, by setting up units with an expiration date, among other things. Independent of the incorporation, basic academic structures—faculties and graduate schools—are, regardless of the type of control (national, local public, or private), regulated by the School Education Law and Standards for the Establishment of Universities and subjected to government approval for any modifications (except for slight ones), which constitutes restriction on academic freedom.

By contrast, nonbasic units have continuously been placed on reform agendas since the incorporation.

Concerning the basic academic units, although it still seems difficult for most universities to significantly reallocate internal resources from the areas of least need to those of greatest need, certain universities have reviewed their entire academic structures. In 2008, Kanazawa University integrally reorganized its academic structure, by regrouping its 8 faculties and 25 departments into 3 academic domains and 16 subdomains, to offer diverse programs crossing disciplinary borders and to allow students greater choice of courses and of future careers.

In addition, national universities have been increasingly cultivating interdisciplinary research programs to better meet the needs of society and to maintain and strengthen their scientific excellence. In many universities, no small part of the resources has been devoted to developing interdisciplinary approaches that cross the borders of existing faculties, gathering researchers from different units and outside. The University of Tokyo, for example, set up a Comprehensive Project Group in 2004 directly under the auspices of the president, aimed at combining several disciplines and opening up new horizons of knowledge. At Yamaguchi University, with its "Research Initiative" scheme, 43 interfaculty research bodies were set up by the end of FY 2007.

Student Services and Student Participation

Student Services. In Japanese universities, particularly in national universities, student services have long remained underdeveloped (Oba forthcoming). However, massification of higher education demands that administrators focus more on the issue. Among efforts undertaken are the establishment of positions in student services, improvement of counseling activities, appointment of advisers, and organization of peer support groups. Sometimes, these services have been concentrated in student support centers. In addition, many universities have set up their own scholarship programs, and extended tuition exemptions.

At Yamagata University, for example, one academic staff adviser has been appointed for every 20 students, and academic advisers are placed in an advising center. In cooperation with neighboring universities and industry, in 2008, Nagoya University set up a Non-research Career Development Center for supporting postdoctoral individuals in employment in the business community. In 2008, the University of Tokyo decided to significantly enhance its financial aid to students. In particular, fees for doctoral students have been set effectively free (Maruyama 2007).

Student Participation. In contrast to the decrease in academic staff involvement, participation of students in university governance is a newly observed phenomenon. Traditionally, students have not been regarded as full members in the campus community, and have rarely represented themselves in decision-making processes at any level; whereas in many European countries and the United States, they often have a voice in the university governance structures, although very seldom as a major

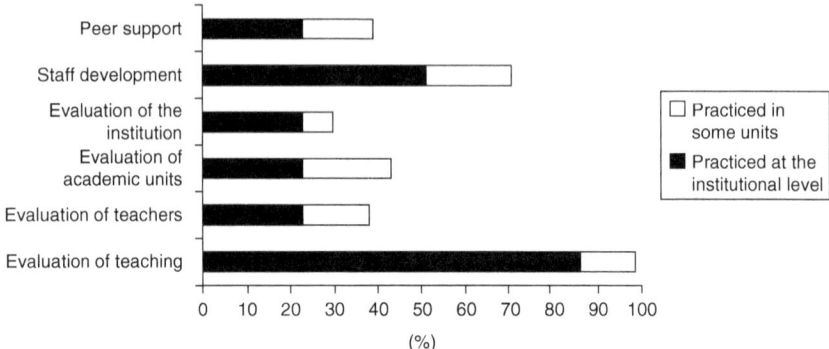

Figure 5.3 Participation of Students in Diverse Campus Activities in National Universities
Source: RIHE (2007).

influence in these structures (Altbach 1998). After incorporation, in some national universities, students have been involved as full members in evaluation committees and other decision-making organs.

At Okayama University, for example, students and staff members (both academic and nonacademic) sit conjointly on a Student–Staff Committee on Educational Improvement, where 37 students are present among 56 members. The committee has implemented academic staff development activities largely inspired by students, including the establishment of new courses and improvement of student questionnaires on teaching. According to a survey conducted in 2006 among the NUC presidents (RIHE 2007), students are involved in evaluating instruction in almost all universities and participating in staff development activities in more than half of the universities (see figure 5.3). However, in other activities studied in the same survey, student participation remains confined to a limited number of universities.

Evaluations

Academic Staff Evaluation in Universities. After incorporation, an increasing number of NUCs have developed their academic staff evaluation systems. Traditionally, evaluation of academic staff members has been carried out almost exclusively through peer review in Japanese universities. Although peer review remains the most effective and important evaluation means, NUCs have been implementing evidence-based periodical evaluations, being pushed by third-party evaluations including those of national university corporation evaluation committee (NUC-EC). For example, Okayama University put in place an evaluation system in 2004 to classify academic staff into four groups (excellent, good, fair, and poor) based on multiple performance indicators. In 2004, among 1,280 participating academic staff members, 897 were classified in the overall performance evaluation as excellent but 20 as poor.[6]

> According to a survey completed in January 2008 (Okawa and Okui, 2008), nearly 90 percent of the NUCs have introduced evaluation systems for academic staff. This was a huge increase since the introduction rate in 2006 was just 68 percent. As for their objectives, 72 percent of the NUCs aim at reactivating their activities, 71 percent of them aim at improving education, and improvement of research is being aimed at by the same percentage of NUCs. However, the introduction rate is lower in the larger universities—slightly more than 70 percent in universities with more than 1,000 academic staff. With regard to use of evaluation results, few NUCs link them with pay scales or promotion of staff.

Institutional Evaluation by MEXT. Every NUC has to submit a self-evaluation report annually to NUC-EC in MEXT. Based on the self-evaluation reports, NUC-EC assesses the extent of attainment of mid-term goals (MTG)/mid-term plans (MTP)[7] of each NUC and compiles an annual evaluation report of the overall performance of the NUCs. All the reports—self-evaluation reports and NUC-EC's report—are published. Although in their first annual report (FY 2004), NUC-EC pointed to several problems, the committee highly appreciated the efforts made by the NUCs to enhance administrative and managerial capacity under the leadership of the presidents. The FY 2005/2006 reports pointed to problems including underdevelopment of staff evaluation systems, unfinished risk-management manuals, and an inappropriate management of administrative councils in some NUCs, although they highly appreciated the NUCs' reform efforts as a whole.

It should be noted that every NUC-EC's annual reports includes not only overall performance assessment results but also some "characteristic practices" reported by NUCs. Although NUC-EC stresses that these practices are merely examples that do not necessarily have to be followed by all the NUCs, it is clear that these are shown as good practices that MEXT recommends NUCs employ to meet accountability requirements. Ironically, in spite of the fact that one of the main objectives of incorporation is to increase the diversity of national universities, diffusion of good practices by NUC-EC has promoted isomorphic change in NUCs, as seen in the case of academic staff evaluation, which risks homogenizing institutions (DiMaggio and Powell 1983), at least in each stratum of institutions.

After the tenure of the first MTG/MTP (2004–2010), overall performance of each NUC will be assessed by NUC-EC. Prior to this final evaluation, for the purpose of contributing to drawing the next MTG/MTP and of reflecting the results in the next term budget allocation, NUC-EC assessed the first-term performance of NUCs based on their activities of FY 2004–2007, and published the evaluation results in March 2009.[8] In the report summary, the president of NUC-EC expressed his satisfaction, asserting that NUCs had well implemented their MTP and that they had performed the role of public institutions supported by taxpayers. However, at the same time, he pointed to several problems observed in some

Table 5.1 Results of the Evaluation by NUC-EC for FY 2004–2007

	Excellent status	As planned	Largely as planned	Slightly behind the plan	Much improvement needed
Education	1	10	79	0	0
Research	3	27	60	0	0
Administration	11	56	18	5	0
Finance	3	83	1	3	0

Note: n=90 (86 NUCs and four inter-university research institute corporations).

national universities, including underutilization of enrollment capacities and unsatisfactory levels of education and research. Evaluation results regarding education, research, administration, and finance are provided in table 5.1.

Major Challenges for National University Governance

The Issue of Financial Resources

The largest source of revenue for national universities comes from MEXT as an operational grant. It represented 47.7 percent of the total revenue (including external resources) of all the national universities in FY 2004. The operational grant has been reduced, however, by 1 percent every year except for the component corresponding to salaries of academic staff members,[9] which has been only partially compensated by the special grant allocated on a competitive basis. As a result, the proportion of operational grant in the total revenue has continuously decreased (see figure 5.4).

In spite of such critical conditions, no NUCs have so far increased their tuition fees over the standards fixed by MEXT, except for two professional graduate courses, although they are authorized to raise registration and tuition fees by as much as 10 percent over the standard amounts set by the ministry. On the contrary, vis-à-vis the rise of standard tuition fees determined by the government in 2005, some universities have opted to freeze their tuition fees, even partially (notably for graduate students).

In the process of budget preparation for FY 2007, the Ministry of Finance had asked MEXT to revise the standards again. This proposal was subsequently withdrawn in the face of howls of protest from NUCs, and it was agreed between both ministries that the standards would be frozen during the current MTG/MTP period. However, it was also agreed that the maximum surcharge rate for the next period would be increased from the current 10 percent to 20 percent.

Against such severe circumstances, NUCs have made great efforts to rationalize their administration and to multiply resources. However, additional resources

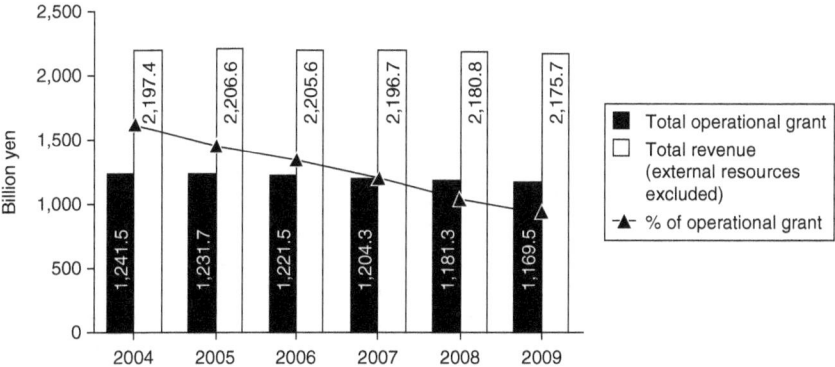

Figure 5.4 Operational Grants and Total Revenues (External Resources Excluded) of NUCs
Source: MEXT.

are limited and very unevenly distributed (Kitagawa and Oba 2009). In FY 2004, external resources, including income from commissioned research, donations, and others, represented only 6.2 percent of the total revenue of national universities. In addition, major national universities, represented by seven former imperial universities and another three research universities, collected more than 60 percent of the external resources obtained by the NUCs. The Ministry of Finance envisages distributing the operational grant based largely on the performance evaluation, to which many NUCs take objection because of the risk of aggravating unjustified disparity among national universities.

On the other hand, the cost-sharing measures such as student payments to the university, recently implemented or currently studied in many countries where public universities are dominant, are unlikely to be further applied to Japanese national universities. The fees that students must pay to public institutions are already exceedingly high and often dissuade enrollment from lower- and even middle-class society. Yano (2008) argues that, in view of the stagnation of the access rate to higher education, many have decided not to go on to universities because of high tuition fees; he strongly recommends lowering fees instead of expanding loans.

Developing Effective Leaders and Support Staff

The new decision-making framework was designed to enable rapid decisions, reflecting opinions from outside the university, among a small circle of high officers. However, in reality, it is impossible for them to assume every responsibility in administration in a loosely coupled organization such as universities (Weick 1991). Osaki (2009) points to problems associated with centralized administration in NUCs and calls for devolution to academic units. On the other hand, it is difficult to expect academic staff executives to have competence and expertise in university administration, where presidents are selected on the basis of their academic achievement and where most academic staff members try to escape from managerial work.

In preparation for incorporation, national universities have tried to construct perfect administrative structures, particularly in the larger research universities that were too sophisticated to be operational (Ikoma 2004). This observation should be critically considered in the light of a repeated statement that a specific arrangement in governance structure of a university versus another has little implication for its performance (Kerr 2001; Lombardi et al. 2002; Kaplan 2004; Henkel 2007). Kerr (2001) states that changes in formal governance have generally made little difference, and that where they have, this has been mostly for the worse. An example is that, with the disappearance or diminution of the integrated secretariat in some NUCs, even miscellaneous issues requiring coordination began frequently going to the presidents, thus reducing the efficiency of the university management (Isoda 2005).

A conclusion drawn from these assertions and experiences is that organizational culture and SD are critically important. In fact, an OECD (2004) report called for a need to develop professional strategic managers in the key nonacademic functions of finance, personnel, estates, and so on, and much effort has been made in this area throughout the world. However, in Japan, SD is still underdeveloped, and there have been very few programs for the development of presidents and other senior administrators, whereas such programs are commonplace in the United States and some other countries. More importantly, SD should address the entire organizational culture of each institution (London 1995), but its programs consist mainly of technical issues (specialized knowledge in administration, teaching proficiency, etc.) and involve few elements relating to organizational cultures.

Participation of the Campus Community and Stakeholders

Although a genuine institutional policy cannot be developed without involving academic staff members, their involvement in the decision-making process has been significantly reduced by the incorporation arrangements. In many countries, the importance of academic staff involvement in personnel decisions, selection of administrators, preparation of budget, and determination of academic policies has been emphasized. Birnbaum (2004) underlines the fundamental need for shared governance in academic institutions, and regards it as the most effective process through which academic institutions may achieve their goals. The French experience also shows that participation of the campus community in the decision-making process is a key factor for successful implementation of institutional strategies (Frémont et al. 2004). Similarly, in the United Kingdom, the strength of a university is considered to depend significantly on the commitment of academic staff and their identification with their university (Henkel 2007).

In Japan, although the initial NUC system design provided for a system placing much importance on top-down decision making, presidents have acknowledged the need for academic staff participation. According to a survey (RIHE 2007), although they have recognized a reduction in the authority of collegial bodies and academic

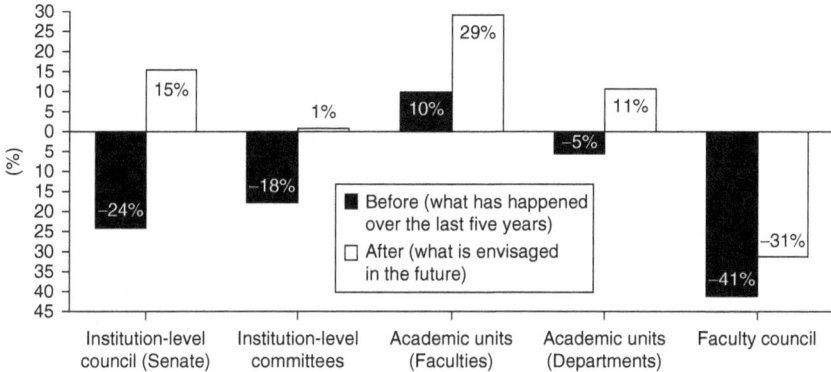

Figure 5.5 Evolution of the Authority of Collegial Bodies and Academic Units in National Universities

Note: The data are based on responses by presidents. Each column corresponds to the difference between percentages of affirmative and negative responses concerning an enhancement of the authority of each collegial body. Vertical bars with a negative value indicate that a majority of respondents have recognized or wish an abridgement of the authority of each body.
Source: Research Institute for Higher Education (2007).

units (except for faculties) over the past years, they now wish to see an enhancement rather than a reduction of this authority (except for that of faculty councils) (see figure 5.5). Many of the more recent studies stress the importance of consensus building and bottom-up approaches (Amano 2008; Osaki 2009; Uesugi 2009).

As shown above, participation of external persons is still problematic. A survey conducted in 2006 of all the external members (directors, AC members, and auditors) points to multiple issues raised by them regarding university administration including relationship between the managements and themselves. A recent study (Uesugi 2009) reports that there is still much frustration between external members and NUC administrations: many external members complain that they go merely through pro forma deliberations, whereas the latter expect external members to know more about the university and to provide more relevant advice.

Plans and Evaluations

The MTP/MTG scheme and evaluation constitute key elements of the NUC system. However, there are many problems with them, and it is difficult to carry out a "Plan, Do, Check, Act" cycle, which is a prerequisite for an enhancement of the institutional effectiveness (Hata 2009).

An evaluation system centered on institutions as it is now should be questioned. Universities, especially large and comprehensive ones, are very complicated organizations that can be evaluated as a whole only with extreme difficulty (Kaneko 2007). In addition, preparatory works for definition of MTG/MTP and evaluations have proved to be so burdensome that there is a strong concern that this would result in degradation of education and research in national universities (Kaneko 2007; Osaki 2009). Sawa (2003) described the incorporation as a "Soviet-style" reform because of similarities between the NUC system and the Soviet system, which had failed because of difficulty in economic manipulation in terms of evaluation and resource allocation scheme. As Shattock (2003) suggests, planning should not be detailed, and in turn, the evaluation process of NUC-EC should be alleviated and transformed into enhancement-oriented one.

Furthermore, allocation of the operational grant should not be tightly linked with its evaluation. In principle, evaluation linked with resource allocation should be implemented on an individual or project basis, exposing researchers to a strict but constructive review and criticism by their peers. In the United States, although funding schemes based on institutional performance were adopted in some states, faced with multiple difficulties, the number of states adopting this practice has decreased (Herbst 2007). The NUC evaluation system is not robust enough to be used for resource allocation (Tanaka 2009). The government should offer multiple funding programs to respond to a diversified higher education system lest competitive funds should concentrate in a small number of universities.

Concerning staff evaluation, although evidence-based evaluations may seem more objective than assessments by political process, they also have their limitations. Especially for academic staff, evidence-based performance assessment is only a partial measure. For this type of evaluation, peer review is essential and it constitutes a fundamental premise of academic freedom, where decisions concerning the quality of scholarship and teaching should be made by reference to the standards of the academic profession, as interpreted and applied by the community of scholars (AAUP 2003). In this context, the link between evidence-based staff evaluation and remuneration should be sufficiently loose.

Conclusion: The Future of National Universities

In an age of knowledge, the need for advanced education and knowledge is becoming increasingly pressing and it calls for a more complicated decision-making process (Eckel and Kezar 2006). Higher education institutions should meet such demands, adapting themselves to an ever-changing society, just as the university has done over time (Sporn 1999). Reforms undertaken in a vast majority of countries during the past few decades have encouraged institutions to be more responsive to such changing societal demands with fewer resources, by according greater autonomy to institutions, rationalizing their governance, and enhancing evaluations (OECD 2003). The incorporation of Japanese national universities adheres *grosso modo* to the same logic.

Now, after the first-term evaluation is completed, even though it is still at an interim stage, implications of the incorporation have largely come into view. However, as seen in the previous section, there are a number of challenges and the incorporation is still in progress. Furthermore, the future of national universities remains quite unclear in the midst of ongoing government reforms. In fact, the Law for Promotion of Administrative Reforms adopted in 2006 stipulates that government personnel expenditures—including those of the NUCs—should be reduced by 5 percent by 2010. A preliminary calculation of the operational grant distribution based on a competition model was presented by the Ministry of Finance in May 2007, which planned to completely change the financial scheme of the NUCs. According to this preliminary report, only 13 NUCs out of 87 would increase their grant, and the rest would see their operational grant decrease up to 90.5 percent. Although this plan was withdrawn in the face of strong opposition, the Ministry of Finance envisages applying a drastic performance funding scheme for distribution of the operational grant of the next term MTG/MTP. The concentration of competitive funds in a small number of universities will critically undermine the viability of noncompetitive national universities that are often located in peripheral areas with few opportunities for external resources from local communities or specialized in areas that are little connected with fund-raising activities but essential for society, such as teachers' education (Yuki 2009). Sugiyama (2009) calls for the development of multiple competitive public funding programs adapted to different types of institutions.

On the other hand, although the national universities have become largely autonomous, they were set up by law and are still significantly subsidized by the government. The ultimate responsibility for their operation continues to reside with the government, and therefore they still retain a public character. Without firm commitment from the government, which should be supportive rather than directive in nature, most of the national universities would not be able to respond to the needs of society, which should not be solved by market forces or privatization. In fact, in many other East Asian countries where similar reforms have been made in their higher education systems, the state's capacity has not been weakened but enhanced to manage the public sector efficiently from a distance (Mok 2007).

Finally for Japan, a new governance model—more decentralized than before, in which both government and national universities share a joint responsibility in ensuring the quality of higher education offerings—should be established, particularly through refining diverse indirect policy tools, such as evaluation systems, and enhancing institutional management with the participation of the campus community. In addition, under politically unstable circumstances, it is essential to develop a culture of dialogue between universities and MEXT and to build a community in which all stakeholders collaborate for further development of higher education.

Notes

1. Specific examples and other information cited in this chapter, unless otherwise noted, come from diverse reports of the NUC evaluation committee in MEXT and performance reports of the NUCs.
2. See Oba (2007) for the legal framework.
3. Competitive funds of the MEXT (managed by the Japan Society for the Promotion of Science) are open primarily to university-based researchers for the purpose of basic scientific studies.

4. A venture capital recognized by the University of Tokyo, which provides support for entrepreneurial activities.
5. A professor accounts for 100 points, an associate professor, 78 points, an assistant professor, 73 points, and an assistant, 60 points (one point corresponds to approximately 100,000 yen). Each component determines how to utilize its points.
6. Report presented at the seminar on the academic staff evaluation system, organized by the Evaluation Committee of Hiroshima University on December 22, 2005.
7. Strategic goals and plan of action of each NUC, conjointly defined by the NUC and MEXT for a period of six years, based on the budget (operational grant) allocated to the NUC. They constitute a kind of contracts between MEXT and NUCs.
8. The evaluation of NUC-EC consists of assessment of each NUC's performance in the improvement of the quality of education and research as well as in the administration. For the former, NUC-EC receives assessment reports of academic units of national universities prepared by the National Institution for Academic Degrees and University Evaluation.
9. NUCs are not required to spend that part of the budget entirely on academic staff members' salary, but they can adjust the salary scale as necessary.

References

Altbach, Philip. 1998. "Politics of Students and Faculty." In *Education: The Complete Encyclopedia*, eds. B. R. Clark, and G. Neave. Oxford: Pergamon Press.
Amano, Ikuo. 2008. *Future of National Universities and Their Incorporation: Caught between Autonomy and Disparity* [in Japanese]. Tokyo: Toshindo.
American Association of University Professors (AAUP). 2003. *Academic Bill of Rights*. Washington, DC: AAUP.
Birnbaum, Robert. 2004. "The End of Shared Governance: Looking Ahead or Looking Back." *New Directions for Higher Education* 2004 (127): 5–22.
Centre for National University Finance and Management (CNUFM). 2007. *A Study on Finance and Management of National Universities after Incorporation* [in Japanese]. Tokyo: CNUFM.
DiMaggio, Paul J., and Walter W. Powell. 1983. "The Iron Cage Revisited: Institutional Isomorphism and Collective Rationality in Organizational Fields." *American Sociological Review* 48 (2): 147–160.
Eckel, Peter D., and Adrianna Kezar. 2006. "The Challenges Facing Academic Decision Making: Contemporary Issues and Steadfast Structures." In *The Shifting Frontiers of Academic Decision Making: Responding to New Priorities, Following New Pathways*, ed. P. D. Eckel. Westport: Praeger.
Frémont, Armand et al. 2004. *Les universités françaises en mutation: la politique publique de contractualisation (1984–2002)* [in French]. Paris: Documentation française.
Hata, Takashi. 2009. "Rethinking National University Corporations in Japan." [In Japanese.] *CAHE Journal of Higher Education* 4: 1–12.
Henkel, Mary. 2007. "Changes in the Governance and Management of the University: The Role of Governments and Third-Party Agencies." *RIHE COE Publication Series* 29: 3–14.
Herbst, Marcel. 2007. *Financing Public Universities: The Case of Performance Funding*. Dordrecht, The Netherlands: Springer.
Honma, Masao. 2005. "The Necessary Development of Managerial Abilities within National Universities." [In Japanese.] *Nikkei News*, August 15, 21.

Honma, Masao et al. 2007. *Use of External Human Resources in the National University Corporations* [in Japanese]. Tokyo: Association of National University Management.
Ikoma, Toshiaki. 2004. "The Essence of the University and Industry-Academy Co-operation." [In Japanese.] *IDE* 462: 25–35.
Isoda, Fumio. 2005. "One Year as an Executive: From the Standpoint of an Executive from MEXT." [In Japanese.] *IDE* 475: 52–55.
Japan Association of National Universities (JANU). 2004. "The Frontline of Incorporation of National Universities." [In Japanese.] *JANU Quarterly Report* 1: 3–10.
Kaneko, Motohisa. 2007. "Incorporation of National Universities in Japan: Design, Implementation and Consequences." Paper presented at the International Conference on Education Research, Seoul, South Korea, October 23–25.
Kaplan, Gabriel E. 2004. "Do Governance Structures Matter?" *New Directions for Higher Education* 2004 (127): 23–34.
Kerr, Clark. 2001. *The Uses of the University Fifth Edition*. Cambridge, MA: Harvard University Press.
Kitagawa, Fumi, and Jun Oba. 2009. "Managing Differentiation of Higher Education System in Japan: Connecting Excellence and Diversity." *Higher Education* DOI 101007/s10-DOI 101009–926.
Kojima, Makoto. 2009. "Increasing 'Management gap' among National Universities in the Seventh Year after Incorporation." [In Japanese.] *ZAITEN*, July 2009: 17–25.
Lombardi, John V., Diane D. Craig, Elizabeth Capaldi, and Denise S. Gater. 2002. *The Top American Research Universities: University Organization, Governance, and Competitiveness*. Gainesville, FL: TheCenter.
London, Manuel. 1995. *Achieving Performance Excellence in University Administration: A Team Approach to Organizational Change and Employee Development*. Westport, CT: Praeger.
Maruyama, Fumihiro. 2007. "Recent Developments Regarding the Tuition Fees of The University of Tokyo: Progress Towards Diversification and Individualisation?" [In Japanese.] *Kyoikugakujutsushinbun* 2293: 2.
Mok, Ka-Ho. 2007. "The Search for New Governance: Corporatisation and Privatisation of Public Universities in Singapore and Malaysia." *RIHE COE Publication Series* 29: 37–60.
Oba, Jun. 2007. "Governance Reform of National Universities in Japan: Transition to Corporate Status and Challenges." *The Journal of Comparative Asian Development* 6 (1): 45–86.
Oba, Jun. forthcoming. "Managing Academic and Professional Careers in Japan." In *Academic and Professional Identities in Higher Education*, ed. C. Whitchurch and G. Gordon. London: Routledge.
Okawa, Kazuki, and Masaki Okui. 2008. *Empirical Study of Development and Management of Academic Staff Evaluation in National Universities* [in Japanese]. Report of Grants-in-Aid for Scientific Research.
Organisation for Economic Co-operation and Development (OECD). 2003. "Changing Patterns of Governance in Higher Education." In *Education Policy Analysis*, ed. OECD. Paris: OECD.
———.2004. *On the Edge: Securing a Sustainable Future for Higher Education*. Paris: OECD.
Osaki, Hitoshi. 2009. "The National University Corporation System Revisited." [In Japanese.] *IDE* 511: 4–9.
Research Institute for Higher Education (RIHE). 2007. *Transforming Universities in Modern Japan* (COE Publication Series 27) [in Japanese]. Hiroshima: RIHE.

Sakimoto, Tatsuro. 2005. "On the Leadership of the University President." [In Japanese.] *IDE* 475: 10–14.
Sawa, Takamitsu. 2003. "'Soviet Style' Reforms Won't Improve National Universities." *The Japan Times*, June 10.
Shattock, Michael. 2003. *Managing Successful Universities*. Berkshire: Open University Press.
Sporn, Barbara. 1999. *Adaptive University Structures: An Analysis of Adaptation to Socioeconomic Environment of US and European Universities*. London: Jessica Kingsley Publishers.
Sugiyama, Takehiko. 2009. "Competitive Resource Allocation: More Attention Needed to the Smaller Institutions." *Nikkei News* August 10, 21.
Tanaka, Hideaki. 2009. *Evaluation and Resource Allocation in Higher Education: Potentialities and Problems of Performance-Based Grant* [in Japanese]. Tokyo: RIETI.
Uesugi, Michiyo. 2009. "Corporate and Governance Issues." [In Japanese.] *IDE* 511: 49–55.
Weick, Karl E. 1991. "Educational Organizations as Loosely Coupled Systems." In *Organization and Governance in Higher Education*, ed. M. W. Peterson. 4th ed. Needham Heights, MA: Ginn Press.
Yano, Masakazu. 2008. "Equalization of Educational Opportunity is Efficient." [In Japanese.] *Kyoikugakujutsushinbun* 2302: 2.
Yokoyama, Shinichiro. 2004. "A Survey among External Members of the Administrative Councils of the National University Corporations." [In Japanese.] *Nikkei News* August 3, 34.
Yokoyama, Shinichiro. 2005. "A Survey among External Members of the Administrative Councils of the National University Corporations." [In Japanese.] *Nikkei News* May 9, 23.
Yuki, Akio. 2009. "From Vice-Minister of MEXT to National University President: NUCs on the Edge of Financial Crisis due to Continuing Reduction of Operational Grant." [In Japanese.] *Nikkei News* March 21, 21.

Chapter 6

Entrepreneurialism in Higher Education: A Comparison of University Governance Changes in Hong Kong and Singapore

William Yat-Wai Lo

Introduction

Entrepreneurial culture or entrepreneurialism has become a driving philosophy of higher education governance across the world. This entrepreneurialism is characterized by commercialization of teaching and research and introduction of quality assurance system in the higher education subsector. "Pursuit of excellence" and "quality education" are the themes on which these are based. Such a business-style management leads to a debate on the core values of university. What is the chief goal of the university? Does the market-model/corporate-style university serve this goal? What kind of university does the society want? These questions are essential in the discussion on changing university governance.

This chapter aims to review the rationale for entrepreneurialism in higher education by examining the changing university governance in Hong Kong and Singapore. It has four main sections. The first is an account of the global trend of university entrepreneurialism. The second section discusses and examines how the entrepreneurial culture has changed university governance with a focus on the implementation of entrepreneurialism and managerialism in the two cities. The third then turns to compare these changes by assessing the agendas and attitudes underlying the relevant policies in the two city-states. The chapter concludes with a reflection on entrepreneurialism in higher education.

The Global Trend of University Entrepreneurialism

Competition, a normal and widely accepted phenomenon among universities throughout the world (Clark 2002) today has been initiated by the growing entrepreneurial culture in the higher education subsector. This culture is generated by a global force, by which individuals in an organization are under a tightly integrated regime of managerial discipline and control (Deem et al. 2007). "Quality" and "accountability" are the themes commonly used in the adoption of the new managerial culture. This cultural globalization is seen as a progressive shift toward managerialism in the public sector and also a part of the public sector reforms, which primarily aim to restructure the state through deregulation of legal and financial controls, opening of markets and quasi markets, and reinventing the role of states (Enders and Fulton 2002; Mok and Welch 2003). These ideological changes have led to the introduction of private sector techniques into public management and the engagement of nonstate sectors in public service delivery in the name of "economy, efficiency and effectiveness." Tertiary education, an area of public policy, is not immune from the onslaught of managerialism, which has been introduced as part public sector reforms. In line with management efficiency and effective use of resources, business-like principles, mechanisms, and practices have been introduced in running universities. In response to the call for the running of education like the running of a business (Currie and Newson 1998), universities in many countries have been deeply engaged in implementing structural reforms to be more efficient and effective in decision making and operations, and to optimize use of limited resources available (Ball 1990, 1998; Bridges and McLaughlin 1994).

Two developments, namely, encouragement of value for money and of achieving public accountability, have contributed directly to the changing university governance alongside entrepreneurialism. This is particularly true during periods of financial stringency. Meanwhile, universities are required to reduce their financial dependence on the state and become more financially proactive (Currie et al. 2002). Therefore, they have diversified their income sources across the state and nonstate sectors. Nontraditional sources of finance such as capital endowment, commercialization of teaching, research and services, loans at privileged interest rates, and grants from business tycoons and charity organizations, have become increasingly common and important.

This diversified financing base has altered the traditional structure of universities. Peripheral units, which promote outreach activities such as industrial liaison, technology transfer, consultancy, and continuing education, have become basic units parallel to departments of various disciplines (Clark 2002). These units act as mediating institutions that link the university to outside organizations. Moreover, the enhanced peripheral units tend to integrate with the departments in daily operations. This causes the blurring of the distinction between university departments and peripheral units.

The changes in university finance and structure have altered the relationship among government, university, business, and industry, and transformed the university into a seller of services in the knowledge industry (Williams 2003). In response to the call for quality excellence from the government and the request for industry-centered knowledge, universities are compelled to fulfill varying expectations from the community. Consequently, they are required to accommodate many types of accountabilities, such as market, political and bureaucratic to establish and maintain connections with other social actors. Indeed, universities have to move toward the new "university-academic-productive sector relations" (Sutz 1997) and the adoption of notions such as "corporate academic convergence" (Currie and Newson 1998), "entrepreneurial universities" (Marginson 2000), "campus inc." (White and Hauck 2000), and "corporate ethos" (Gould 2003). More importantly, academic values are now encircled by managerial and budgetary interests (Clark 2002).

Questing for Entrepreneurialism in Hong Kong

The higher education system in Hong Kong transformed itself into a mass higher education system during the early 1990s and has been moving from quantity to quality, and from increasing resource inputs to enhancing effectiveness from the mid-1990s (Cheng 2001). Managerial elements were brought in to reform Hong Kong's education sector with the publication of the *Education Commission (EC) Report No. 7*. Efficient and cost-effective measures and accountability to the stakeholders were introduced as an integrated strategy for building a quality culture in the education sector (EC 1997). In the *Review of Education System Reform Proposal* published in 2000, the Hong Kong government pointed out that there was an urgent need to provide opportunities for Hong Kong people to develop global skills and competencies to sustain Hong Kong's competitiveness in the knowledge-based economy (EC 2000). This policy proposal brought about a new wave of massification in Hong Kong's higher education. The government then decided to expand the higher education subsector by doubling subdegree places by the year 2010 (Tung 2000). Meanwhile, the government started a series of reforms, which brought in managerial elements such as quality assurance and accountability to stakeholders to the higher education subsector. In its review report, *Higher Education in Hong Kong*, in 2002 the University Grants Committee (UGC) proposed a role differentiation, through which a small number of institutions would be strategically identified as the focus of public and private sector support to ensure their capacity for competition with other international institutions at the highest levels (UGC 2002). It then released another report in 2004 entitled *Hong Kong Higher Education: To Make a Difference, To Move with the Times*, in which a clear distinction on the role differentiations among the various universities was made by providing them with different role statements and missions (UGC 2004). In addition, other managerial approaches were proposed and later implemented; these included decoupling the salary pay scale of academic staff from that of the civil service to enhance the freedom and flexibility of institutional management to determine the appropriate terms and conditions of service; and increasing the proportion of public funding based on how well they fulfill the distinctive role of the institutions (UGC 2002). Beyond this, the UGC sought to develop a differentiated yet interlocking system, in which different institutions are expected to operate in distinctive roles but to work in deep collaboration (UGC 2004). These policy initiatives reflect how the UGC has played a strong role in steering the degree-awarding sector of higher education in the process of reviewing the whole university system in the context of the rise of managerialism. The following section specifies some entrepreneurial endeavors of Hong Kong's higher education to show how the system is changing with the global trends of managerialism and entrepreneurialism.

Imposing a Quality Assurance Mechanism

Developing the entrepreneurial culture of higher education involves a shift toward bureaucratic accountability in universities, and regulation on assessing input-process-output is widely adopted as a technique for bureaucrats to uphold accountability (Burke 2005). In Hong Kong, although the UGC seeks to avoid undue intervention in the affairs of the institutions, the imposition of a quality assurance system with an emphasis on role differentiation is seen as a means of regulation in the higher education subsector, in response to the request for public accountability in the society. The Research Assessment Exercise (RAE), for example, was developed as a new funding methodology in 1991, by which resource allocation was linked to performance of individual university departments. To date, four RAEs have been carried out in 1993, 1996, 1999, and 2006. In the assessment, the number of active researchers and the quality of research outputs in each cost center were used as indicators for resource allocation. The term "active researchers" referred to the faculty members in a cost center with research output above the threshold set by the UGC, and the quality of research outputs was based only on the quantity of articles published in international peer-reviewed journals (Chan 2007). The RAE was criticized for bringing a "publish or perish" phenomenon into the academic profession because university departments were assessed and rated as cost centers in RAE 1993 and 1996 (Cheng 1995).In response to this critique, the UGC dropped the idea of active researchers and evaluated the performance of the entire cost center in RAE 1999 and 2006. The UGC also claimed that it would strike a balance between basic research and applied research, and therefore included applied research in RAE 1999 and 2006 by adopting a broader definition of research and scholarship (UGC 2000, 2007). Even though Professor Roland Chin, chairman of the Research Grants Council under the UGC, said that "it is neither fair nor appropriate to compare directly the institutions' performance in research" (UGC 2007), the RAE has successfully legitimated the UGC's initiative of role differentiation through highlighting the outstanding research results of three research-intensive universities, namely, the Chinese University of Hong Kong, the University of Hong Kong, and the Hong Kong University of Science and Technology.

Apart from research, the UGC has also adopted various initiatives and provided incentives to institutions to ensure quality in both teaching and research, commensurate with the role of the institution. These initiatives include Management Review (1998–1999), Teaching and Learning Quality Process Reviews, the Performance and Role-related Funding Scheme, Common English Proficiency Assessment Scheme, Teaching Development Grants, and Language Enhancement Grants. Furthermore, the Quality Assurance Council (QAC) was established in 2007 to function as a semi-autonomous body under the UGC to assist the UGC in ensuring the quality of programs offered by UGC-funded institutions at first-degree level and above (QAC 2009).

In these many quality assurance initiatives, the UGC has reiterated the fulfillment of unique roles by the institutions. The role differentiation indeed functions as a continuous sanction upholding bureaucratic accountability. This shows that although the UGC is not involved in the day-to-day operations of universities, it plays a strong role in innovating the landscape of tertiary education through quality assurance and resource allocation. This is a reflection of the managerial approach, mentioned earlier, toward the new relationship between the government and the university.

Diversifying the Funding Base

The notion of "value for money" has been borrowed from corporate culture and has become a key driver of higher education development. It is implemented in terms of new financial strategies by which Hong Kong's universities have attempted to diversify the financial sources through three major strategies, namely, the adoption of the user-pays principle, commercialization of research, and mobilization of the community's resources. The user-pays principle has been adopted since the government set a minimum fee level for UGC-funded institutions to recover 18 percent of costs, starting from 1997 onward. Because of this new policy, universities started to raise their tuition fees. The policy is associated with a change in the Grants and Loans Scheme. Under the new scheme, approval of grants is on a more stringent basis. Meanwhile, students can choose to apply for the Non-means Tested Loan Scheme, which operates on a full-cost recovery basis, which means that higher interest rates and administrative fees are charged. The user-pays approach has also been adopted at both the subdegree and the postgraduate levels. For example, the number of graduates in full-time accredited self-financing postsecondary program has increased from 1,068 in 2002 to 15,220 in 2008 (see figure 6.1). Meanwhile, the number of full-time accredited self-financing postsecondary programs has also grown from 41 in 2001–2002 to 347 in 2008–2009 (see figure 6.2). The rapid growth of these non-first degree programs was owing to the government's position that sees these programs as the major measure to support the aggressive increase in postsecondary education opportunities. Yet, it has decided to withdraw its funding to the subsector that awards non-first-degree programs.

To fulfill the market needs for continuing education, the government has spent HK$5 billion on establishing the Continuing Education Fund (CEF) for subsidizing working adults with learning aspirations to pursue continuing education and

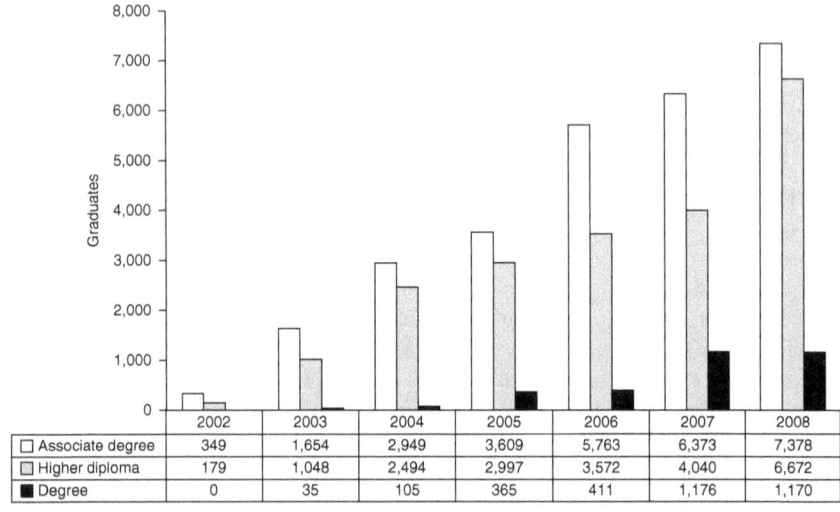

Figure 6.1 Numbers of Graduates of Full-time Accredited Self-financing Postsecondary Programs, 2002–2008
Source: IPASS (2009).

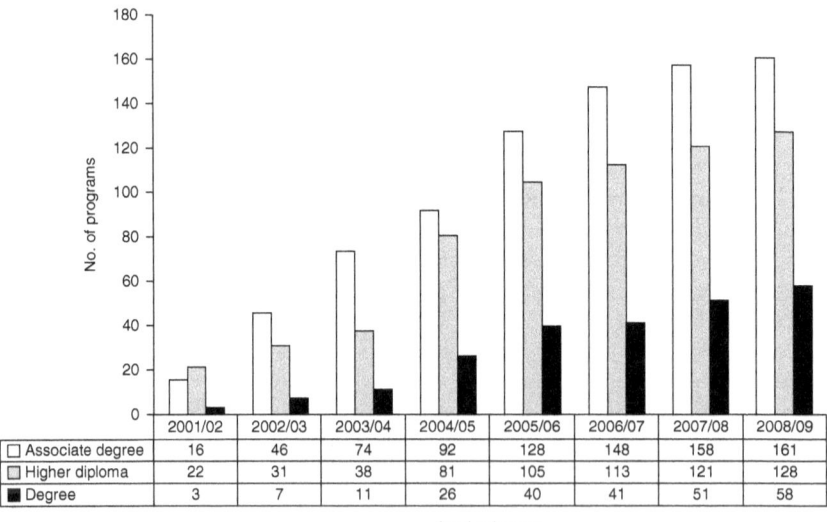

Figure 6.2 Numbers of Full-time Accredited Self-financing Postsecondary Programs, 2001/02–2008/09
Source: IPASS (2009).

training courses. Applicants are eligible for reimbursement of up to 80 percent of their tuition fees, subject to a maximum sum of HK$10,000, upon the successful completion of their training programs. While these initiatives taken to cater to market demand have further facilitated the growth of the education market, they will also lead to the commercialization of education. On the one hand, in line with the fee-charging principle, Hong Kong's universities and their commercial extensions have started to run various kinds of distance learning courses, conversion courses, commissioned courses, and continuing education programs at different levels on a commercial basis, either by themselves, or in collaboration with overseas universities or with the private sector. On the other, a wide range of choices, with limited but accessible subsidies, encourage students to take courses in the education market instead of through the traditional enrollment channels.

For mobilization of nongovernment funding, fund-raising has become a widely accepted method of gaining new financial resources for universities in Hong Kong. They have become progressively active in seeking donations from social organizations and individuals. Nowadays, every university in the territory has established a donation committee for raising funds. There have been a few representative cases of generous donations to the tertiary education in the local community. For instance, the Li Ka Shing Foundation donated HK$1 billion to the University of Hong Kong's (HKU) Faculty of Medicine (*Ming Pao,* May 6, 2005, A05); and the Fok Ying Tung Foundation donated HK$500 million to develop HKUST's Nansha Information Technology Park in Guangzhou (*Sing Tao Daily,* March 20, 2006, A21).

To foster a fund-raising culture, a HK$1 billion Matching Grant Scheme (MGS) was established in 2003 for awarding grants to UGC-funded institutions to match private donations.. The MGS primarily aims to diversify funding sources for higher education and to increase the momentum for developing a stronger philanthropic culture in the community toward investment in education. The general principle of the scheme is that both the matching grant and the corresponding private donation must be used for activities within the ambit of UGC recurrent grants. The matching grant was disbursed on a dollar-for-dollar matching basis up to the "floor" amount of HK$45 million, beyond which HK$1 was granted for every HK$2 donation, up to a ceiling of HK$250 million of grant on a first-come-first-served basis. Yet, the early phase of the scheme shows that universities with a longer history and a larger group of alumni are more capable of generating revenue through fund-raising than others. Thus, funding which has not been matched by the concerned institutions in a 12-month period would be opened for application by all institutions on a first-come-first-served basis. By the end of 2008, there were four rounds of MGS under which the eight UGC-funded institutions had together secured over HK$6.7 billion of donations, and a total sum of HK$4 billion has been allocated to match the donations (UGC 2009).

Diversifying the Provision

In the past, the UGC-funded institutions played a dominant role in the provision of higher education in Hong Kong. Private institutions constituted only a very small proportion of the higher education provisions. However, this situation has changed in recent years. For instance, Shue Yan University, a private tertiary education institute with a 35-year history, has been newly recognized and renamed, and it became the first private university in Hong Kong. Shue Yan's elevation to private university status breaks the monopoly on degree awarding held by publicly funded universities or programs run in association with overseas universities. It is hoped that this new development would mark the way for more private tertiary institutions offering degrees (Lam and Hui 2006).

Moreover, the government has decided to undertake further massification of higher education in recent years, so that 60 percent of secondary school leavers will be able to receive tertiary education by the year 2010. "In achieving this target, the government will facilitate tertiary institutions, private enterprises and other organizations to provide options other than the traditional sixth form education, such as professional diploma courses and sub-degree courses" (Tung 2000, 23). In response to the government's call for further massification of higher education, the Education Commission (EC) proposed three major components in its *Review of Education System Proposal;* universities, that is, degree-awarding educational institutions; postsecondary colleges, that is, institutions that offer courses above secondary level; and continuing education institutions, that is, continuing education institutions that provide different types of courses above the secondary level (EC 2000).

The proposal indicates that privatization, as an efficient way to diversify the higher education system and to allow students more choices, will be a likely trend with the expected rapid growth of associate degree programs by community colleges that are not funded by the government. In fact, in recent years, numerous community colleges have been established to provide subdegree programs, including associate degree, higher diploma, professional diploma, and other postsecondary programs of equivalent standard on a self-financing basis. Currently, there are 20 institutions offering full-time accredited self-financing subdegree programs, and all the UGC-funded institutions have joined this new market by establishing their community colleges or continuing education units, which can be seen as "semi-private" institutions in themselves. Though these subdegree programs are operated on a self-financing basis, the government provides a package of financial assistance schemes to eligible students, including means-tested grants, low-interest loans, non-means-tested loans, and travel subsidies (EMB 2006). This demonstrates that in privatizing higher education, the Hong Kong government has adopted a "public-aided approach" to transform the higher education landscape from a public dominance to a public-private mix.

In addition, the continuing education units of the UGC-funded institutions are active in developing distance learning courses, conversion courses, and other continuing education programs in collaboration with overseas universities. Unlike Singapore and Malaysia, where the government directly intervenes in shaping the development of joint programs, the Hong Kong government has adopted a far more liberal approach to allow the market forces to decide the higher education market. Foreign universities can easily enter the Hong Kong market. Currently, all courses conducted in Hong Kong leading to the award of nonlocal higher academic qualifications (including subdegree, degree, postgraduate or other postsecondary qualifications), or professional qualifications, must be properly registered or be exempted from registration. An overseas institution is required to obtain accreditation, or other formal permission, from the Education Bureau (EDB) prior to its operation. This category is diverse, ranging from compulsory registration to formal assessment of academic criteria. The EDB will normally seek independent expert advice from the Hong Kong Council for Academic Accreditation (HKCAA) as to whether a course meets the criteria for registration or it may be exempted from registration. However, the relevant requirements are considered straightforward and nonburdensome. The Hong Kong government tends not to directly curb and regulate the quality, content, level, and cost of courses offered by foreign educational institutions. Instead, it heavily relies on the market mechanism, where its main role is to provide sufficient information for consumers to make a choice (Yang 2006).

The rapid expansion of subdegree and continuing education programs has diversified the provision of higher education in Hong Kong. As a consequence, a new market has emerged and it is becoming more mature in the higher education subsector. Universities are now required to compete with each other and, therefore, tend to reform their curricula design in accordance with the market needs. Vocation-oriented studies have become popular in universities. To increase their competitiveness, some universities have started to revise their program structures and to provide more international student exchange programs, internship programs, and double major programs. These curriculum changes have given students many more choices in courses than before, and thus they attract students with varied needs and expectations. All these changes are considered as a sort of marketization, which represents a move from the traditional teacher-oriented paradigm to a learner-oriented one (Mok 2005).

Parallel Developments in Singapore

To enhance its competitiveness in the globalized economic environment, Singapore has attempted to reform and streamline its education sector in line with managerialism and entrepreneurialism. The launch of the national vision of "Thinking Schools, Learning Nation" (TSLN) in 1997 was viewed as a major milestone. The vision, the central force behind the development of education, has been guiding the government's subsequent educational initiatives. The primary goal of the TSLN is to introduce greater flexibility and autonomy in the education sector to maximize students' potential through developing their ability of thinking independently and innovatively (FitzPatrick 2003), as the Singapore government has viewed creativity as a crucial ingredient in enhancing the competitiveness of the country's economy (Tan and Ng 2007). As Tao Chee Hean, the then minister for education, said, "we hope to better develop each of our students to his full potential, so that he will be ready to face the challenges of the New Economy" (cited in Tan and Ng 2007, 164). The Singapore government's attitude demonstrates how education reforms in the country are linked with the emergence of the knowledge-based economy.

Following the launch of the TSLN vision, universities in Singapore have been granted in the past decade more autonomy and more accountability than ever before. According to the report entitled *Fostering Autonomy and Accountability* published in 2000, more autonomous power in fiscal and personnel matters would be granted to the two state universities, namely the National University of Singapore (NUS) and the Nanyang Technological University (NTU). The autonomization is aimed at ensuring that public funds can be used in an efficient and effective but accountable way. Meanwhile, by restructuring schemes and introducing quality audit and control, universities in Singapore have moved toward a businesslike model. In this section, a few examples are given of the changes that have been taking place in Singapore characterized by managerialism and entrepreneurialism

Imposing a Quality Assurance Mechanism

Business management concepts and practices have been introduced to the university sector in Singapore in response to the demand for accountability and efficiency in the society since the mid-1990s. This has been done by introducing the strategies of role differentiation and quality audit and control to ensure the quality of teaching and research with a rational distribution of resources (Lee and Gopinathan 2007). It has designed a three-tiered university system, in which the first tier would be the elite universities whose primary aim is to carry out world-class research and development, while the second and third tiers would be the bedrock of the university segment. According to the policy paper entitled *Developing Singapore's Education Industry* published by the Ministry of Trade and Industry (MTI) in 2002, the first tier of the university system would comprise top "world-class universities" across the world. The government thus invited nine top "world-class universities" to establish their offshore campuses in Singapore (MTI 2002). The introduction of transnational education to the city-state was due the government's keenness to develop Singapore as a "regional hub of higher education." This point is elaborated fully below.

The policy paper expects that the second tier of the university system would mainly consist of the existing local universities (namely NUS, NTU, and Singapore Management University [SMU]), while the third tier would constitute additional private universities focusing on teaching and applied research. With the expansion of the university system, the government targeted to raise the university cohort participation rate from 21 percent in 2003 to 25 percent by 2010 (SMOE 2003). Despite the plan for building "world-class university" by bringing in renowned foreign universities, the three local universities continue to play a predominant role in Singapore's tertiary education. Among them, NUS and NTU have been developed as comprehensive universities, which "initiated a number of innovative programmes, including the broadening of undergraduate education, the introduction of a core curriculum, collaborations with top foreign universities, and the establishment of inter-disciplinary centres" (SMOE 2007), while SMU has been positioned to be a business and management university that mainly offers business curriculum. These three are seen as the top-tier universities in the city-state, while SIM University, a private comprehensive university, and six private specialized universities/institutions, including local branches of foreign universities, constitute the second tier. The polytechnics are responsible for professional education and are regarded as the third tier in the present system (SMOE 2007).

Apart from role differentiation, the Singapore government has strengthened its quality assurance mechanism by working out a Quality Assurance Framework for Universities (QAFU). To execute the auditing process, SMOE set up an external panel called Higher Education Quality Assurance Unit (HEQAU) to evaluate and validate the universities' self-assessments of their institutional goals and performance targets. The universities would develop their own performance indicators used in QAFU. Then, each university would make a self-assessment, once every three years, on the basis of 32 institutional goals covering five areas, namely, governance, management, teaching, research, and service. Individual universities are thus required to evaluate the extent to which they have achieved the targeted goals. This would then be followed by external challenge and validation. An external review panel would visit the university and conduct wide-ranging consultations with the management, internal quality assurance managers, academic staff, students, and external stakeholders. Finally, at the feedback and development stage, the university would report about what it has learnt from the auditing exercise (SMOE 2001, cited in Lee and Gopinathan 2007, 117–122). To sum up, quality assurance was first introduced and then it became embedded in Singapore's higher education subsector when its landscape was restructured by implementing regular auditing exercises.

Corporatizing Public Universities

The Singapore government has comprehensively reviewed the university sector in 2003. In the report *Restructuring the University Sector—More Opportunities, Better Quality*, the government indicated its will to restructure the landscape of the university sector by developing NUS and NTU into comprehensive universities, while maintaining SMU's niche of business management. This restructuring exercise follows the logic of assigning stratified missions to individual institutions to maximize the effective utilization of public resources. Nevertheless, the government is also aware of the need to retain limited scale of interuniversity competition, because "managed" competition is seen as conducive to improving the quality of Singapore's higher education (Lee and Gopinathan 2007, 130). The government therefore decided to further autonomize the university sector in finance and governance through corporatization.

NUS and NTU, the two publicly funded comprehensive universities, have been transformed from statutory boards to university companies since the promulgation of the University Corporatization Act in 2005, while SMU was founded as a private company in 2000. By being corporatized, universities were made further autonomous as "not-for-profit" companies. The Singapore Ministry of Education (SMOE) hopes that after becoming autonomous universities, NUS, NTU, and SMU will have greater flexibility in deciding on matters such as internal governance, budget utilization, tuition fees, and admission requirements, given that these flexibilities enable the universities to differentiate themselves and pursue their own strategies to bring about the most optimal outcomes for their stakeholders (SMOE 2005b). These reforms also intended to cultivate a greater sense of ownership among the larger university community to engender a mind-set change and instill a greater sense of pride among the key stakeholders of the university who therefore would be more active in shaping the unique culture and identity of their universities (SMOE 2005b).

In fact, corporatizing of public universities can be traced back to the establishment of SMU, the third university in Singapore. Given that public universities were built as an extension of the government in the past, the Singapore government intended to adopt the U.S. model in SMU, which is seen as more flexible and more capable to cope with the highly dynamic global environment. The SMOE thus has been watching over the development and operation of SMU's corporatized model very closely since its establishment. When such a model is seen to be successful, it will be further promoted in the other two comprehensive universities. This is the rationale behind the recent corporatization of public universities in Singapore.

It is noteworthy that though each institution is assigned a role in the university system, corporatization encourages institutions to brand themselves differently. For instance, SMU is positioned as a business management institution and therefore is pursuing an advantaged position among the business schools in Singapore. The case of SMU rationalizes the recent actions of corporatization in the context of the policy of role differentiation and the associated stratified missions. On the one hand, universities have been granted more autonomy to compete with each other in the newly emerging higher education market. On the other, they are required to follow an agreed role in the subsector. Indeed, corporatization and the associated competition among universities are adopted as the ways to prevent higher education institutions from becoming static in their development. There is a contractual relationship between universities and the SMOE, in which the government insists on maintaining its control. As the University Autonomy, Governance and Funding Steering Committee says,

> Even as we seek to devolve greater autonomy to NUS, NTU and SMU, we remain mindful that our universities are vital national institutions and they have a public obligation to fulfill.... Hence, we need to ensure that our universities' missions remain firmly aligned with our national strategic objectives. At the same time, our Steering Committee proposes that the Minister for Education appoint the university Council members. In addition, the Steering Committee recommends that an enhanced accountability framework for universities be introduced, comprising the existing Quality Assurance Framework for Universities (QAFU), and the proposed Policy and Performance Agreements between MOE and each university. (SMOE 2005a)

Diversifying the Provision

As said earlier, developing Singapore as a "regional education hub" was set as a target for the nation. The government tactically and strategically invited "world-class" and "reputable" universities from abroad to set up their Asian campuses in the country in the mid-1990s. In fact, SMU's attempt at collaboration started with its adoption of the U.S. model in setting up the collaboration with the Wharton School of the University of Pennsylvania in 1999. Later, two foreign business schools namely, INSEAD and University of Chicago Booth School of Business (formerly the Chicago Graduate School of Business), came to Singapore to set up their branches in Asia. INSEAD is an international business school offering postgraduate programs in management, including MBA, Executive MBA, and PhD. It has campuses in Singapore and France, and one center in Abu Dhabi. The Asian campus in Singapore shares an equivalent status with the European campus in France and both are "fully connected" (INSEAD 2009). The University of Chicago Booth School of Business provides postgraduate courses in business management and has campuses in Chicago, London, and Singapore. Its Executive MBA program provides courses to combine students from all three campuses to provide them a wider global network (University of Chicago Booth School of Business 2009).

The government also encourages local universities and institutes to partner with overseas universities. For example, the Singapore Manufacturing Federation's (SMF) School of Management NUS has tied up with Australia's Murdoch University to provide joint programs and operate an International Study Centre. The Lee Kuan Yew School of Public Policy of the NUS offers a double master's degree in collaboration with Columbia University's School of International and Public Affairs, London School of Economics and Political Science, and the Institut d'Etudes Politiques de Paris. A dual-degree educational doctorate is jointly run by the Singapore National Institute of Education and the Institute of Education at the University of London (Ng and Chan 2008).

While developing transnational education has been accepted as a strategy to internationalize Singapore's higher education and to pursue "world-class" status, it has diversified the provisions of higher education in the country as well.

Comparing Entrepreneurial Endeavors in Higher Education in Hong Kong and Singapore

While Hong Kong and Singapore adopted a relatively centralized model in their education systems, in which the state plays a dominant role vis-à-vis the private sector (Mok and Tan 2004), the higher education reforms discussed above have shown how the governments in the two cities have subsequently promoted private and managerial elements in their higher education so as to incorporate universities. Nevertheless, flourishing alongside managerialism and entrepreneurialism does not necessarily mean a decline of state role in the higher education subsector. On the contrary, the adoption of a businesslike model might provide new and rational means to strengthen state control in university governance. The RAE, teaching and learning quality review and management review exercised by UGC in Hong Kong, and the QAFU exercised by HEQAU in Singapore, for example, are recognized as a series of efficient instruments to build up a quality assurance mechanism to sustain the quality of teaching and research of universities. This mechanism was meant to drive the universities toward developing the roles that governments wanted them to play. The two governments have no plans to withdraw their steering role in higher education, despite the transformation from centralization to decentralization. A more decentralized governing setting, which has been built through strengthening the quality assurance mechanism, enables the governments to govern from a distance (Jayasuriya 2005, 24).

Although Hong Kong and Singapore have a similar perspective on the government's role in stratifying the higher education subsector, they seemingly have different perspectives on the government role as the funder. From the perspective of the Hong Kong government, private and nonstate sectors can be additional financial sources for providing education services (Tung 2000). Given the fact that the Hong Kong has a long history of public dominance in education, it seems that the society is yet to have a culture of accepting a private-dominated education sector. The government hence has adopted a "public-aided approach" to transform the higher education landscape from a public dominance to a public-private mix. By facilitating fund-raising activities for universities and encouraging a philanthropic culture in the community, the MGS helps to change the tradition of sole reliance on government funding in higher education subsector. The adoption of the fee-charging and user-pays principle then can be viewed as the methods to locate new financial sources for the university sector.

The Singapore government similarly intends to develop a public-private mix, which however has a different meaning in terms of government funding strategy. For example, while SMU, as a private company, is allowed to raise endowment fund and charge tuition fee, the government provides full financial support to its facilities and part of its operating budget. Indeed, Singapore launched the university endowment fund as early as in 1991 to diversify sources of university funding. NUS and NTU had to raise SG$250 million on their own to net another SG$250 million to match the SG$500 million of start-up funds from the government, thus making a total of SG$1 billion within a five-year period (Gopinathan and Morriss 1997). Meanwhile, universities also set up spin-off companies to garner extra financial resources. NUS, for example, established its enterprise in 2001 as a university-level cluster to provide an entrepreneurial and innovative dimension to education and research. Its mission is "to be an agent of change, to promote the spirit of innovation and enterprise within the NUS community, and to generate value from university resources through experiential education, industry engagement and partnerships and entrepreneurship support" (NUS 2007).

All these changes functionally fit into the public-aided approach implemented in Hong Kong. However, with a different rationale, the corporatization of higher education in Singapore is not primarily taken as a method to generate additional funding, though the NUS and NTU, as the university companies, are required to achieve their missions and objectives within the limits of financial resources available to them. Indeed, according to the speeches of the Singaporean officials, financial constraint is not a key consideration when they are planning the future development of higher education. Instead, they repeatedly stress the importance of innovation and diversity in higher education for nurturing students to be creative and innovative (Ng 2007). In contrast, the generation of nonstate input was set as a major goal, when the then chief executive of Hong Kong, Tung Chee Hwa called for further expanding and reforming the higher education subsector in 2000 (Tung 2000). These two standpoints project different mind-sets of leaders of Hong Kong and Singapore. For Hong Kong's leaders, corporatization of higher education would mean the maximization of "value for money" and cost-effectiveness in higher education. "Academic entrepreneurship" (Leydsdorrff and Etzkowitz 2001), therefore, has been upheld by the government to transform the governance framework of the education sector into that of the business sector. In contrast, for Singapore's leaders, the incorporation reforms would merely mean a rational instrument to streamline the higher education subsector in the face of the global tide of managerialism. Quality control would be the primary consideration in granting autonomous power. So keeping the higher education subsector regulated through a more businesslike model (i.e., external quality assurance requirements) becomes a possible way to achieve the dual goal of autonomization and re-regulation set out by the Singapore government. Such an argument is empirically supported by the two governments' reactions to the problems of financial stringency and resource shortage after the Asian Financial Crisis. While the Hong Kong government continuously reduced the recurrent grant for tertiary education from the late 1990s to early 2000s, the Singapore government, on the contrary, increased its recurring expenses on universities (Singapore Department of Statistics 2001; UGC 2004).

The argument of different agendas in the implementation of similar reform approach is further supported by different attitudes in the introduction of overseas tertiary education providers. Hong Kong provides a free market in this part of the higher education subsector. Any institution may enter the Hong Kong market if it wants to, but the government would neither intervene nor support any foreign higher education providers. Such an attitude stems from the belief in the effectiveness of market mechanism. However, considering the government's retreat in its financial commitments in subdegree level of higher education and local institutions' eagerness for collaborating with foreign partners, it is believed that the introduction of transnational education in Hong Kong is seen as an instrument for "profit-seeking" investments. In Singapore, the government, however, is proactively involved in this emerging part of higher education. It sees collaboration as a way to realize the strategic goals of internationalization of higher education and building of world-class universities and not as a profit-making venture. Therefore, the number of institutions entering the Singapore higher education market is limited and controlled. Only those regarded as renowned universities would be invited to set up their branches in the city-state, while the government would close those seen as underperforming. The closure of the Division of Biomedical Sciences of John Hopkins University in Singapore in 2006 was one such example that demonstrated the government's strong position on this issue (Lee and Gopinathan 2007, 128).

Summing up, though universities in both Hong Kong and Singapore are pushed to move toward a more businesslike model, their entrepreneurial agendas and attitudes are not the same..

Critical Reflections on Entrepreneurialism in Higher Education

The higher education reforms in Hong Kong and Singapore have been carried out through a combination of styles and controls, which consists of various business-style management skills, including management and productivity development systems, budget controls, market strategies, the redistribution of labor, the development of research and ancillary enterprises, and customer service orientation (Gould 2003). The introduction of these skills has brought a marketized and diversified funding mechanism to universities. We live at a time when a utilitarian rationality that stresses cost effectiveness and value for money has come to dominate societies No wonder then that today's university culture is economically rational or entrepreneurial. Therefore the need for accountability to the general public and productivity of the university sector in terms of economic values have become a strong rationale for the adoption of managerial skills such as performance-based finance and salary systems and the use of market mechanisms. Meanwhile, while more people are pushed to seek for tertiary education by the tide of lifelong learning and continuous education in the society, students' choice has become an important factor in the consideration of launching courses and programs. This has also led to the rise of consumerist culture, which has brought a tremendous increase of courses and programs in the higher education market.

These changes have fundamentally altered the academic atmosphere, in which cultural changes toward entrepreneurship have dominated university governance. This would plausibly make the university more flexible, productive, and creative in coping with the dynamic environments, given that a business modeled on managerial stratum would be more proactive in facing changes, exercise more discretionary power in financial arrangements and decision-making processes, and enjoy more freedom to innovate their organizations (Currie and Vidovich 1998; Bottery 2000). In this sense, academia might not totally veto the values of managerial and market elements and of corporatization in the transformation of the higher education susbsector as well as of the relationship between universities and the state, or even that of society.

Some fundamental ideas and values underlying the establishment of a university, like democracy, liberty, and humanity however may be phased out in the progress toward entrepreneurialism. As Scott (2004) argues, if universities are defined as centers that promote these values and their primary function is to cultivate citizenship in students and enable them to live in a responsible way socially, culturally, economically and politically, as well as by professional codes and practices, instead of managerial/bureaucratic ones, they are in a better position to achieve academic excellence. The introduction of an entrepreneurial culture in higher education is seen to be causing an erosion of the conduct of higher education and would send a wrong message to students. The consumerist culture on campus then makes the students unable to distinguish the role of citizen from that of the consumer. Even the academics would collapse the distinction between education and job training, or scholarship and grant getting, and so on (Giroux 2005). The managerial reforms or the growth of the corporate culture, in universities are, therefore, being criticized as a sort of "mis-education" (Lustig 2005), "deprofessionalization of academics" (Readings 1996) and "anti-humanity" (Scott 2004). In Toni Morrison's (as cited in Giroux 2002, 456) words,

> If the university does not take seriously and rigorously its role as a guardian of wider civic freedoms, as interrogator of more and more complex ethical problems, as servant and preserver of deeper democratic practices, then some other regime or ménage of regimes will do it for us, in spite of us, and without us.

Morrison rightly cautions all members of the academia to be aware of the changing meanings and purposes of higher education. Yet higher education is undergoing a more rapid progress of depublicization owing to its high potential for profit generation. This is especially clear when we consider the strong mind-set that favors learning and education and rationalizes the eagerness to pay for better education, commonly shared among the East Asian societies.(Cummings 1996). Higher education is a big business venture in the region. However, higher education reforms in Hong Kong and Singapore are not merely developments toward a more diversified model for funding, and education provision, but also are ways of promoting the cities as regional education hubs and of transforming higher education into a sort of service industry for export to generate revenue for the national treasury. Therefore it seems impossible to reverse the tide of entrepreneurialism and its implications for higher education.

Striking a balance between the fundamental values of university education and the advantages of entrepreneurialism is perhaps the biggest challenge that academia faces today.

Conclusion

The discussion above indicates that recent higher education developments in Hong Kong and Singapore are in line with entrepreneurialism. The new dispensation requires universities to fulfill a more complex mission, which consists of the traditional goals of providing general liberal education, research and scholarship, service to society, as well as the new objective of giving support for the economy through the provision of useful knowledge within the context of a knowledge-based economy (Gould 2003). Though critics point out that there are conflicts between the old and new missions of the university, it is not necessarily a choice between good and evil. Universities are no doubt required to sacrifice some of their traditions in the process of transition, but this can be a way to revitalize higher education. However, the changes involved in this transition should be achieved through a democratic process. As Elizabeth Kelly (1995, 88–89) points out,

> [University] is where much of the collective historical memory of particular culture is generated, collected, analyzed, and preserved. As institutions, universities are distinguished from other public and private arenas because of venerable traditions of intellectual autonomy and academic freedom, which have formally, if not always substantively, shaped the quest for knowledge and truth. Although this history had hardly been unproblematic, the institutional constellation of higher education offers an existing framework within which individuals can work toward thinking, debating, and implementing a praxis if democracy public knowledge to inform a much larger, and ongoing, process of recognizing and extending the range of social, economic, and political possibilities and choices.

This quotation provides a guideline for a truly diversified development of tertiary education. This is a criterion much to be prized for a regional hub of higher education.

References

Ball, Stephen J. 1990. *Politics and Policy Making in Education.* London: Routledge.
Ball, Stephen J. 1998 "Big Politics/Small World: An Introduction to International Perspectives in Education Policy." *Comparative Education* 34 (2): 119–130.
Bottery, Mike. 2000. *Education, Policy and Ethics.* New York: Continuum.
Bridges, David, and Terence H. McLaughlin, eds. 1994. *Education and the Market Place.* London: Falmer Press.
Burke, Joseph C. 2005. "The Many Faces of Accountability." In *Achieving Accountability in Higher Education: Balancing Public, Academic, and Market Demands*, ed. J. C. Burke. San Francisco: Jossey-Bass.
Chan, David K. K. 2007. "Global Agenda, Local Response: The Changing Education Governance in Hong Kong." *Globalization, Education and Societies* 5 (1): 109–124.
Cheng, Yin-Cheong. 1995. "School Education Quality: Conceptualization, Monitoring, and Enhancement." In *Quality in Education: Insights from Different Perspectives*, eds. P. K. Sui and T. K. Tam. Hong Kong: Hong Kong Education Research Association.
Cheng, Yin-Cheong. 2001. "Education Reforms in Hong Kong: Challenges, Strategies and International Implications." Plenary speech presented at the International Forum on Education Reform: Experiences in Selected Countries, Bangkok, Thailand, July 30–August 2, 2001.
Clark, Barton R. 2002. "*Entrepreneurial University* (Comparative Education Policy Research Unit Occasional Paper Series No. 1). Hong Kong: Comparative Education Policy Research Unit, City University of Hong Kong.
Cummings, William K. 1996. "Asian Values, Education and Development." *Compare* 26 (3): 287–304.
Currie, Jan, and Janice Newson, eds. 1998. *Universities and Globalization: Critical Perspectives.* Thousand Oaks, CA: Sage Publications.

Currie, Jan, and Lesley Vidovich. 1998. "Micro-economic Reform through Managerialism in American and Australian universities." In *Universities and Globalization: Critical Perspectives*, eds. J. Currie, and J. Newson. Thousand Oaks, CA: Sage Publications.

Currie, Jan, Richard DeAngelis, Harry de Boer, Jeroen Huisman, and Claude Lacotte. 2002. *Globalizing Practices and University Responses: European and Anglo-American Differences*. Westport: Praeger.

Deem, Rosemary, Sam Hillyard, and Mike Reed. 2007. *Knowledge, Higher Education, and the New Managerialism: The Changing Management of UK Universities*. Oxford; New York: Oxford University Press.

Education and Manpower Bureau (EMB). 2006. Hong Kong: EMB. http://www.emb.gov.hk.

Education Commission (EC). 1997. *Education Commission Report No.7: Quality School Education*. Hong Kong: EC.

EC. 2000. *Review of Education System Reform Proposal*. Hong Kong: EC.

Enders, Jürgen, and Oliver Fulton, eds. 2002. *Higher Education in A Globalising World: International Trends and Mutual Observations: A Festschrift in Honour of Ulrich Teichler*. Dordrecht, The Netherlands: Kluwer Academic Publishers.

FitzPatrick, Paul. 2003. "Reinventing Singapore: Changing a Country's Mindset by Changing Its Education System." *International Higher Education* 31 (Spring): 22–23.

Giroux, Henry A. 2002. "Neoliberalism, Corporate Culture, and the Promise of Higher Education: The University as a Democratic Public Sphere." *Harvard Educational Review* 72 (4): 425–463.

Giroux, Henry A. 2005. "Academic Entrepreneurs: The Corporate Takeover of Higher Education." *Tikkun* 20 (2): 18–22.

Gopinathan, Saravanan, and Susan B. Morriss. 1997. "Trends in University Reform in the Context of Massification." *RIHE International Seminar Reports* 1: 55–71.

Gould, Eric. 2003. *The University in a Corporate Culture*. New Haven, CT: Yale University Press.

Information Portal for Accredited Self-financing Post-secondary Programmes (IPASS). 2009. "Statistical Information." Hong Kong: IPASS. http://www.ipass.gov.hk.

INSEAD. 2009. "Who We Are." New York: INSEAD. http://www.insead.edu/home.

Jayasuriya, Kanishka. 2005. "Capacity beyond the Boundary: New Regulatory State, Fragmentation and Relational Capacity." In *Challenges to State Policy Capacity: Global Trends and Comparative Perspectives*, eds. M. Painter and J. Pierre. Basingstoke, UK: Palgrave Macmillan.

Kelly, Elizabeth A. 1995. *Education, Democracy, and Public Knowledge*. Boulder, CO: Westview Press.

Lam, Agnes, and Polly Hui. 2006. "College Made First Private University." *South China Morning Post*, December 20, City 1.

Lee, Michael H., and Saravanan Gopinathan. 2007. "University Restructuring in Singapore: Amazing! Or a Maze?" *Journal of Comparative Asian Development* 6 (1): 107–141.

Leydsdorrff, Loet, and Henry Etzkowitz. 2001. "The Transformation of University-Industry-Government Relations." *Electronic Journal of Sociology* 5 (4): 1–17.

Lustig, Jeff. 2005. "The University Revisioned: An Alternative to Corporate Mis-Education." *The Review of Education* 27 (1): 17–52.

Marginson, Simon. 2000. *Entrepreneurial Universities*. Comparative Education Policy Occasional Paper Series No. 1. Hong Kong: Comparative Education Policy Research Unit, City University of Hong Kong.

Ming Pao. 2005. "Li Ka Shing Donated HK$1 billion to HKU for Helping the University Become the World's Top 25 Universities." [In Chinese.] May 6, A05.

Ministry of Trade and Industry (MTI). 2002. *Developing Singapore's Education Industry.* Singapore: MTI.
Mok, Ka-Ho. 2005. "Fostering Entrepreneurship: Changing Role of Government and Higher Education Governance in Hong Kong." *Research Policy* 34 (4): 537–554.
Mok, Ka-Ho, and Jason Tan. 2004. *Globalization and Marketization in Education: A Comparative Analysis of Hong Kong and Singapore*. Cheltenham: Edward Elgar.
Mok, Ka-Ho, and Anthony Welch, eds. 2003. *Globalization and Educational Restructuring in the Asia Pacific Region.* Basingstoke, UK: Palgrave Macmillan.
National University of Singapore (NUS). 2007. "Enterprise." Singapore: NUS. http://www.nus.edu.sg.
Ng, Pak-Tee. 2007. "Quality Assurance in the Singapore Education System in an Era of Diversity and Innovation." *Educational Research for Policy and Practice* 6 (3) 235–247.
Ng, Pak-Tee, and David Chan. 2008. "Similar Agendas, Diverse Strategies: The Quest for a Regional Hub of Higher Education in Hong Kong and Singapore." *Higher Education Policy* 21 (4): 487–503.
Quality Assurance Council (QAC). 2009. Hong Kong: QAC. http://www.ugc.edu.hk.
Readings, Bill. 1996. *The University in Ruins.* Cambridge, MA: Harvard University Press.
Scott, Dane. 2004. "Transforming the 'Market-model University': Environmental Philosophy, Citizenship and the Recovery of the Humanities." *Worldview* 8 (2–3): 162–184.
Sing Tao Daily. 2006. "To Guarantee Sufficient Research Grant, HKU Will Not Be Privatized in the Short Run." [In Chinese.] March 20, A21.
Singapore Department of Statistics. 2001. *Yearbook of Statistics Singapore 2001.* Singapore: Singapore Department of Statistics.
Singapore Ministry of Education (SMOE). 2003. "Restructuring of Singapore's university sector." *Press Release*, 28 May 2003. Singapore: SMOE.
SMOE. 2005a. "Autonomous Universities–Towards Peaks of Excellence." Press release, January 6, 2005. Singapore: SMOE.
SMOE. 2005b. *Milestone 2004–2005.* Singapore: SMOE.
SMOE. 2007. "Education System: Post-secondary." Singapore: SMOE. http://www.moe.gov.sg/corporate/post_secondary.htm.
Sutz, Judith. 1997. "The New Role of the University in the Productive Sector." In *Universities and the Global Knowledge Economy: A Triple Helix of University-Industry-Government Relations*, **eds.** H. Etzkowitz and L. Leydesdorff. London: Pinter.
Tan, Charlene, and Pak-Tee Ng. 2007. "Dynamics of Change: Decentralized Centralism of Education in Singapore." *Journal of Education Change* 8 (2): 155–168.
Tung, Chee-Wah. 2000. *The 2000 Policy Address: Quality Education, Policy Objective for Education and Manpower Bureau.* Hong Kong: Government Printer.
University Grants Committee (UGC). 2000. *Research Assessment Exercise 1999—Local Universities Achieve Remarkable Research Results.* Hong Kong: UGC. http://www.ugc.edu.hk.
UGC. 2002. *Higher Education in Hong Kong: Report of the University Grants Committee.* Hong Kong: UGC.
UGC. 2004. *Hong Kong Higher Education: To Make a Difference, To Move with the Times.* Hong Kong: UGC.
UGC. 2007. *Excellent Results from the Research Assessment Exercise 2006.* Hong Kong: UGC. http://www.ugc.edu.hk.
UGC. 2009. *Results of the Fourth Matching Grant Scheme Announced.* Hong Kong UGC. http://www.ugc.edu.hk.
University of Chicago Booth School of Business. 2009. "About Chicago Booth." Chicago: Booth School of Business. http://www.chicagobooth.edu.

White, Geoffry D., and Flannery C. Hauck, eds. 2000. *Campus, Inc.: Corporate Power in the Ivory Tower.* Amherst, NY: Prometheus Books.

Williams, Gareth. 2003. "An Honest Living or Dumbing Down?" In *The Enterprising University: Reform, Excellence and Equity*, ed. G. Williams. Buckingham, UK: Open University Press.

Yang, Rui. 2006. "Transnational Higher Education in Hong Kong: An Analysis." In *Transnational Higher Education in Asia and the Pacific Region*, ed. F. Huang. Hiroshima: Research Institute for Higher Education, Hiroshima University.

Chapter 7

University Governance Structure in Challenging Times: The Case of Malaysia's First APEX University (Universiti Sains Malaysia)

Morshidi Sirat and A. R. Ahmad

Introduction

The current era of globalization and the subsequent internationalization of higher education are undoubtedly the two main influencing factors determining the developmental path of higher education systems and institutions in both developed and developing countries. Apparently, many higher education systems and institutions, especially those from the emerging economies, are positioning themselves in the global higher education landscape through networks, student mobility programs, and other academic exchanges with developed countries. Generally, globalization induces competition between high-ranking education systems and institutions, rather than inspiring capacity building wherein 'capacity building' refers to intentional, coordinated, and mission-driven efforts aimed at strengthening the management and organizations to improve their performance and impact. This occurs through development, strategic planning, program design and evaluation, board development, financial planning and management. There is an increasing desire among higher education institutions (HEIs) and governments for data that compares institutions and indicates standards as they attempt to attract the best students and academic staff (Hazelkorn 2008a). In addition, for the consuming public, there is a demand for transparency and information that have not been forthcoming from the HEIs and governments (Hazelkorn 2008a). Naturally, this environment led HEIs to devise and implement global rankings to facilitate status-building ambitions while providing information to the public. Many HEIs are not particularly keen on global rankings, as evidenced by the reactions of many vice chancellors and university presidents who are highly critical of the attempt to rank their institutions based on some questionable methodology. But their governments are in favor of ranking systems and have introduced higher education strategies premised on the outcomes of these rankings. What is more telling is that governments use rankings as policy instruments to influence reform of higher education and HEIs use them as management tools to support reorganization, resource allocation, and changes in academic work (Hazelkorn 2008b). World rankings have been adopted in order to "push" academics to embrace global profiling of their respective higher education institutions through research based on overseas/external grants and publications in high-impact, internationally referred foreign journals. Ranking has also brought with it the need to internationalization curriculum and research, which requires academics to have foreign research students and research collaborators. Then there is an emerging trends towards community engagement. In other words, academic works has become more complex and varied, involving various spatial scales ranging from local, regional, national to international.

Governments have responded to global rankings and relevant policies have been put in place that are aimed, first, at creating greater vertical (reputational) and horizontal (functional) differentiation of HEIs, as done in Japan and Germany, and second, establishing a diverse set of high-performing, globally focused HEIs, as in Australia (Hazelkorn 2008c). Apparently, the obsession with ranking has consumed many HEIs and governments. They perceived world-class status as beneficial not only to the HEIs but, more importantly, to the nation. The Malaysian central government and politicians have long expressed interest in the outcome of the annual global ranking exercise. The fates of Malaysia's four main universities and their vice chancellors in particular have been debated in the Malaysian Parliament as a result of global rankings.

Admittedly, the path of transformation to world university status and global ranking recognition would normally involve external players and factors as well as elements that are internal to the institutions concerned (Salmi 2009). With respect to the external determinants and influences, the role of the government is very important, particularly in the context of aspiring universities in the developing countries. It is the government's responsibility to provide abundant resources for such an endeavor; and even more so when public universities are involved. Equally important is the role of government in empowering universities to create a favorable environment in which to conduct their core activities, particularly with respect to allocation and spending of resources and recruitment and concentration of talents. Arguably, this would normally require a reassessment of the government-university relationship in terms of institutional and financial autonomy. The universities must also be ready to transform their internal governing structures and talents to meet the challenges associated with achieving world-class status.

Governments generally use one of the following three strategies to establish a world-class university (Salmi 2009). (1) They can upgrade a small number of existing universities that have the potential to excel. While this "picking of winners" approach is considered to be less expensive, there are insurmountable difficulties associated with it. For instance, changing a university's mode of operation is very difficult when they have always functioned within the same regulatory framework. Such change is often met with resistance. (2) Governments can encourage a number of existing institutions to merge, forming a new university that would achieve the synergies appropriate to a world-class institution. This approach, the so-called hybrid formula, is considered neutral in terms of cost, but it is likely to work as the legal status of the new institution is different from that of existing one. This should be compared with a situation where there is neutral cost but institutions involved have historical baggage that prevent the new arrangement to work effectively. In this later case, while there is no additional cost (positive point), it is not likely to work as there is no change in the legal status of institutions involved. (3) Governments can create new world-class universities from scratch. This clean-slate approach is very expensive to implement but it has many advantages; it creates an opportunity to formulate appropriate regulatory and incentive frameworks without the weight of historical baggage.

In Malaysia, a result of the government's preoccupation with global rankings and the desire for world-class stature for some of the country's universities is a commitment to the creation of research-focused universities. There are currently four such institutions in Malaysia. Of these four research universities, one, Universiti Sains Malaysia, was selected in 2008 to participate in the government's Accelerated Programme for Excellence (APEX) and was subsequently elevated to the status of APEX university. APEX universities are adequately endowed and empowered to achieve world-class status. The hope is that APEX universities will be ranked among the top 100 global institutions by 2013 and in the top 50 by 2020. We argue that in order to achieve this objective the government must review and reassess several aspects of the current government-university relationship, in particular as the governance structure. Change to the governance structure is of particular interest in this case as the government is challenged with establishing an APEX university by upgrading an existing university. However, contrary to what Salmi (2009) has indicated, we are of the opinion that the cost involved in such upgrading exercise will be high. Harvard University and other top-ranked universities have demonstrated that this exercise is too expensive for a developing country to undertake, as there are many competing socioeconomic objectives in an emerging higher education system. Equally important is the fact that the elevated university has to operate within the existing regulatory framework, maintaining the government–university relationship. Realizing this potential entanglement, Universiti Sains Malaysia is working on a modified governance structure that will enable it to transform while satisfying the government, which is the main sponsor of the program.

This chapter examines Malaysia's APEX initiative and the selection of Universiti Sains Malaysia as the first APEX university. We also discuss Universiti Sains Malaysia's struggle to put in place a governance structure that would enable it to meet the challenges that it will have to overcome. Being the first to chart new territory in terms of the state-university relationship is challenging and sometimes frustrating for Universiti Sains Malaysia.

World-Class University Status and Governance System

Even without the added pressure of achieving world-class status, any university, and in particular public universities, would have to deal with a myriad of pressing issues relating to efficiency, effectiveness, participation, leadership, and responsiveness to the environment. In order for universities to be able to cope with the ever-changing environment in which they operate, there must be appropriate regulatory framework to govern them. For world-class universities, apart from institutional governance with set context for the principal-agency nature of the state-university relationship, it is equally important to have significant internal self-governance and an entrenched tradition, usually buttressed by statutes, to ensure that the academic community (usually professors, but sometimes including students) has control over the central elements of academic life: the admission of students, the curriculum, the criteria for the award of degrees, the selection of new members of the professoriate, and the basic direction of the academic work of the institution (Altbach 2003).

One of the key elements of a higher education law is its definition of a public university's legal status (Fielden 2008). The law should determine the type of governance. Models range from state controlled to completely independent (Morshidi 2009). Within this continuum of state-controlled and independent status are semiautonomous and semi-independent public universities the definitions of which depend on national legal framework. But generally, in the context of Malaysia, a state-controlled public higher education institution is in effect an agency of either the Ministry of Education (MOE) or the Ministry of Higher Education (MOHE). An independent public university on the other hand is a statutory body; a charity or nonprofit corporation with no government participation the control of which is linked to national strategies that may or may not receive public funding. Semiautonomous public universities can agencies of the MMOE or MOHE, a state-owned corporation, or a statutory body. Semi-independent public universities are statutory bodies, charities, or nonprofit corporations subject to MMOE and MOHE control (Fielden 2008). Interestingly, as Fielden (2008) notes, there is a strong international trend to increase the autonomy of public institutions by making them independent, self-governing organizations along the lines of the semi-independent model or the independent model. In other words, there is a trend in many developed and developing higher education systems away from a governance system based on state control to one that is only supervised by the state. In such instances, three changes occur. First, central government delegates power to another tier of government, but the former still retains some coordinating policy function. This is typical of European institutions. Second, in the United Kingdom, India, and Pakistan the state delegates a range of powers and functions to a specialized buffer body or in some instances to several buffer intermediaries. Typically, however, the central government retains central control over national strategy and the overall size and shape of higher education, while the buffer body or bodies undertake funding and operational management. In some cases, these buffers are purely advisory in nature. One such example is the Council on Higher Education in South Africa (Fielden 2008). Arguably, having a buffer body generally encourages greater institutional autonomy. The third option for Malaysia is for the MMOE or MOHE to continue managing the universities directly and delegating considerable power to university administrators so that the government's role becomes a more strategic one.

In the context of Malaysia's APEX University the authors support the model that involves delegation of considerable powers to the universities as we believe this approach nurtures selected institutions toward achieving world-class stature. In this respect, Fielden's (2008) statement that the basic principle behind institutional autonomy involving direct delegation of powers to universities is that these universities operate better if they are in control of their own destiny is very relevant. Arguably, universities have an incentive to change if they can benefit from their actions; they can be entrepreneurial and reap the rewards. We acknowledge that there are areas where delegation is not always simple and the government may fear that universities are not fit to exercise power effectively, in particular with respect to financial management. In view of this, while there is a tendency toward less direct control by the central government of the universities the former seems to have developed more complex supervisory and reporting regimes, particularly in the area of performance. For instance, governments are often reluctant to relinquish control of selecting or appointing university presidents, vice chancellors, or the chairs and members of university boards. In the context of APEX University, legislation defining this type of university needs to be clear about the role of the government and the powers of the university and the relevant governance issues. Ultimately, the latter must encompass or cover powers of the university board, selection of the chair and members and board composition, appointment of the vice chancellor, and the role of the university senate.

Interestingly, in Malaysia, the government's control of the public universities by way of circulars (that are issued by the central authorities to public universities from time to time) and administrative directives has raised many issues. These government directives have no legal status, unless they are derived from a specific provision of an act of parliament. As such the universities are not bound by them. In fact, public universities such as Universiti Sains Malaysia have the power to accept, reject, or modify a circular. But many public universities adopt government circulars and administrative directives, especially from the Ministry of Finance (MMOF), which holds the purse strings.

Universiti Sains Malaysia as an APEX University

Universiti Sains Malaysia, established in 1969 on Penang Island, is the second oldest university in Malaysia after Universiti Malaya in Kuala Lumpur. By definition, Universiti Sains Malaysia, as a public university, is state-controlled and incorporated as a statutory body. As a statutory body, the university implements duties and responsibilities in line with the government's objectives and aspirations (Morshidi 2009). Following a myriad of education reforms in 1996, the Malaysian government introduced corporate governance for state-controlled universities in 1997 by amending the 1971 University and University Colleges Act (UUCA). With the passage of a law on the incorporation of state-controlled universities, Universiti Sains Malaysia was subsequently incorporated in 1998. The new governance structure implied that the university would operate as an efficient, transparent, and financially able entity. It is important to note that even though Universiti Sains Malaysia is incorporated, it is not an independent administrative entity. The government still retains explicit control of the institution. Admittedly, for various reasons, some of which are political in nature, many public universities have allowed themselves to be controlled by central authorities.

Universiti Sains Malaysia and three other premier universities with excellent track records in research and innovation were designated as research universities in 2006. In 2008, Universiti Sains Malaysia was selected as Malaysia's first APEX university based on its readiness to transform itself to fulfill the nation's ambition (or obsession) to have a public university listed among the world's top 100 universities by 2013. With this APEX university status, Universiti Sains Malaysia envisioned that it would pave the way for other research universities to be elevated as APEX universities with full autonomy in finance, service scheme, management, student intake, and student fees among other things. For Universiti Sains Malaysia to move from state-controlled to semi-independent status under APEX, careful planning is required. In general, the university community welcomes more institutional autonomy, favorable APEX governance structure, abundant resources, better scheme of service and compensation, and talent concentration. But is this just wishful thinking?

Toward a Governance System for APEX University

When Abdullah Badawi, the former prime minister of Malaysia, unveiled the National Higher Education Strategic Plan 2020 and the National Higher Education Action Plan 2007–2010, he expressed the government's commitment to establishing "the Malaysian version of Ivy League or Oxbridge universities" (*The Star Online* 2007), which "will be given the autonomy to allow them to focus on becoming the very best" (*The Star Online* 2007). The government's ambitious plan of transforming one of the most promising public higher learning institutions into a globally recognized university is part of the higher education transformation exercise undertaken by the MOHE to help Malaysia's transition into a knowledge- and innovation-based economy. However, to achieve this goal requires a massive investment of financial and human resources and, more importantly, the political will to provide a bold and vibrant new legal and regulatory framework that is radically different from the current regulatory framework under the UUCA of 1971.

The higher education subsector is tied to the state because of the need for public funding and its reliance on legislation, which is the product of a sovereign power (Rochford 2006, 150). The incorporation of any public university requires the sanction of the Malaysian cabinet and the university must have its constitution drafted in accordance with Schedule 1 of the UUCA of 1971. However, the quickly changing landscape of the higher education system has resulted in the emergence of a new relationship between the government and the university, so a different form of governance is essential to cope with the challenges that confront the nation's higher education system.

The UCCA of 1971 set out the objectives and functions of the university: the ministerial powers and duties, the appointment of the vice chancellor and senior management of the university, the composition of the board of directors, and a description of its function, the composition of the senate and its role, matters relating to finance, student development, and other affairs of the university not directly related to teaching, research, and service to the community. Examining the provisions of the act makes one realize that the public university in Malaysia is indeed an extension of a government bureaucracy and the idea of an independent, free, and self-governing institution is indeed a myth. The government's dominance and influence over the university, legitimized in the form of a legal instrument such as the UCCA of 1971, has led to the politicization of the idea of university. As argued by Lee, the Malaysian government's concerted efforts to provide higher education opportunities for Malays and other indigenous group is a clear manifestation of how the government viewed access to higher education as an instrument for social engineering and the restructuring of society (Lee 1997). The establishment of the Ministry of Higher Education in 2004 is another example of government intervention in the higher education system.

In December 2008, after more than 37 years in existence, the UCCA was amended. A new law was enacted on February 1, 2009. The move to amend the UCCA was meant to provide new impetus for rejuvenating the public universities; unfortunately the amendment did not address government's interest in establishing the much talked-about APEX University. The establishment of the APEX University was announced in September 2007, but the government did not introduce the new framework for its governance until December 2008. It is possible that the government was sceptical of the university's ability to govern itself as an autonomous institution. The reluctance of the government was also probably due to their fear of losing control and influence over the new APEX universities. Admittedly, the government has an interest to ensure that APEX universities progressed according to the government's agenda and not the university concerned.

One of the fundamental changes promised by the government was to allow APEX universities to be autonomous entities by empowering the board of directors (MOHE 2007, 34). However Section 3 of the UCCA (2008 amendment) provides that the minister "shall be responsible for the general direction of higher education" (Government of Malaysia 2008). Such power gives the minister a mandate over directives, policies, and regulations issued by the Ministry of Higher Education, which inevitably leads to government interference in university affairs. Intervention by the minister or the MOHE compromises the independence of the university's board of directors. Any such intervention would surely stifle innovative policies and "out of the box" initiatives by university management.

Section 3 further provides that the universities are subject to "national policies, strategies and guidelines...formulated...by an authority established under any written law." The provision gives the minister the right to interfere in university affairs and extends power to other authorities and institutions established under any written law. This could result in other institutions or authorities demanding the right to guide the universities, making a mockery of the university's autonomy, politicizing the institution and compromising its independence. We are of the opinion that a university program that aspires to transform a Malaysian institution into one that is globally competitive should never be controlled by any authority other than the board of directors, which is entrusted with this responsibility by the university's stakeholders. For Malaysia's APEX to succeed, the strategic direction must be based on global outlook and international trends and must go beyond national policies and strategies. In the new higher education system, the future of the universities has more to do with the markets and global needs than past iterations have (Duke 2004).

However, we do not intend to suggest that Malaysia's APEX university program should distance itself from the national agenda and strategic interests of the country. The government, as the major stakeholder in an APEX university, is properly represented on the university board and its representative must be able to influence and convince the other board members of the strategic needs of the country and that the university can help to realize it. Presenting the government's case to the board would allow the university to function in accordance with the principle of good governance and eliminate external intervention, allowing the board to execute their mandate as entrusted.

Section 4A of the UCCA 1971 provides that "for the purpose of selecting a qualified and suitable person for the post of Vice Chancellor... the Minister shall, from time to time, appoint a committee to advise him on such appointment." This provision means that the APEX University will continue the practice of appointing vice chancellors and senior university management and the minister has the sole authority to make an appointment. The 2008 amendment to the UCCA has made it mandatory for the minister to appoint a search committee whose mandate is to assist in the selection of a potential vice chancellor. Section 4A clearly sets out a new mechanism for the selection process, an obvious departure from the previous practice although the minister retains absolute discretionary power in making the appointment. Some have argued that a global search should be conducted by a search committee commissioned by the board of directors and the decision must be made by the board rather than a minister. The board of directors must be given a mandate to commission the search and make the appointment because is the board members are the best judges of the kind of talent needed to provide leadership for an APEX university. The appointment of the vice chancellor should never be seen as a political appointment, so it is best for the appointment to be made by the board, which represents the interest of the stakeholders.

Section 4B of the act provides the minister with the power to, "with the consent of the employee, issue a direction for the secondment or transfer of the university employee to the service of the requesting university... and it shall be the duty of the university of the said employee to carry out that direction whether or not the university agrees to the secondment or transfer." The intention of the parliament was to accelerate the promotion of research and educational development where the more established universities should be willing to share their expertise with the newly established universities. Since Malaysian universities are considered statutory bodies, the university has to consent to any request for secondment or transfer to another university, statutory organization, or organization in Malaysia. However, some argue that such power could undermine the authority of the university as a statutory body and the provision regards the university as part of a government department or agency and is at the mercy of the ministerial directive. The act also does not define the notion "in the interest of higher education or the promotion of research and educational development" which would lead to the politicization of such transfer or secondment. The need of any university for expertise in an area of their interest should be resolved through the rigorous process of recruitment or head hunting, compatible with the international good practices. A ministerial intervention could lead to serious conflict of interest and, in the case of an APEX university, such an intervention would put the university board in the difficult position of having to strike a balance between addressing the strategic needs of the university and being seen as defiant by the political master.

An important concept that has surfaced in the debate on the university and the public good is the notion of public sphere. Pusser (2006, 17) argued that the university itself is a public sphere, "a space that is at once physical, symbolic, cultural, political and semantic, not in relation to the state or the broader political economy but as a site of complex, autonomous contest in its own right." As further contended by Giroux (2002), fundamental to the rise of a vibrant democratic culture is the recognition that education must be treated as a public sphere where students gain a public voice and come to grips with their own power as individuals and social agents. The government must envision the APEX University as a public sphere where public interaction, conversation, and deliberation can take place and where the nature of state interest and private demands can be debated. This requires the government's commitment to academic freedom, that is, the right to free expression. To categorize faculty and staff of public universities in Malaysia as civil servants and subjecting them to the Statutory Bodies Discipline and Sur-Charge Act 2000 (Act 605) has created a culture of fear among academics. As a result, the right to free expression is severely compromised. Some provisions, such as Act 605, Schedule 2, Sections 18, 19, and 20, threaten disciplinary measures against criticism of official policies. Unfortunately, official discussions about the APEX University have centered on the issues of funding and structure and not on the protection of academic freedom and freedom of enquiry.

The new governance mechanism for an APEX university should provide autonomy and preserve the university as a public sphere. At the same time efforts must be made to ensure that no single group influences the direction of the university. The conferment of autonomy should be comprehensive, encompassing all levels—the individual, the institution, and society. Demands for control would have to give way to contest, collaboration, and consensus. In an APEX university, faculty members must be assured of their freedom to promote critical engagement, students must be provided with the institutional support for their role as critical actors in enacting and promoting the public sphere in the university, and university administrators must rise to the challenge of protecting the university from state and private intervention as well as from institutional control.

The greatest impediment to the conferment of autonomy to an APEX university is Section 8 of the UCCA. The section required the constitution of the university to "contain provisions for all matters set out in the First Schedule of this Act." Section 8 also compels the board of directors to amend the constitution if it does not contain provisions set forth in the Schedule 1. It is hard to imagine how the new APEX universities would be able to operate under a new governance system when it is mandatory for its constitution to comply with the Schedule 1 of the UCCA. Section 8 of the UCCA further empowers the *Yang di Pertuan Agong* (the constitutional supreme king of Malaysia) to amend the constitution of the university so it aligns with UCCA's Schedule 1. The power of the Yang di Pertuan Agong refers to the power of the minister, because the Yang di Pertuan Agong, a constitutional monarch must act on the advice of the appropriate executive, which in this case is the minister of higher education. This power can stamp out any attempt to blaze new trails and may disallow any effort by an APEX university to depart from the regulatory mechanisms of Schedules 1 and 2 of the UCCA. There is no guarantee that APEX universities would not be subject to the provision of the UCCA. To date, no initiatives have been taken to amend the UCCA and make APEX universities exempt from the act. As it stands, the governance of an APEX university is founded on the provision of the UCCA. Any effort to reform and introduce "the new governance system" is a futile exercise until an amendment to exclude it from UCCA is made.

The state's dominance in the governance system of Malaysian public universities has resulted in a centralized governance and management system that has granted some degree of autonomy to the universities but not the authority to manage key aspects of their operation (World Bank 2007).[1] The World Bank observed that the current governance regime is restrictive, especially with respect to three critical decision-making capacities crucial to competition at the international level. Malaysian universities must (a) be able to select students on their own terms; (b) have the freedom to offer competitive compensation packages to attract the most talented and the brightest faculty from around the world; and (c) have the authority to appoint highly qualified and capable university leaders (World Bank 2007, 35–36).

On the ability of APEX universities to select the students n their own terms, the Universiti Sains Malaysia was recently given the mandate to select their students based on its own criteria rather than from the centrally managed student admission system administered by the MOHE. However, Universiti Sains Malaysia is still bound by limitations imposed by the MOHE such as restrictions on international students in critical areas such as engineering and medicine.

Another notable constraint is the inability of public universities to offer remuneration packages comparable to the international standard. Therefore it is difficult for them to attract and retain the best talent. As long as the governance system is subjected to the present regulatory framework, in which faculty members are regarded as civil servants and their salaries are based on the current civil service compensation scale, APEX universities will not be able to attract talent cutting across university's academic and administrative services. Since the establishment of the APEX University depends on the hiring of internationally renowned academics and eminent scientists, the reform of the recruitment process is extremely urgent and necessary. The first step toward such reform is new legislation.

In Malaysia, recent higher-education reforms have seen a shift toward a more intense pattern of centralization rather than a move toward devolution. The corporatization of public universities conducted in 1997/1998 with a view to limit the state's dominance and intervention in the provision of higher education in Malaysia was never fully implemented and the movement was completely abandoned during the 1997 economic crisis. Since then, the role of the state in matters related to the governance of public higher learning institutions has been strengthened rather than reduced. Mok (2007) argued that although Malaysia adopted a softer approach of governance for the higher education subsector, which is less authoritative and less interventionist, the critical role of the state in the regulations and supervision of the universities can never be underestimated. Such a trend is in fact detrimental to the healthy development of APEX University, which requires the space and freedom to transform into a higher learning institution of a world-class stature.

This chapter argues that the present mechanism is not sufficient to accommodate the interests of the new APEX University. However there are a few mechanisms that the government could explore. Section 28 provides that the Yang di-Pertuan Agong may exempt a university from the provisions of Schedules 1 and 2 or allow them to vary any provisions of the same schedules. This provision only allows partial exemption; it is not an exemption from the rest of the act. However, partial exemption can be utilized by the Ministry of Higher Education and Universitii Sains Malaysia to establish a new charter for the purpose of regulating the new APEX University.

Another alternative is to provide a new UCCA Schedule 3, which would allow Parliament to exclude all APEX universities from the provision of Schedules 1 and 2. This new Schedule 3 could be a bold move forward in providing a governance system for APEX universities.

The government should also consider drafting a new Universities Act to accommodate the rapidly changing global landscape of higher education. The higher education subsector requires fresh thinking and innovative ways to regulate universities. The UCCA could be repealed and a new act introduced in which innovative measures regarding university governance, autonomy, and accountability would be incorporated. Prior to the enactment of the UCCA, the University of Malaya was regulated by the University of Malaya Ordinance 1949 and the University of Malaya Act 1961. Both acts were repealed when UCCA was enacted in 1971.

Another alternative would be to create an APEX University Act. This act could follow other similar legislation, such as the University Teknologi Mara Act and the governance of the International Islamic University. Both universities are public universities that are not subject to the provisions of the UCCA. Interestingly the International Islamic University of Malaysia was incorporated under the Companies Act of 1960. The new act could provide for a vibrant system of governance or leave the matter of drafting the university charter to the Board by way of subsidiary legislation.

Conclusion

This chapter was developed on the premise that the transformation of APEX University into a world-class institution would normally involve the commitment of the state as well as the university itself. It has been shown that the role of the government is very important as it provides abundant resources and must empower universities before the process can begin. A favorable environment must be created where universities can conduct core activities, particularly with regard to the allocation and spending of resources and the recruitment and retention of world-class faculty. There is a need for a reevaluation of the government-university relationship in terms of institutional and financial autonomy. In addition, the state has to provide an environment that is conducive to the flourishing of academic freedom and the freedom to question for academic staff and researchers. With future generations in mind, students must be allowed to explore their potential and test their leadership and organization skills. The selected universities must be ready to transform their internal governing structures and talents (the extra-ordinary abilities of the university's staff in academic, administrative, and support spheres) to meet the challenges associated with achieving world-class status.

An innovative legal framework and national environment will enable the APEX University to be creative and innovative when transforming their internal governing structure. Failures and hiccups in implementation by the APEX universities are to be expected as they explore ways and means to move forward as autonomous bodies. The government should not overreact to minor reverberations in the implementation process. The government should accept that the APEX experiment involves risk and the learning process is very valuable to the institution. More importantly, the government should trust and support the APEX University in its implementation of the transformation plan. This should come in the form of autonomy, both institutional and financial.

Note

1. This study published by the World Bank was prepared at the request of the Economic Planning Unit to help develop a strategic vision for the evolution of the country's universities toward gaining world-class status.

References

Altbach, Philip G. 2003. "The Costs and Benefits of World-Class Universities." *International Higher Education* 33 (Fall): 5–8.
Duke, Christopher. 2004. "Is There an Australian Idea of a University?" *Journal of Higher Education Policy and Management*, 26 (3): 297–314.
Fielden, John. 2008. *Global Trends in University Governance. Education Working Paper Series, No. 9. Washington, DC: World Bank.* http://www.worldbank.org.
Giroux, Henry A. 2002. "Neoliberalism, Corporate Culture and the Promise of Higher Education: The University as a Democratic Public Sphere." *Harvard Educational Review* 72 (4): 425–63.

Government of Malaysia. 2008. *University and University Collages Act 1971 (Amended 2008)*. Putrajaya: Government of Malaysia.
Hazelkorn, Ellen. 2008a. *Global Obsession with Rankings*. Dublin: Dublin Institute of Technology. http://www.slideshare.net.
———. 2008b. *The Rising Popularity of University Rankings: Lessons and Implications*. Melbourne: University of Melbourne. http://*www.cshe.unimelb.edu.au*.
———. 2008c. *Are Rankings Reshaping Higher Education?* Paris: UNESCO. http://www.unesco.org.
Lee, Molly. 1997. "Public Policies Toward Private Education in Malaysia." Paper presented at the First International Malaysian Studies Conference, University Malaya, Kuala Lumpur, November 17–18 .
Ministry of Higher Education (MOHE). 2007. *Pelan Tindakan Pengajian Tinggi Negara 2007–2010*. Putrajaya: MOHE.
Mok, Ka-Ho. 2007. "The Search for New Governance: Corporatisation and Privatisation of Public Universities in Malaysia and Thailand." *Asia Pacific Journal of Education* 27 (3): 271–290.
Morshidi, Sirat. 2009. "Strategic Planning Directions of Malaysia's Higher Education: University Autonomy in the Midst of Political Uncertainties." *Higher Education*, DOI 10.1007/s10734–009-9259–0.
Pusser, Brian. 2006. "Reconsidering Higher Education and the Public Good, The Role of Public Spheres." In *Governance and the Public Good*, ed. G. W. Tierney. Albany: State University of New York
Rochford, Francine. 2006. "Is There Any Clear Idea of a University?" *Journal of Higher Education Policy and Management* 28 (2): 147–158.
Salmi, Jamil. 2009. *The Challenge of Establishing World-Class Universities*. Washington, DC: The World Bank.
The Star Online. 2007. "Reaching for the Top." *The Star Online*, September 2. http://thestar.com.my.
World Bank 2007. *Malaysia and the Knowledge Economy: Building a World-Class Higher Education System*. Washington, DC: The World Bank.

Chapter 8

Shifting Governance Patterns in Taiwanese Higher Education: A Recentralized Future?

Sheng-Ju Chan

Introduction

A successful university is generally believed to be heavily dependent upon a well-designed governing structure that is able to facilitate decision making and tackle problems faced by higher education institutions (HEIs). However, based on the experience of universities around the world, it is not clear whether or not this is true (Birnbaum 2004). It is possible to detect the major differences between university and nonuniversity HEIs by looking at how they are governed and the different regulatory procedures they adopt. In general, nonuniversity institutions tend to fall under tighter scrutiny by external regulations compared to their counterparts in the university sector, which usually enjoy the protection of "academic freedom" with less external intervention (Teichler 2008). This major variation highlights the fact that a common adopted governance pattern cannot be found among higher education institutions.

Governments around the world continue to search for the best options for their own countries. A wide range of governance reforms has taken place across the globe (Amaral et al. 2003). Japan observed neighboring countries implementing comprehensive restructuring of the legal status of public universities. In 2004 Japan followed suit, turning their public universities into independent judicial entities—a move that granted them more flexibility and autonomy, essential ingredients to success in the competitive global market (Chen 2005). Likewise, the Australian federal government, which lacks direct control of its universities, initiated a debate regarding the appropriateness and sufficiency of university governance by publishing the discussion paper "Meeting the Challenges: The Governance and Management of Universities" (Nelson 2002). Such reform initiatives and intentions signify that the previous arrangements concerning university governance and management are outdated and inadequate in the modern sociopolitical setting.

Since the 1990s, higher education governance in Taiwan has changed its approach dramatically by adopting various philosophical rationales. A centralist model for governing every aspect of society was adopted since the late 1940s (Husen and Postlethwaite 1985). Higher education, being a very important means of social and ideological control, was tightly monitored by the government (Law 1998). In the late 1980s educational authorities began to grant HEIs greater autonomy in line with the deregulation that occurred with the lifting of martial law in 1987. The main aim of this change to governance strategy was closely related to the slogan "social democratization movement," which suggests a transfer of power and decision making to lower social or political units and organizations. Globalization and global economic competition has intensified since the late 1990s, which has caused the Taiwanese government to begin rethinking how to restructure the governance relationship between the state and universities. A Sustainable Development Committee in Higher Education was established in 2008 to advise central authorities on major issues such as university governance (TMOE 2008a). The main argument of this chapter is that although the governance reforms in Taiwan have made some improvement by transforming universities into more democratic and autonomous facilities, the increasing need to be competitive in the global marketplace poses a serious threat to the recently established institutional autonomy and "shared" governance of the higher education subsector. The latest policy reforms in the Taiwanese higher education subsector may "recentralize" its power arrangement.

Diverse Theoretical Discourse on Governance in Higher Education

Before turning the focus directly to Taiwan's experiences, the following theoretical and conceptual analysis and review serves to inform understanding of the evolving nature of governance issues. Due to the long and prestigious history of excellent universities, people tend to have a fixed belief that universities should retain wider control of their own management and internal operation, which derives from the spirit of institutional autonomy or self-management. This ideal form of governance authority was somehow modeled upon the prestigious Oxford and Cambridge universities, which were famous for faculty domination of decision making—what Clark (1983) terms "academic oligarchy." Within this model, internal faculty retain the final right to decide the major issues regarding personnel, finance, teaching, curriculum, and research (Middlehurst 2004). In other words, the institution has the "independent" right to be the final judge of its internal management without the constraints imposed by other religious and political entities (Shattock 2006). Such control by the academic staff over governance was primarily justified by the need to sustain the grand "cultural" mission of the university—that is, to generate, disseminate, and reserve knowledge (Barnett 1990). This cultural need created the necessity for academic freedom and institutional autonomy to avoid the intervention of political forces on self-management (Braun and Merrian 1999).

This academic domination in governance structure is not prevalent in European countries, where a more "state-controlled" pattern prevails (van Vught 1989). The state-control model has been characterized by a strong authority of state bureaucracy on the one hand and a relatively strong position of the academic community within universities on the other. Indeed, the state ultimately interferes to "regulate the access conditions, the curriculum, the degree requirements, the examination systems, the appointment and remuneration of academic staff, etc." (van Vught 1994, 331), while the academic faculty maintains considerable authority over the regulation of content and research. In other words, governance power is shared between the state and faculty guilds rather than being dominated by the academic oligarchy as in traditional British universities.

However, since the 1980s, both conventional models have eroded and been gradually replaced by a rather "managerial" or "remote-controlled" model (Amaral et al. 2003). Traditionally, the collegial model—although benefiting by being free from the external interruption of a wider environment—has been the focus of serious criticisms in the face of rapidly changing demands of higher education (Amaral et al. 2003; Duderstadt and Womack 2003). In general, two assumptions were behind these attacks: "under existing governance arrangements institutions have not been responsive enough and the speed of institutional decision making is doubtful" (Birnbaum 2004, 7). The most recent governance reforms in the Australian higher education subsector even pointed out that,

> Traditional structures are unwieldy and poorly positioned to respond to a rapidly changing higher education environment. A key assumption is that streamlined smaller bodies, with more external expertise and less internal faculty involvement, can best provide focused whole-of-institution leadership. (McInnis 2006, 121)

Despite the recognition of the importance of faculty participation in hiring and tenure evaluations, Duderstadt and Womack (2003, 152) still assert that, "when faculty members do become involved in university governance and decision making, often they tend to become preoccupied with peripheral matters such as parking or intercollegiate athletics rather than strategic issues such as academic programs or undergraduate education." Criticism has centered on full-time academia's inefficient decision-making procedures and the subsequent ineffective quality of their decisions. Such claims have led to the conclusion that a collegial dominance or shared governance pattern is outdated and insufficient.

Solutions proposed to overcome such weaknesses focus on market competition and managerial-oriented strategies (Birnbaum 2000; Amaral, Jones, and Karseth 2002). In fact, since the 1980s these two interrelated concepts have been regarded as effective tools to ease the problems posed by traditional governance models. Advocates of the former (free market) asserted that the triumph of the market mechanism would be the solution. By creating market or market-like environments, education organizations including universities tend to behave more effectively and efficiently than their public sector counterparts since organizations are more responsive to environmental changes (Amaral, Magalhães, and Santiago 2002, 134). Consequently, according to Maroy (2009, 67), "we are witnessing the advancing of 'liberalization,' or privatization and the market. The result is the rise of new public actors or the mobilization of actors from the world of business or civil society in the production and management." Such managerial-oriented strategies can address the problem of inefficient and ineffective decision-making mechanisms discussed above because a university will not necessarily operate in line with the public's wishes without external monitoring and outcome control or evaluation. By adopting this approach, governments do not intervene in the internal matters, thereby devolving more autonomy to the operating units while remotely examining the accountability and performance of intended groups (Ferlie et al. 2008). The primary task of the government in this model is to redesign the "regulatory regime" and monitor the "outcome" of service delivered. As Deem, Hillyard, and Reed (2007) state, new managerialism is both an ideology and a set of management practices and techniques widely applied to the public sector, including universities.

Governance discourses continue under dramatic transformation. Traditionally protected faculty participation and self-management have been cited as inappropriate and proponents of the new managerialism believe they should be replaced by market forces claimed by the neoliberalism and managerial monitoring techniques. Although unsure of the result of these new governance strategies, it is apparent that many countries have adopted these policies and measures (Amaral, Jones, and Karseth 2002). The following sections examine the shifting governance patterns in Taiwan from a historical perspective.

Prior to 1987: A Bureaucratic Centralized Past

From the perspective of a political regime, Taiwan was a typical authoritarian system before the mid-1980s, using direct control from the top to regulate or monitor every aspect of the public life and leaving very limited autonomy for the local organizations or units. The same was true in the higher education subsector. In order to preserve the cultural and national identity rooted in mainland China, universities were regarded as part of the "administrative machine of government" with extremely tight regulation from the central government (Chen 1993). This allowed no room for institutional autonomy or academic freedom—features enjoyed by many modern Western universities. Such a high level of control over the university means that HEIs are not allowed to voice opinions different from the ruling government. Such institutions are not for creating new thought or knowledge for widespread acceptance, but instead are followers or accepters of administrative orders from the political regime of the time—namely, the Kuomintang. This grand ideology prevailed throughout society, and all HEIs were forcedly subjected to tight government control.

The Ministry of Education (TMOE) at the time took the role of central command by setting up nearly all important regulatory and statutory arrangements in the higher education subsector. The TMOE had direct control of the establishment of institutes (both public and private); decisions related to the founding, increase, and decrease of departments and colleges; assignment of the presidents of public universities; determinations of the student enrollment quota; examination of the qualification of university teachers; and even implementations of the universal compulsory course of higher education (Chen 2007). Faculty personnel structures and funding systems were required to be in accordance with governmental regulations and administrative orders. Furthermore, accounting systems and personnel offices were part of the bureaucratic system and had to obey all administrative rules. Once again, universities did not maintain autonomy over funds or recruitment of suitable people, as complicated administrative processes had to be followed. With regard to the curriculum, natural science departments were highly preferred since political leaders did not wish to produce scholars of "democratic thought." Living in this sociopolitical environment, academics viewed intellectual autonomy and academic freedom as very remote (Morris 1996).

This governance structure design in Taiwan's higher education originated from the idea of political authoritarianism, which tends to concentrate authority at the top level and leave very limited variations for local discretion. The negative impacts of such a bureaucratic centralized arrangement were noticeable. As the General Consultation Report on Educational Reform[1] put it,

> An apparent maladjustment happening in our education system was that there was too much unnecessary binding...judging from the surface, all the educational control measures aim to ensure and enhance the quality. However, after long-term operation, the side effects of tight control are gradually emerging. Particularly some non-educational factors also intervening in the schooling system urgently need to be "deregulated," such as the indoctrination of political ideology, human planning orientation educational policies, the cultural and sexual bias, credentialism, and the needs of military training, etc. (Council on Educational Reform 1996, 14)

The drawbacks in the Taiwanese educational system caused by biased political ideology became evident after the revocation of martial law in 1987. The public lessened the tight controls, retained more self-determination, and returned to the original purpose of education in general. Since policy change and reform were introduced in the late 1980s, HEIs in Taiwan have experienced a wave of change in governance patterns from a nationalization model to one that is more democratic and accompanied by political reform (Mok 2002). This development in policy reform has completely reshaped the nature of how higher education systems are governed and regulated and ultimately redefined the relationship between the state and the higher education subsector.

The 1980s to the Late 1990s: In Search of Institutional Autonomy

Initiated by democratic political reform, the education sector sought to break from the past and enter a new situation in which lower units and organizations retained greater power for self-management. Some educators and scholars in universities asserted that they wished to bring "democracy" to higher education campuses

(Chang 1987). Institutional autonomy, academic freedom, and faculty governance suddenly moved to the heart of public debate and discussion (Ho 1990, 1993). One major idea, *song-bang* (i.e., liberalization or deregulation), was introduced and advocated in 1994 by the Council on Education Reform, a special commission review committee. The council argued that the education sector should be granted more "autonomy" without inappropriate and unnecessary intervention and regulation from upper administrative agencies. In this open and innovative atmosphere, institutional autonomy became the primary goal of policy reform. This spirit of change was perfectly interpreted by a white paper on higher education:

> Autonomy of higher educational institutions is reflected mainly in the interaction between universities and state. Universities are public institutions, and must therefore obey national laws whilst government retains only a supervisory role, leaving the rest entirely up to each individual institution to exercise without constraints. For universities to become more democratic and effective, they must have more autonomy and self-determination. In other words, in university curricula, budgets, expenditures and personnel deployment, they must be given far greater autonomy and flexibility. (TMOE 2001b, 18)

The whole idea of deregulating and liberalizing the higher education system had to do with the institution of democratic and autonomous governance structures at the university level. The revised University Law published in 1994 realized a few fundamental ideas that had been forbidden a decade earlier. This new regulation allowed each university or college to select its own president, set up a University Affairs Council composed of elected senior academic faculty to serve as the highest policy-making body, and institute faculty councils to deal with the recruitment, promotion, and dismissal of teachers (Mok 2000). Granting self-decision power to the universities was meant to assist each institution in running its internal management smoothly as previously, government control meant that the government possessed relatively limited knowledge about the individual universities while making decisions. The earlier bureaucratic centralization structure of university governance has led to rather weak and rigid institutional internal management while the new governing mechanism is said to be facilitating in strengthening the specialization and feature of each university. Another important dimension of deregulation and autonomy is the relaxation of financing systems. In 1996, a limited trial (involving five universities) of relaxed financial management was launched in order to increase the flexibility and efficiency of using state appropriations. The introduction of the new University Development Fund indeed gave individual public universities more autonomy in managing their budgets. Under the new scheme, the selected institutions could spend money raised from nonstate sources as they saw fit and even keep such financial sources for future use instead of returning them to the TMOE (Chiang 2004). Furthermore, the more flexible arrangement of financing mechanisms encouraged the generation of additional funding from multiple channels, such as tuition fees, provision of extension education services, the sale of intellectual property rights, and research grants. Being primarily dependent upon public taxes made public institutions less innovative and more ineffective in the use of limited financial sources. Such types of financial devolution and flexible arrangements are deemed to be meaningful instruments for enhancing the performance of the sector as a whole (TMOE 1995).

Such moves gradually approached the elements of academic oligarchy, where faculty participation and involvement are required for institutional internal governance. However, Taiwanese universities and their members did not yet enjoy sufficient autonomy. Even after a decade of deregulation, the Taiwanese nation-state still maintained a wide range of control over universities. Judging from the diverse theoretical orientations previously outlined, traditional privilege, such as institutional autonomy adopted by many Western universities, had been more or less realized in the Taiwanese context, although it had not yet achieved the level of British institutions. Having deepened democratic participation and self-management within the university campus, these new initiatives and policy reforms apparently resulted in a new type of governance pattern under the joint coordination of governmental and institutional forces. However, the increasing economic globalization and competition of the late 1990s coupled with restricted public budgets meant that new governance reform ceased and governmental control was reinstated.

Latest Governance Reforms: A Reverse Development?

In the twenty-first century, Taiwanese higher education has faced another major governance challenge. Internally, overpopulated HEIs have posed a serious threat to educational quality. Meanwhile, increasing financial burdens for the state government and decreasing unit costs per student have led the educational authority to demand higher accountability for the higher education subsector (Wang 2003). Externally, the nation-state has found itself involved in a giant economic race at the global level, in which universities are the "engine" boosting national economic development (TMOE 2008b). University league tables or institutional ranking became an important indicator of the "competitive advantage" of each country (Deem et al. 2008).

In this context, Taiwanese educational authority shifted the direction of governance reform. In 2001, a merger plan was introduced that suggested integrating small-scale public universities with larger ones. The primary rationale for implementing such a plan was the "effective use of limited resources" and the benefits of "economies of scale" rather than the "enhancement of educational quality" (TMOE 2001a). Although enthusiastically endorsed by the TMOE, the outcome has been limited, with only three successful merger cases to date. Nevertheless, this economic rationalism was not only applied to the merger policy, but also to the world-class university policy. In order to combat fierce global competition, in 2003 the government declared that ten Taiwanese research centers or academic fields would reach the top levels in Asia within five years and at least one university would be ranked in the world's top 100 within a 10-year period. The government offered extra financial incentives to those very limited number of institutions that could achieve the stated objectives. In order to select qualified institutions and examine their subsequent performance, value for money and site supervision or outcome evaluation became the primary tools for monitoring the performance of HEIs from a distance. Thus, universities turned into agencies whose purpose was to fulfill the objectives prescribed by the state in accordance with principal-agent theory. This policy has become a managerial tool to "attract" institutions into complying with the strategic development desired by the TMOE. But while the means for achieving these specific goals may be in the hands of university, the ultimate achievement depends on the "examination" or "interpretation" conducted by the external authority. To use the jargon of Berdahl (1990), "procedural autonomy" is allowed in these cases while "substantial autonomy" has been lost under the scrutiny of the "supervising state" (van Vught 1989).

Another recent development concerning governance reform relates to how or whether public universities should be transformed into legally independent entities. Despite educational deregulation undertaken during the 1990s, university governance continued to be criticized for its lack of innovation and competitiveness. Rigid and strict systems prevented flexible internal management and hindered human resource deployment, financial operations, and administrative decision making (TMOE 2004). With the hope of assisting prestigious public universities in competing with their foreign counterparts, a 2005 amendment to the University Law was proposed that focused on "corporatization"—a legal status that allows public HEIs to own their assets and buildings, enjoy financial freedom, and employ personnel independently. As such, becoming a corporation was said to raise the institutional autonomy of universities (Chen 2006). However, the amendment did not pass because HEIs were concerned about the drawbacks of "administrative corporation" (this is a very unique way to corporatize; for a detailed analysis, see Chen 2007). Without independent judicial status, public universities still maintain a special regulatory link with the government. Efforts toward corporatization continue as institutions remain eager for greater autonomy.

On the other hand, universities are increasingly subject to external assessment as a result of the emergence of quality assurance mechanisms (Kezar and El-khawas 2003). Over-provision in higher education and the force of marketization led to the implementation of "university subject evaluation" in 2005, the results of which were even used as determinant of student admission quota. Overwhelming concerns about declining educational quality since the late 1990s created reasonable room for the government to steer or monitor the process and products of educational services. This managerial-oriented evaluation aimed not only to be the safeguard of learning quality, but also an accountability system from the perspective of the institution. Such evaluation measures have been proven to diminish institutional autonomy (Tapper 2007). Moreover, due to continual financial constraints, the emergence of competitive governmental funds has often been utilized to ease the problem of underfunding as well as improve the use of resources in an effective and efficient manner. In addition to fixed educational expenditures allocated according to a specific formula, up to 70 percent of extra funds are distributed based on outcome or performance-based management.

In addition to the introduction of "remote steering" strategies, the increasing force of marketization has played a key role in shaping governance patterns in Taiwanese higher education (Chou 2008). Although the language of market force has not been the dominant discourse in official white papers or documents, the formation of market-oriented mechanisms does come from different sources in Taiwan's higher education setting (Mok and Lo 2002). One prominent driver is closely related to the rapid growth of the number of institutions (from 76 in 1987 to 163 in 2008), echoing the increasing demand for access to higher education. However, this over-supply reform policy also created a situation in which each institution must operate in an increasingly competitive environment for students, governmental budgets, research grants, and even industry cooperation. Under the dogma of neoliberalism, state provision has been regarded as an ineffective measure in the education sector. Therefore, private HEIs have been expanding since the lifting of martial law, with more than two-thirds of college students enrolled in these institutions. Furthermore, the decreased public budget for higher education became an impetus for policy makers to require institutions to search for more diverse funding sources, such as tuition fees. All these initiatives contributed to the realization of marketization in Taiwan's higher education subsector.

Education officials have said that higher education reforms in Taiwan aim to deregulate unnecessary controls and increase flexibility and innovation. Actually, these practices are closely linked to market competition or economic rationalism. Neoliberal tools are used to stimulate motivation and inspire efficiency improvement. Meanwhile, managerial measures such as indicators, evaluation, and competitive funds have been the core tools used to ensure that services provided by HEIs meet the needs and requirements of students, parents, industries, and governments. It seems that a combination of different philosophical elements have been used simultaneously in Taiwan's higher education subsector.

Discussion: Shifting Governance Patterns in Taiwanese Higher Education

Generally speaking, three phases can be identified in governance reforms in Taiwan. An authoritarian style of governance was adopted prior to 1987, when central domination prevailed. Later, from the late 1980s to late 1990s, changes in governance centered on the deregulation or devolution of power to lower organizations or units. The government's priority was to establish a framework in which the university was capable of retaining greater power for decision-making processes and management. This period of governance reforms sought to grant substantial autonomy to HEIs, giving them more freedom to choose. Finally, recent governance reforms have paid particular attention to competition, quality assurance, and efficiency rather than empowerment of faculty and institutions Strong, state-led reforms also characterize the period of policy change in the early twenty-first century. The comprehensive involvement of the government in defining the role, function, and performance of HEIs indicates a trend toward recentralization of university management.

Relating the changing patterns of the Taiwan case to diverse theoretical debates on university governance provides meaningful insight. These changing governance patterns in Taiwan may more or less reflect theoretical concerns and notions. Although the first wave of governance reform was inspired by the political democratization movement and the educational deregulation of the late 1980s, the rationales adopted to guide the transformation of university management can be traced back to the Oxbridge tradition of faculty/academia retaining a greater decision-making power. The most popular slogan or reform jargon at the time was "professor rules the campus" and "campus democracy," as advocated by the Nobel Laureate Yuen-Tseh Lee, who led a comprehensive review group on education in 1994. Followers believed that a true university should enjoy wider freedom in order to fulfill the ultimate objective in pursuit of knowledge truth, preventing interventions from religious or political regimes. In this context, the status of the university must be altered from a centrally controlled institution to an organization that steers its own development based on the decisions of insiders (i.e., academic faculty). However, despite endeavors to promote institutional autonomy since the late 1980s, the freedom that each Taiwanese HEI possesses is far from complete and less comprehensive than counterparts in the United Kingdom and the United States (Chen 2007). The abandonment of the authoritarian governance type does not mean the automatic appearance of the academic oligarchy model outlined. On the contrary, in continental European countries, state bureaucracy is still strong and regulates the access conditions, the curriculum, the degree requirement, and so forth, while leaving other roles to be fulfilled by faculty. This state-controlled pattern remained a feature of the governance structure in Taiwan even after the 1990s.

The increased pressure of market forces and international competition that stems from economic globalization has caused Taiwan's government to shift its governance reforms to adopt combined solutions that range from neoliberalism to new managerialism. The practices and techniques endorsed by the former governance philosophy resulted in the formation of certain market mechanisms in Taiwanese higher education. The adoption of these measures aimed to improve the performance of institutions or enhance the use of limited public funds or resources. The overarching objective was clearly related to the pursuit of efficiency, economy, and effectiveness (Amaral et al. 2003). Rather than be sorely reliant upon the market force to steer the development of its higher education subsector, Taiwan also depended heavily on managerial techniques advocated by new managerialism. Many outcome- or performance-based monitoring strategies and remote-steering strategies have been introduced and implemented since 2000. By allowing individual institutions to operate and compete in a market environment, the Taiwanese government intended to make universities more autonomous. Consequently, market strategies and a quasi-market environment were turned into instruments or platforms manipulated by the state. Differing significantly from the separate rationales of neoliberalism and new managerialism, market forces in Taiwan were introduced in accordance with the guidance and command of the state, combining these two different forces (market and state) together to direct the development of higher education. In other words, the market did not work alone, but served as a facilitator to achieve the objectives that the government prescribed for universities.

Thus, the institutional autonomy pursued in the 1980s by the Taiwanese government and universities is an end in itself, whereas after the late 1990s it became merely an instrument or precondition enabling HEIs to aim for greater competitiveness and accountability. This situation explains why the greater autonomy that the central authority promised (e.g., corporatization reform) was simply lip service. What the central authority really delivered was procedural autonomy—a situation in which institutions are free to choose the means while the goals are predetermined by governments or other stakeholders (not the institutions themselves). In order to cope with increasing demands from the outside world, senior leaders in Taiwanese universities requested greater executive power to carry out strategic planning and responses, which may have caused further erosion of shared governance and faculty participation. This observation seems to be consistent with the findings of Mok (2009) on Singapore and Malaysia:

> Although the senior management of corporatized/incorporated universities in these Asian states has been given more discretion to decide how to operate their universities, most of the front line academics have not experienced major differences in university governance after the reforms took place. Instead of feeling "emancipated" and "empowered," many academics feel more pressures and control from the university administration and government ministers.

Such shifts of governance reforms created a tension between autonomy and accountability (Tierney 2006). Governance reforms after the late 1990s in Taiwan shifted to market and managerial orientations, which are related to the appeal of the 3 E's: efficiency, effectiveness, and economy. Accountability was the main concern driving policy initiatives and may have created a danger of reducing institutional autonomy. After two decades of endeavors, higher education governance in Taiwan has seemingly begun to shift its patterns from deregulation or decentralization of power back to recentralization, where central authority can easily achieve its wishes through market measures and the use of managerial strategies proposed by both neoliberalism and new managerialism. A recentralized pattern may be realized with the advancement of these governance philosophies in the near future.

Conclusion

Traditional governance in higher education emphasized the importance of faculty participation and institutional autonomy, by which individual academic staff could enjoy more freedom to decide their own affairs on campus. At the time, the university was one important component of the cultural sphere and, as such, needed such a design to protect it from political disturbances. However, today's modern university has to meet a wide range of external challenges, such as globalization, economic competition, and limited governmental funds. Therefore, the dominant discourse in governance structure contends that market competition and managerial techniques or measures are regarded as more effective and efficient ways to steer universities.

Governance reforms in Taiwan's higher education subsector have also undergone dramatic changes since political liberation in 1987. Bureaucratic centralization was once a feature of this system, but the 1994 amendment to the University Law changed this. For a while, Taiwan was on the way to accepting the idea of deeper faculty participation—an early model appreciated by many in academe. Nevertheless, this democratic governance reform was soon replaced by the central steering model, encompassing the core ideas of new managerialism and market forces. Accountability and performance became the main concerns of the government in the face of diverse pressures. Inevitably, this transformation in governance caused a serious concern about the further development of institutional autonomy and even faculty participation. If this trend continues, what was cherished before the late 1990s can gradually erode and a new type of centralization governance may come to power.

Note

1. The General Consultation Report on Educational Reform was produced by the Council on Educational Reform, a mission-oriented committee established in 1994 to review all major issues confronting the Taiwanese education system and to advise the government on how to respond to them.

References

Amaral, Alberto, Glen A. Jones, and Berit Karseth, eds. 2002. *Governing Higher Education: National Perspectives on Institutional Governance.* Dordrecht: Kluwer Academic Publishers.
Amaral, Alberto, António Magalhães, and Rui Santiago. 2002. "The Rise of Academic Managerialism in Portugal." In *The Higher Education Managerial Revolution*, eds. A. Amaral, V. L. Meek, and I. M. Larsen. Dordrecht: Kluwer Academic Publishers.
Amaral, Alberto, Vicent L. Meek, and Ingvild M. Larsen, eds. 2003. *The Higher Education Managerial Revolution?* Dordrecht: Kluwer Academic Publishers.
Barnett, Ronald. 1990. *The Idea of Higher Education.* Buckingham: Open University Press.
Berdahl, Robert O. 1990. "Academic Freedom, Autonomy and Accountability in British Universities." *Studies in Higher Education* 15 (2): 169–180.
Birnbaum, Robert. 2000. *Management Fads in Higher Education: Where They Come From, What They Do, Why They Fail.* San Francisco: Jossey-Bass.
———. 2004. "The End of Shared Governance: Looking Ahead or Looking Back." *New Directions for Higher Education* 127 (Autumn): 5–22.
Braun, Dietmar, and François-Xavier Merrien, eds. 1999. *Towards A New Model of Governance for Universities? A Comparative View.* London and Philadelphia: Jessica Kingsley Publishers.
Chang, Chun-Hsing, ed. 1987. *The Sound of Campus* [in Chinese]. Taipei: Dun-Lee Publisher.
Chen, Der-Hwa. 2006. "A Reflection on the University Education Reforms from the Perspective of the Amendment to University Law." [In Chinese] *Higher Education Bulletin*, Issue 178.
Chen, Hung-Wen. 2005. "The Content and Implications of Corporatisation of National Universities in Japan." [In Chinese] *Comparative Education* 55 (1): 35–65.
Chen, Shun-Fen. 1993. *Essays on Higher Education* [in Chinese]. Taipei: Normal University Bookstore.

Chen, Wei-Jao. 2007. *The Dilemmas and Responses of Taiwanese Higher Education* [in Chinese]. Taipei: National Taiwan University Press.
Chiang, Li-Chuan. 2004. "The Relationship between University Autonomy and Funding in England and Taiwan." *Higher Education* 48 (1): 189–212.
Chou, Chu-Ing. 2008. "The Impact of Neo-liberalism on Taiwanese Higher Education." In *The Worldwide Transformation of Higher Education*, eds. D. P. Baker and A. W. Wiseman. Oxford: Elsevier Science Ltd.
Clark, Burton. 1983. *The Higher Education System: Academic Organization in Cross National Perspective*. Berkeley: University of California Press.
Council on Educational Reform. 1996. *General Consultation Report on Educational Reform* [in Chinese]. Taipei: The Executive Yuan.
Deem, Rosemary, Sam Hillyard, and Mike Reed. 2007. *Knowledge, Higher Education, and the New Managerialism*. Oxford: Oxford University Press.
Deem, Rosemary, Ka-Ho Mok, and Lisa Lucas. 2008. "Transforming higher education in whose image? Exploring the Concept of the 'World-Class' University in Europe and Asia." *Higher Education Policy* 21 (1): 83–97.
Duderstadt, James J., and Farris W. Womack. 2003. *The Future of the Public University in America: Beyond the Crossroads*. Baltimore: The Johns Hopkins University Press.
Ferlie, Ewan, Christine Musselin, and Gianluca Andresani. 2008. "The Steering of Higher Education: A Public Management Perspective." *Higher Education* 56 (3): 325–348.
Ho, De-Fen. 1990. *The Rebirth of University* [in Chinese]. Taipei: China Times Press.
———. 1993. *Taiwanese Higher Education White Paper* [in Chinese]. Taipei: China Times Press.
Husen, Tusén, and T. Neville Postlethwaite. 1985. *The International Encyclopaedia of Education: Research and Studies 2*. Oxford: Pergamon Press.
Kezar, Adrianna, and Elaine El-khawas. 2003. "Using the Performance Dimension: Converging Paths for External Accountability?" In *Globalization and Reform in Higher Education*, ed. H. Eggins. Maidenhead: Open University Press.
Law, Wing-Wah. 1998. "Higher Education in Taiwan: The Rule of Law and Democracy." *International Higher Education* 11 (Spring): 4–6.
Maroy, Christian. 2009. "Introduction to the Sub-issue 'New Modes of Regulation of Education Systems.'" *Compare* 39 (1): 67–70.
McInnis, Craig. 2006. "Renewing the Place of Academic Expertise and Authority in the Reform of University Governance." In *Governance and the Public Good*, ed. W. G. Tierney. Albany: State University of New York.
Middlehurst, Robin. 2004. "Changing Internal Governance: A Discussion of Leadership Roles and Management Structures in UK Universities." *Higher Education Quarterly* 58 (4): 258–280.
Mok, Ka-Ho. 2000. "Reflecting Globalization Effects on Local Policy: Higher Education Reform in Taiwan." *Journal of Education Policy* 15 (6): 637–660.
———. 2002. "From Nationalisation to Marketization: Changing Governance in Taiwan's Higher Education System." *Governance: An International Journal of Policy, Administration, and Institutions* 15 (2): 137–159.
———. 2009. "When State Centralism Meets Neo-liberalism: Managing University Governance Change in Singapore and Malaysia." Paper presented at the 2009 Asian-Pacific Forum on Sociology of Education, Tainan, Taiwan, May 6.
Mok, Ka-Ho, and Eric H. C. Lo. 2002. "Marketization and the Changing Governance in Higher Education: A Comparative Study." *Higher Education Management and Policy* 14 (1): 51–82.

Morris, Paul. 1996. "Asia's Four Little Tigers: A Comparison of the Role of Education in Their Development." *Comparative Education* 32 (1): 95–109.

Nelson, Brendan. 2002. *Meeting the Challenges: The Governance and Management of Universities*. Canberra: Department of Education, Science, and Training, Commonwealth of Australia.

Shattock, Michael. 2006. *Managing Good Governance in Higher Education*. Maidenhead, England: Open University Press.

Taiwan Ministry of Education (TMOE). 1995. *Report on Education of the Republic of China: An Educational Prospect Towards The 21st Century* [in Chinese]. Taipei: TMOE.

———. 2001a. *The Plan for Integration of Regional Resources for National Universities* [in Chinese]. Taipei: TMOE.

———. 2001b. *White Paper on Higher Education* [in Chinese]. Taipei: TMOE.

———. 2004. *A Statement on the Transformation of National Universities into Administrative Corporations* [in Chinese]. Taipei: TMOE. (In Chinese)

———. 2008a. *Sustainable Development Committee in Higher Education* [in Chinese]. Taipei: TMOE. http://140.111.34.181/h_group.php.

———. 2008b. *A Proposal for Developing World-Class Universities and Top Research Centres* [in Chinese]. Taipei: TMOE. http://www.edu.tw.

Tapper, Ted. 2007. *The Governance of British Higher Education: The Struggle for Policy Control*. Dordrecht, The Netherlands: Springer.

Teichler, Ulrich. 2008. "Diversification? Trends and Explanations of the Shape and Size of Higher Education." *Higher Education* 56 (3): 349–379.

Tierney, William G. 2006. "The Examined University: Process and Change in Higher Education." In *Governance and the Public Good*, ed. W. G. Tierney. Albany: State University of New York.

van Vught, Frans A., ed. 1989. *Governmental Strategies and Innovation in Higher Education*. London: Jessica Kingsley Publishers.

———. 1994. "Autonomy and Accountability in Government/University Relationships." In *Revitalizing Higher Education*, eds. J. Salmi and A. M. Verspoor. Oxford: IAU Press.

Wang, Ru-Jer. 2003. "From Elitism to Mass Higher Education in Taiwan: The Problems Faced." *Higher Education* 46 (3): 261–287.

Chapter 9

Southeast Asian Higher Education in the Global Knowledge System: Governance, Privatization, and Infrastructure

Anthony Welch

Introduction

Higher education in Southeast Asia is a heady mix of ambition and constraint. Notwithstanding the considerable diversity among the five nations treated in this chapter (Indonesia, Malaysia, Philippines, Thailand, and Vietnam), the mix of a young demographic profile, rising aspirations, and limited state finances represents a common challenge, albeit to differing degrees. The late 1990s regional financial crisis also struck the region hard, as did the worldwide economic crisis of 2008–2009, although the specific impact of the latter on regional higher education was as yet not fully clear at the time of writing. A further common element is the current ambition to develop Accelerated Programme for Excellence (APEX) universities that are able to take their place among the leading higher education institutions (HEIs) of the world, although the capacity to reach this goal, especially in the shorter term, again differs appreciably among the five systems (Welch 2010a). Against this background, changing modes of governance in higher education, as well as issues of transparency, are key elements. Tensions between moves toward greater devolution and greater demands for accountability occur against a background of increasing privatization, including of public sector HEIs. This is arguably sharpening issues of governance in regional higher education.

The Functions of Higher Education

According to Manuel Castells, all societies throughout history designate specific roles and functions for universities (Castells 1993). Not only do these roles and functions change over time, depending on a given society's prevailing historical culture, ideology or politics, but they are also not always congruent and hence Castells refers to "universities as dynamic systems of contradictory functions" (1994, 25). He identifies four principal functions:

1. Universities may be assigned the responsibility for training bureaucracies and the provision of a highly skilled labor force. Most clearly evident in classical China, this was also Vietnam's primary goal in its early Confucian period, for example, when institutions of higher learning were devoted to preparing students for the imperial system of examinations which, for the successful, led to key posts as scholar-officials in the state bureaucracy.
2. A somewhat different function of universities can be to act as social sorting mechanisms to select and train scientific, economic, political, and educational elites. In such cases, the selection, socialization, and the development of networks among other cadres all help to distinguish these élites from the rest of the society. Historically speaking, the French example is pertinent here, just as its paler colonial imitation in Vietnam. Santo Tomas University, the Philippines institution founded in 1611, also served this function, albeit for the colonial elite.
3. Universities are often assigned the duty of acting as ideological apparatuses, responsible (among other institutions) for the formation and dissemination of the societal, or state ideology. Here again, the role of Ho Chi Minh thought and Marxist Leninist thought in contemporary Vietnam, and the national ideology of *Pancasila* in Indonesia since independence, are arguably illustrative.
4. Universities also function to generate new knowledge. This is a more modern trend attributable to the successful incorporation by German universities of the research seminar, and maths, science and technology into their curriculum in the nineteenth century and, somewhat later, U.S. science-oriented universities' close involvement in scientific and technological (including military) development, and economic growth. Here too, the context among the five nations differs appreciably, but each is a potent mix of ambition and restraint. Illustrative are Malaysia's recent designation of *Universiti Sains Malaysia* as its first APEX university, and Vietnam's current plans to develop equivalent institutions, although the former is better placed to achieve this goal (Welch 2010a).

Castells' taxonomy of roles and functions provides a broad outline of goals that are set for universities to perform:

- train skilled labor as demanded by the society,
- cultivate élites,

- generate and transmit ideology, and
- create and apply new knowledge.

Here however, while ambitions and aspirations among developing countries are usually great, they often suffer from something of a disadvantage, relative to their counterparts in the developed world, where, as indicated below, the concentration of various kinds of resources and a longer history of research and development give the latter important competitive advantages.

The ongoing ability to successfully manage the sometimes contradictory functions of Castells is a crucial index of success for developing countries in achieving growth, reform, equity, and social integration. Castells does not distinguish here between public and private institutions, but the addition of private universities into this sometimes volatile mix, including the regulation of this developing sector, further complicates an already difficult task, as is seen below.

Despite the developing country status of four of the five Southeast Asian countries, (Malaysia's GDP per capital level now places it in a middle-income category), all have ambitious plans to extend higher education to larger proportions of their populace, who are in turn pressing their governments for more and more places for their children, and more institutions of higher education. This is for at least two reasons, each of which relate to Castells' taxonomy above.

The first is that higher education is seen by governments and international organizations such as the Organization for Economic Co-operation and Development, World Bank, and Asian Development Bank, as critical to the supply of the highly skilled personnel that, in a more post-Fordist world, are said to be the foundation of the new knowledge economies. As World Bank (2000b, 9) notes,

> The quality of knowledge generated within higher education institutions, and its availability to the wider economy, is becoming increasingly critical to national (and one could add international ARW) competitiveness.

Just as countries such as China have recently implemented ambitious schemes to extend provision of higher education to substantially greater proportions of its populace, many less populous developing countries have equally ambitious schemes. Governments of developing nations tend to see universities, not merely as institutions of great national and international prestige (and also as important repositories of national culture), but crucially, also as springboards to the future, perhaps in concert with key industries such as information technology (IT), engineering, and science, with which many of its better established universities are now engaged in cooperative or contract research. Just as information and communication technology is seen as critical to development priorities, so too higher education is increasingly seen (especially in a more neoliberal, economically rational world, see Pusey 1991) as a driver of economic growth, putatively even enabling developing nations to leap ahead in their ongoing quest for development. (As seen below, however, the parallel with higher education goes no further, since this fervent aspiration is not so easily achieved, at least not in the shorter term.)

As indicated, however, this rationale for higher education is not limited to states (termed the "social rate of return"), but also obtains at both the level of the individual (the so-called individual rate of return). Many individuals see university education in the developing world as a chance to secure a good white-collar job, and perhaps even a passport to a postgraduate opportunity at an overseas university, and/or the chance to work and live abroad. While this does not hold true for all who wish to pursue higher education—after all, significant numbers of students still pursue degrees in music or philosophy such as in the fine arts, or in the less remunerative areas of the humanities such as history, languages, or philosophy that are almost bound to keep them poor—it is more likely to hold true for those who enroll in the key areas such as engineering, the sciences, IT, and business.

However, there are important differences in poorer, developing countries where, as in Vietnam, public universities can provide places for at most 10 percent of qualified applicants, fuelling a demand for private universities that is likely only to increase, and perhaps lead to some distortions in fields of study. Thus, for example, the intense pressure to gain entry leads to that goal becoming an end in itself and a large huge number of students end up studying subjects in which they have little interest, thus adding to the concerns about efficiency and quality of the higher education system. Or private institutions only offer a restricted range of subjects, particularly languages, IT, and Business Studies.

Compared with lower levels of education, tertiary education is particularly expensive to provide, and even more so in the mission-critical departments and faculties of IT, engineering, and science:

> By their very nature, science and technology have always demanded significant and ongoing investment to establish, maintain and expand the "engine" of physical infrastructure—including laboratories, libraries and classrooms. They also need a rich (and expensive) fuel of textbooks, computers, equipment, and other supplies. (World Bank 2000b, 71)

This is less so in business education, although even here, to establish an internationally reputable, well-staffed business school takes both time, and a considerable investment. To develop Stanford Business School, or INSEAD in France, to their current level, took time, planning and a considerable, ongoing injection of resources, some or all which are often unavailable in developing countries.

The Southeast Asian Context

To understand Southeast Asian higher education, it is important to remind ourselves here of basic Asia facts, such as the following: As recently as the end of the twentieth century, 900 million Asians (75 percent of the global total) were still forced to survive on less than US$1 per day. In addition, 75 percent of the world's illiterates, two thirds of whom are poor women, lived in Asia, millions of children who complete primary school could neither read nor write, and millions more dropped out every year because of poverty. Half of all children in the region, most of them poor, were not enrolled in secondary school, while almost 40 percent of children aged below five were malnourished, and hence unlikely to achieve their full intellectual potential. Nonetheless, some regional governments expended more on their military than on their children. Only 6 percent of total Asian Development Bank spending has been on education (ADB 2001, 3).

More specifically, the Southeast Asia region embraces around 540 million people, with a combined Gross Domestic Product (GDP) of US$610 billion (or US$1.9 billion in PPP$), and with very wide disparities—both across the region, and within countries. Per capita GDP ranged from US$9,120 (Malaysia) to US$2,300 (Vietnam) in 2005 (UNDP 2005, 20). Women constitute 49 percent of the total population over 56 percent of which still inhabits rural areas. Almost half of the substantial numbers employed in agriculture are women; Human Development Index (HDI) ranks ranged from 59 (Malaysia) to 112 (Vietnam) in 2002 (UNDP 2005). Poverty rates ranged from 16.6 percent in Indonesia (in 2004) to 14.1 percent in the Philippines (in 2005) (ADB 2005).

Southeast Asia and the Global Knowledge System

The facts detailed in the section above help to explain why, while the ambition and commitment of developing countries to expand opportunities for higher education in these key areas (including the desire to build world-class departments and institutions) is undoubted and ubiquitous, there are genuine questions about how far and fast they can move on this front. This is more so in the case of many developing countries, including the majority of the countries in this survey (with the exception of the Philippines whose impressive tertiary enrollment ratio of 30 percent in 1995 included many higher educational institutions [HEIs] of low quality), which had a tertiary enrollment ratio in the second lowest category internationally (between 5 and 15 percent) in 1995 (World Bank 2000b, 12–13), while quality among many HEIs is still problematic in all five countries.

When we take into account the concerns about the ability of developing countries to expand opportunities in higher education, it becomes obvious that the existing scientific gap between South and North is huge, and growing, exacerbated by trends that are examined below. This comes as no surprise when we examine some simple statistics. The North, for example, has around ten times the proportion of research and development (R&D) personnel (scientists and technicians) per capita as the South (3.8 percent, compared to 0.4 percent), and spends about four times the proportion of GDP on R&D—2.0 percent compared to 0.5 percent (World Bank 2000b). Most recent data underline major disparities on a variety of knowledge indices, as seen in table 9.1.

Particularly with respect to researchers per million of population, the average difference is more than seventeenfold, while in no Southeast Asian country is the difference from the developed country averages less than twelvefold. Table 9.2 reveals

Table 9.1 National Innovation Indices, by Country, Region, and Level of Development

Countries	Average years of schooling	Researchers per million	Quality of scientific research institutions	University-industry research collaboration
Southeast Asia	6.6	210	4.1	3.6
Indonesia	4.7	207	3.9	3.4
Malaysia	7.9	299	5.0	4.7
Philippines	7.6	48	3.3	2.7
Thailand	6.1	287	4.0	3.6
Developed country average	9.5	3,616	5.1	4.4

Source: World Bank (2006, 134).

Table 9.2 R&D Expenditure Levels, and as Percent of GDP,[a] 2002

Countries	US$ billions (PPP)	Percentage of world	1992	2002
Southeast Asia	3.3	0.4	0.1	0.2
Indonesia	0.3	0.0	0.1	0.1
Malaysia	1.5	0.2	0.4	0.7
Philippines	0.4	0.0	0.2	0.1
Thailand	1.1	0.1	0.2	0.2
Developed country average	645.8	77.8	2.3	2.3

Source: World Bank (2006, 116).
Note: [a] Regional data are sum of R&D divided by sum of PPP GDP.

significant ongoing disparities in R&D, both in terms of spending and as proportion of GDP.

In addition, the North registers approximately 97 percent of all patents registered in the United States and Europe, and, together with the newly industrializing countries of East Asia, accounts for 84 percent of all scientific articles published (World Bank 2000b, 69). Recent data from the United States Patent Office reveal an ever-widening gap in patent-related performance. From 2000 to 2004, while developed countries have been granted an average of 168,017 patents per 100,000 people, which was about 19.58 percent of the overall number, the five Southeast Asian countries have been granted only 140 patents per 100,000 people, which was about 0.04 percent of all patents (World Bank 2006, 123).

It is of course important to acknowledge that such indices as Science Citation Index, Social Science Citation Index, Engineering Index, and the like are skewed in favor of English language journals, thereby adding linguistic disadvantage to the existing disparities of wealth. Notwithstanding this common additional burden for the Southeast Asian Five, there were still appreciable publication and citation differentials among them. In 1995, Thailand had the most number of publications among the five Southeast Asian countries (648), followed by Malaysia (587),

Indonesia (310), Philippines (294), while Vietnam had the least (192). The pattern was the same for number of citations from 1993 to 1997: Thailand (8,398), Malaysia (3,450), Indonesia (3,364), Philippines (2,893), and Vietnam (1,657) (World Bank 2000a, 125–127).

Comparative figures help put this into perspective: Australian publications for 1995 totaled 18,088, and Japanese, 58,910. Citation counts for each of these countries from 1993 to 1997 were 301,320 and 930,981 respectively. More recent data show that higher education across Southeast Asia contributes much less to total R&D performance than among developed nations, as indicated in the table 9.3

As table 9.3 shows, with the exception of Thailand, the higher education subsector contributes little more than half of total R&D performance, relative to the average of developed nations, while in the case of Indonesia it is approximately one-sixth, at 4.6 percent. These stark disparities exist, notwithstanding the existence of traditions of great respect for education and the role of the teacher in society that obtain in much of Asia, and East and Southeast Asia particularly, and despite the venerable forms of learning that long obtained in countries such as Vietnam where Hanoi's Temple of Literature—refurbished some years ago by American Express—contains the stele of scholar-priests of many centuries ago, and Thailand, which exhibits a long-standing Buddhist tradition of commitment to learning (Bovornsiri et al. 1996, 55–57).

The above data reveal that notwithstanding the highest annual GDP per capita growth rate of any world region in recent decades (World Bank 2006, 38–39), very high aspirations for higher education at both individual and social levels, and a high commitment to learning, existing levels of infrastructure in higher education among Southeast Asian nations limit capacity for knowledge creation, indicated by Castells as the fourth key function of the modern university.

Demographic Challenge

It is also important to note in the Southeast Asian context that, in addition to rising aspirations, pressure on tertiary provision also stems from the demographic profile of all five countries, both in terms of the relative youth of their populations, and

Table 9.3 R&D Performance by Sector

Countries	Business	Government	Higher education
Southeast Asia	51.3	22.2	15.7
Indonesia	14.3	81.1	4.6
Malaysia	65.3	20.3	14.4
Philippines	58.6	21.7	17.0
Thailand	43.9	22.5	31.0
Developed country average	62.9	13.3	27.0

Source: World Bank (2006, 120).

the high fertility rates relative to developed nations. From 1975 to 2000, all five countries had a modest average annual population growth rate: Philippines and Malaysia (2.4 percent), Vietnam (2.0 percent) Indonesia (1.8 percent), and Thailand (1.7 percent). As of 2000, in all five countries, populations under 15 were more or less about 30 percent of the whole population: Philippines (37.5%), Malaysia (34.1%), Vietnam (33.4%), Indonesia (30.8%), and Thailand (26.7%) (UNDP Human Development Report 2002).

Simply responding to this demographic pressure and the rising aspiration levels for higher education is a difficult task for each of the Southeast Asian Five, even apart from questions of institutional quality.

The Rise of Private Higher Education

Demography and rising aspirations in Southeast Asia have important implications. Given a young population (only one of the Southeast Asian Five has less than 30 percent of their population under the age of 15, and in the case of the Philippines it is closer to 40 percent), rising levels of aspiration for higher education, and budgetary constraints, the state is less and less likely to be able to satisfy demand for tertiary entry. How far is this likely to fuel demand for private higher education? What does private higher education mean for equity, in countries, where under the influence of globalization and structural adjustment, the gap between the rich and poor, already large, is only widening?

One arguable measure, albeit perhaps somewhat crude, is the differing proportion of private HEIs (PHEIs) that obtained in the Southeast Asian Five countries about a decade ago. In 1997–1998, all students in Malaysia and Vietnam were enrolled in public HEIs. In Thailand too, public HEIs prevailed over private ones with a student proportion of six to four. Yet in Indonesia and Philippines, a majority of students (59 percent and 75 percent respectively) were enrolled in private HEIs (Gonzales 1999, 116).

A striking index of change in Southeast Asian higher education is the extent to which this picture has changed over the last decade, as evident in table 9.4. Notwithstanding the substantial diversity of political system within the Southeast Asian Five, ranging from a socialist polity adapting to the demands of a market economy and recent entry to Word Trade Organization (Vietnam) to long-term crony capitalist regimes (Philippines), private higher education in the region has grown apace. While private higher education in the Philippines was already dominant, it has continued to grow, so that its proportion of the whole is now over 80 percent. Vietnam has announced strikingly ambitious targets to expand higher education, which entail vigorous growth of the private ("People's") HEIs (Welch 2007a, 2009). Effectively, private sector HEIs doubled their share of enrollments in Vietnam from 1996–1997 to 1998–1999 (Welch 2007a), while Le and Ashwill (2004) report that by 2002–2003, there were 23 PHEIs, enrolling 24,500 students (around 12 percent of the total of 200,000 new enrollments). By 2020, government plans are for 40 percent of all enrollments to be private ("non-public") (Hayden and Thiep 2004). In Malaysia, there are now 18 private universities registered, with a

Table 9.4 Numbers and Types of HEIs in Southeast Asia, 2007

Countries	Public			Private			Total
	Degree	Non-degree	Subtotal	Degree	Non-degree	subtotal	
Indonesia	—	—	81	—	—	2,431	2,516
Malaysia	18	40	58	22	519	541	599
Philippines	424	1,352	1,776	1,363	2,045	3,408	5,184
Thailand	66	—	66	54	401	455	521
Vietnam	201	—	201	29	—	29	230

Note: "—" indicates that the data are not available.
Source: ADB (2008, 45), citing SEAMEO (2007).

similar number of colleges, while private enrollments in higher education now significantly outnumber those in the public sector, if diploma and certificate levels are taken into account (MOHE 2006). In Indonesia, private higher education has also grown, although with total private enrollments now estimated to be 1.9 million, of a total of 3.4 million (Buchori and Malik 2004; Welch 2007b), the proportion may not have increased.

Distinct political ideologies make a difference to higher education policies in each of the five cases, although at least three factors moderate these differences. The first is the powerful homogenizing effects of economic globalization and structural adjustment which, as has been argued elsewhere, is moving many systems in a similar direction, albeit at different paces, and to differing degrees (Welch and Mok 2003). The second is the gap between official rhetoric and actual practice in each case. Although, for instance, following the example of its powerful and sometimes troublesome northern neighbor, Vietnam chooses to call its private universities "People's Universities," they are in many ways little different in form and function from private institutions in other countries. The third homogenizing effect is the rise of global English (Crystal 1997; Wilson et al 1998), which is exerting pressure on both teaching and research regimes, not merely regionally.

Reforming Governance in Higher Education

What implications do the data and trends indicated above have for the governance of regional higher education? Clearly, the fact that, with the exception of Malaysia, the other four Southeast Asian nations included here fall in the less developed category, and that in addition, they suffered substantially in the fallout from the regional economic crisis of the late 1990s, imposes limits on both the quality of teaching and learning and the capacity of the public sector to respond to demand. While all five countries still enjoyed substantial GDP growth rates in 1997, the picture turned bleak suddenly in 1998 after the Asian Financial Crisis had just broken out: the GDP growth rate of Thailand has dived from 8.4 to –10.0 percent, Vietnam from 8.2 to 3.5 percent, Malaysia from 7.5 to –7.5 percent, Philippines from 5.2 to

−0.5 percent, and Indonesia from 4.5 to −13.7 percent (IMF 2001, 35; World Bank 2000a). [TS: Please note that highlights are minus symbols.]

While a significant economic renaissance is evident among all the Southeast Asian Five, especially compared to the depths of the late 1990s, the worldwide economic recession of 2008–2009 reverberated strongly through the region, with significant effects in education (Welch 2010a, b, c). None of the universities in the Southeast Asian Five, for example, was listed within the top five hundred universities listed in the Shanghai Jiaotong index of leading research universities (MOHE 2006, 263–73). That said, of course, each country has cherished icons of higher education among its ranks: Vietnam National University, University of the Philippines, University of Indonesia, Chulalongkorn University, and University of Malaysia.

More than knowledge creation is however, limited by relative lack of resources, infrastructure, and training. The lack of income and infrastructure in education also affects regulatory capacity in higher education. While regional higher education systems grow apace, particularly in the private sector, as was seen above, it is not clear that regulatory capacity, and in some cases transparency, has always paralleled this growth.

Internationally, a significant element of higher education reforms in recent years has been changes to governance. As the goals of higher education have been revised, against the background of a complex and shifting environment, so too has the governance of higher education (Amaral et al. 2001, 2003; OECD 2003). A key element, common to many systems of higher education, including in the Asia Pacific, is the move toward devolution, from a pattern of strong centralization. While governments retain a strong interest in higher education, and in particular its capacity to contribute to national economic development, devolution to institutional level is seen as a means to ensure flexibility and diversity. In Indonesia, for example, educational decentralization in higher education was trialed via a pilot scheme in five public HEIs, which were accorded the new status of *Badan Hukum Milik Negera*, or "State Owned Legal Institution" (Welch 2007b). By virtue of this new status, the selected HEIs were authorized to create new patterns of student recruitment, which would, inter alia, have the effect of garnering greater financial support from students and their families.

At the same time, however, HEIs are caught in something of a dilemma. On the one hand, the increasing mismatch between ever-increasing enrollment demand and limited state capacity means that public HEIs are being pressured to diversify their income sources, while the private sector expands to respond to unmet demand. Both trends are evident in the Southeast Asian systems treated here. This may add little if anything to teaching quality or research output however; indeed, there is evidence in several Southeast Asian systems that it may weaken each, with academics from the public sector being either poached to work in the private, or increasingly moonlighting there (Welch 2007b).

On the other hand, while governments tout the virtues of devolution, institutions find themselves pressured by more intricate regulatory architecture, which sets real limits on their capacity to put devolution into effect. While state funding per student plateaus, or is even declining, governments demand more and more accountability; this process has been characterized as more like accountancy, as rule by performance indicator increasingly burdens academic work and life (Welch 1998). In the process, devolution has been characterized as a form of centralized decentralization (Lee and Gopinathan 2004; Mok 2004). Many critics seriously question the extent to which the much-touted institutional freedom to run their own affairs is genuine, or whether it is illusory, against such a backdrop. Certainly, regional evidence shows that decentralization of governance (Aspinall 2004) and even education at other levels have not been without their problems (Surakhmad 2002; Amirrachman et al. 2009). In higher education too, problems persist, as is seen below.

The Impact of Limited Infrastructure

In a curious irony, it can be argued that the increasing demands of governance impose real limits on governability in Southeast Asian universities. While regionally, devolution has been accompanied by increased demands for performance data, and a move to discretionary funding for which HEIs must compete, little or no additional personnel, or other resources, have been made available to respond to such trends. At the same time, governments, too, are under pressure, often with very limited resources available within agencies and ministries charged with the regulation of quality and propriety in higher education. Given the less developed status of all but one of the Southeast Asian Five, personnel with which to perform such regulatory tasks are limited, and the high-level training required of such staff cannot always be assumed.

This has long been problematic, but has become more so, in light of several factors. The rise of mass higher education systems and larger numbers of institutions make the mechanics of ensuring quality control difficult, even in the public system. The rise and complexity of the private sector, sketched above, has made the job even more complex, with in some cases the total number of HEIs nationally rising to more than 1,000. Recent figures for Malaysia show 533 PHEIs of nonuniversity status (MOHE 2006, 257), while in Indonesia, for example, there are two categories of PHEIs, *terakreditasi* (accredited), and *tidak terakreditasi* (nonaccredited). The latter are quite widespread. Geographic dispersal adds to these difficulties, although in the early 1990s, some 25 percent of all PHEIs were still located either in Jakarta (16.4 percent) or East Java (9.6 percent), for example, (Pardoen 1998, 28) the proliferation in recent years of PHEIs well outside the major cities, yields its own difficulties:

> [S]uch a big number of PHEIs presents problems, especially when dealing with the quality control of the education they offer...the controls sound weak due to the fact that monitoring activities are not easy, and necessitate a high cost because some of the PHEIs are in scattered areas. Generally, the problems of monitoring PHEIs lead to several particulars concerning government policies, quality control and financial matters. (Hardihardaja 1996, 42).

Finally, the rise of transnational higher education, and cross-border programs and institutions make the regulatory challenge even tougher, for already hard-pressed national regulatory agencies. While many transnational institutions and programs act ethically, and are of high quality, there are numerous regional examples of bogus "cyber universities" and virtual diploma mills.

The Impact of Corruption

It must also be acknowledged that Southeast Asia is not free of corruption, which also permeates higher education, at times. While most university staff, both academic and administrative (sometimes they are the same individuals) throughout the region work hard under challenging conditions, including the aforementioned poor remuneration rates and very limited resources, there are some who perform less honorably.

Transparency International's 2006 Corruption Perceptions Index (CPI) points to a strong correlation between corruption and poverty, with a concentration of impoverished states at the bottom of the ranking. "Corruption traps millions in poverty," according to the Chair of Transparency International, Huguette Labelle:

> Despite a decade of progress in establishing anti-corruption laws and regulations, today's results indicate that much remains to be done before we see meaningful improvements in the lives of the world's poorest citizens. (Labelle 2006, 1)

The 2006 Corruption Perceptions Index (CPI) (Transparency International, www.transparency.org) is a composite index that draws on multiple expert opinion surveys that poll perceptions of public sector corruption in 163 countries around the world, the greatest scope of any CPI to date. Countries are scored on a scale from zero to ten; zero indicates high levels of perceived corruption, while ten indicates low levels of perceived corruption.

A strong correlation between corruption and poverty, evident in the results of the CPI 2006 affects the Southeast Asian Five significantly. Public sector wages in all but Malaysia are poor and moonlighting common. Indeed, the correlation between poverty and corruption is underscored by the fact that only Malaysia scored 5.0, while others scored much less: 3.6 (Thailand), 2.6 (Vietnam), 2.4 (Indonesia), and 2.5 (Philippines).

Westcott's analysis of corruption in Southeast Asia provides some examples of the general effects of pervasive corruption (Richardson 2001; Westcott 2001). He cites, for example, Thailand's National Counter Corruption Commission's estimate that up to 30 percent of government procurement budgets may be lost because of corrupt practices. At the lower end, this would almost equal the entire budget of the Ministry of Agriculture. At the upper end, it would exceed the combined budgets of Agriculture and Public Health (Westcott 2001, 252) ministries. Data from Vietnam cite reports showing that nearly one-third of Vietnam's public investment expenditure in 1998, equivalent to 5 percent of the GDP, was lost to fraud and corruption, and the situation did not improve in recent years (Westcott 2001, 258). As elsewhere in Southeast Asia, the situation is not helped by poor public sector pay, and widespread moonlighting, as indicated above.

The effects on higher education are revealed in the two following examples. The first occurred within Indonesia, where a PHEI's Faculty of Engineering, which was facing an upcoming evaluation of its facilities by the national regulatory authority, and was well aware that its level of engineering infrastructure was inadequate, adopted a strategy to circumvent the problem. Unwilling to accept the consequences of a poor rating, the Faculty of Engineering borrowed from local engineering firms numerous items of major equipment. The day after the successful inspection, which ultimately yielded a satisfactory B rating, all items of equipment were returned to the firms, leaving students just as bereft of much necessary equipment as before. Such stories are not uncommon: "Many private schools provide engineering education without sufficient equipment to support the curriculum and end up compromising the quality of their graduates" (Buchori and Malik 2004, 262). The need for a more effective regulatory regime is now widely acknowledged, against a background where the widespread culture of corruption (known in Indonesia as *Korrupsi, Kollusi, and Nepotism*) has the capacity to undermine the effectiveness of quality assurance procedures (*Kompas* 2002).

The second set of examples come from Vietnam, where in 2001, serious problems surfaced at certain PHEIs. At least two difficulties became apparent in the course of the official police investigation. Each also arguably related to their status as nonstate institutions, ineligible for public funds. The first issue was that of overenrollment, in a situation where the Ministry of Education and Training (MOET) sets legally defined enrollment limits for such institutions. Dong Do University was found by MOET to have overenrolled to the tune of 2.8 times its MOET quota. Thus for the academic year 2001–2002 alone, Dong Do had enrolled 4,205 students, rather than its allotted 1,500. Curiously, however, the problems had been known for some years:

> The Dong Do University scandal first surfaced in October 1998 when officials of the Ministry of Education and Training found that the number of students admitted to the university far surpassed the permitted figure. (*Vietnam News* 2002a)

The second issue was one of entry standards. While this may be seen as simply an issue of quality, it was alleged in 2001 that the leaders of Dong Do had been routinely accepting bribes from students or their families to secure entry to the institution. This, too, is strictly illegal, but allegedly done to boost numbers of enrollments and income levels.

Once again, the official MOET investigation did indeed uncover substantial breaches; papers were given marks of eight or nine out of ten, at times by unqualified markers, when their real grade was assessed at as low as 0.5. Several dozen students were accepted for enrollment without even being on the list of students for selection. Another 380 had no upper secondary graduation certificates at all. All in all, some 80 percent of students accepted for enrollment at Dong Do were found to have scores lower than that reported by the University Council, while some others had had their marks increased by rescoring. Beyond these serious breaches of procedure, the investigating team also found that the university had failed to build any facilities, offices, or classrooms in seven years of operation, or to invest in enhancing the quality of academic staff. Facilities were assessed as not meeting the standards of a university (Lao Dong 2002).

As a result of this investigation, Dong Do's 2002 enrollments were deemed cancelled, and the university given strict instructions to end such illegal practices. The Hanoi police were called in to conduct an investigation, and if necessary, proceed to prosecutions against the rector and other senior staff responsible. The deputy chair of its board of management was subpoenaed "... for his involvement in of the biggest scandals to date in the education sector" (*Vietnam News* 2002a, b). The former director of its Training Department was also charged.

At times, too, gamekeeper has turned poacher. In a separate case in 2002, two senior MOET officials, both at the level of deputy minister, were reprimanded or sacked, after their involvement in the "Asian International University scam" was revealed. Both officials were linked with the "bogus university, which set up shop in Vietnam, and enrolled thousands, awarding worthless paper degrees" (*Vietnam News* 2002c). After being in operation for five years, Asian International University, which was established in 1995 in cooperation with Hanoi University of Foreign Languages, ceased pretending to be a university. It left more than 2,000 students stranded and lost hundreds of thousands of dollars (Le and Ashwill 2004). In another incident, the so-called American Capital University offered an MBA program, together with a partner, the variously titled Singapore (later Senior) Management Training Centre. Both institutions are now defunct, again leaving a large number of students thousands of dollars out of pocket (Ashwill 2006).

Conclusion: Blurring Borders, Changing Balance

If private higher education is to grow, as is currently the case in many parts of the world (Altbach 1999), the question of the impact of such a new balance on equality must be addressed. According to World Bank (2000a, 57),

> there is another important downside to private financing—it may preclude the enrolment of deserving students who do not have the ability to pay, and often evokes resentment among students who do. Means-tested scholarship and loan programs are one possible approach to addressing this problem, but they have proven very difficult to administer due to the difficulty of assessing ability to pay, sometimes exorbitant administrative costs, corruption and high rates of default.

At the very least, there is a heightened need for regulation and quality assurance, in such a new context where there is likely to be a growing number of local and international private providers, some of whom are worthy, and others little more than shopfronts or (cyber) diploma mills. As indicated above, already, the rector of one of the larger and more long-standing "People's" universities in Vietnam was placed under police investigation, allegedly for both exceeding his enrollment quota by a huge margin, and for taking bribes to allow students with poor marks to enroll. In Indonesia, and in others of the Southeast Asian Five countries, examples of corrupt practices and cheating exist. Such stratagems were driven, at least in part, by the need or greed for funding, as well as poor public sector pay, and a culture in which lack of transparency can continue.

Despite the undoubted need for careful regulation of the higher education subsector, and the importance of promoting quality, it will not be easily or simply accomplished, as World Bank (2000a, 58) notes:

> [I]n most developing countries, no clearly identified set of individuals or institutions is working to ensure that all the goals of the country's higher education sector will be fulfilled. A coherent and rational approach toward management of the entire higher education sector is therefore needed...Policymakers must decide on the extent to which they will guide the development of their country's higher education sector, and the extent to which they think that market forces will lead to the establishment of and operation of a viable system. Overall, the Task Force believes that government guidance is an essential part of any solution.

The case of the Philippines where, as was seen above, more than three quarters of all enrollments are private, illustrates the difficulty clearly. In a political system, where every legislator sees it as part of his or her legacy to create an HEI that will be named after him or her, the proliferation of small and often very poor quality institutions is a long-standing problem. Faced with this difficulty, efforts were made during the 1980s to introduce a national system that regulated the establishment and operations of PHEIs. The ensuing stout opposition by the private sector, many of whom argued that the regulations threatened the financial viability of their institutions, forced the abandonment of the scheme, and a reversion to a laissez-faire pattern occurred. It is for that reason that all but a few HEIs in the Philippines are regarded by both domestic experts and external accreditation agencies as well short of international degree-level standard.

Finally, given the swiftness and the extent of the transformation, which is seeing public HEIs introducing fees, at times quite high, and employing all available strategies and stratagems to diversify their funding base, are the boundaries between public and private likely to be as clear in the future as in the past? Just as transnational HEIs and programs are breaching national borders on an unprecedented scale, are we likely to see a further blurring of borders between public and private in higher education? According to the World Bank (2000a, 58),

> Private higher education is one of the most dynamic and fastest-growing segments of post-secondary education at the turn of the twenty-first century. A combination of unprecedented demand for access to higher education and the inability or unwillingness of governments to provide the necessary support has brought private higher education to the forefront. Private institutions, with a long history in many countries, are expanding in scope and number and are increasingly important in parts of the world that have relied on the public sector. A related phenomenon is the "privatization" of public institutions in some countries. With tuition and other charges rising, public and private institutions look more and more similar.

In such circumstances, the challenge to governance of higher education in Southeast Asia remains substantial.

References

Altbach, Philip G. 1999. "Comparative Perspectives on Private Higher Education." In *Private Prometheus. Private Higher Education and Development in the Twenty first Century*, ed. P. G. Altbach. Westport, CT: Greenwood Press.

Amaral, Alberto, Glen A. Jones, and Berit Karseth, eds. 2001. *Governing Higher Education: National Perspectives and Institutional Governance*. Dordrecht, The Netherlands: Kluwer Academic Publishers.

Amaral, Alberto, V. Lynn Meek, and Ingvild M. Larsen, eds. 2003 *The Higher Education Managerial Revolution?* Dordrecht, The Netherlands: Kluwer Academic Publishers.

Amirrachman, Alpha, Saefudin Syafi'i, and Anthony Welch. 2009. "Decentralisation of Indonesian Education: The Promise and the Price." In *Globalisation, Comparative Education and Policy Research*, ed. J. Zajda. Amsterdam: Springer.

Ashwill, Mark. 2006. "US Institutions Find Fertile Ground in Vietnam's Expanding Higher Education Market." *International Higher Education* 44 (Summer): 13–14.

Asian Development Bank (ADB). 2001. *Education Sector Policy Paper (Draft)*. Manila: ADB.

ADB. 2005. *South East Asia Annual Report 2005*. Manila: ADB. www.adb.org.

ADB. 2008. *Education and Skills: Strategies for Accelerated Development in Asia and the Pacific*. Manila: ADB.

Aspinall, Edward. 2004. "Indonesia: Transformation of Civil Society and Democratic Breakthrough." In *Civil Society and Political Change in Asia*, ed. M. Alagappa. Palo Alto, CA: Stanford University Press.

Bovonsiri, Varaporn, Pornlerd Uampuang, and Gerald Fry. 1996. "Cultural Influences on Higher Education in Thailand." In *The Social Role of Higher Education*, eds. K. Kempner and G. Tierney. New York: Garland.

Buchori, Mochtar, and Abdul Malik. 2004. "The Evolution of Higher education in Indonesia." In *Asian Universities. Historical perspectives and Contemporary Challenges*, eds. P. G. Altbach and T. Umakoshi. Baltimore: The Johns Hopkins University Press.

Castells, Manuel. 1993. "The University System: Engine of Development in the New World Economy." In *Improving Higher Education in Developing Countries*, ed. A. Ranson, S.M. Khoo, and V. Selveratnam. Washington, DC: World Bank.

Castells, Manuel. 1994. "The University System: Engine of Development in the New World Economy." In *Revitalizing Higher Education*, eds. J. Salmi and A. Verspoor. Oxford: Pergamon.

Crystal, David. 1997. *English as a Global Language*. Cambridge: Cambridge University Press.

Gonzales, Andrew. 1999. "Private Higher Education in the Philippines." In *Private Prometheus. Private Higher Education and Development in the Twenty first Century*, ed. P. G. Altbach. Westport, CT.; London: Greenwood Press.

Hardihardaja, J. 1996. "Private Higher Education in Indonesia: Current Developments and Existing Problems." In *Private higher education in Asia and the Pacific*. eds. T-I. Wongsothorn and Y. Wang. Final Report. Bangkok: UNESCO PROAP, and SEAMEO RIHED.

Hayden, Martin, and Lam Quang Thiep. 2004. "A 2020 Vision for Higher Education in Vietnam." *International Higher Education* 44 (Summer): 11–13.

International Monetary Fund (IMF). 2001. *IMF Country Report No.01/59 Viet Nam*. Washington, DC: IMF.

Kompas. 2002. "Tampa Kontrol, Peningkatan Anggaran Pendidikan Bisa Berbahaya [Without Controls, Increasing the Education Budget Could Be Dangerous]." Jakarta: Kompas.com. http://www.kompas.com. August 15.
Labelle, Huguette. 2006. *2006 Corruption Perceptions Index.* Berlin: Transparency International. http://www.transparency.org.
Lao Dong (Labour) Newspaper. 2002. Various Issues. http://www.laodong.com.vn.
Le, Ngoc-Minh, and Mark A. Ashwill. 2004. "A Look at Nonpublic Higher Education in Vietnam." *International Higher Education* 36 (Summer): 16–17.
Lee, Michael H., and Saravanan Gopinathan. 2004. "Centralized Decentralization of Higher Education in Singapore." In *Centralization and Decentralization: Educational Reforms and Changing Governance in Chinese Societies*, ed. K. H. Mok. Dordrecht, The Netherlands: Kluwer Academic Publishers.
Ministry of Higher Education (MOHE). 2006. Report by the Committee to Study, Review and Make Recommendations Concerning the Development and Direction of Higher Education in Malaysia. Putrajaya, Malaysia: MOHE.
Mok, Ka-Ho, ed. 2004. *Centralization and Decentralization: Educational Reforms and Changing Governance in Chinese Societies.* Dordrecht, The Netherlands: Kluwer Academic Publishers.
Pardoen, Sustriso R. 1998. *Assessment of Private Investment in Private Higher Education in Indonesia: The Case of Four Private Universities.* Jakarta: Centre for Societal Development Studies Series, Atma Jaya Catholic University.
Pusey, Michael. 1991. *Economic Rationalism in Canberra: A Nation-Buiding State Changes Its Mind.* Cambridge: Cambridge University Press.
Richardson, Michael. 2001. "In Many Asian Countries, Public Anger at Corruption Is on the Rise." *International Herald Tribune,* January 22, 6.
Southeast Asian Ministers of Education Organisation (SEAMEO). 2002. *Private Higher Education: Its Role in Human Resource Development in a Globalised Knowledge Society.* Bangkok: SEAMEO.
SEAMEO. 2007. *Number of Tertiary Institutions by Sector and Type.* Bangkok: SEAMEO. http://www.seameo.org.
Surakhmad, Winarno. 2002. "Desentralising Education: A Strategy for Building Sustainable Development." Paper presented at the Conference on Autonomy in Education in the Indonesian Context, *Australian National University*, Canberra, September 29, 2002.
Transparency International. 2006. *Corruption Perception Index.* Berlin: Transparency International. http://www.transparency.org.
UNDP. 2002. *Human Development Report 2002 Deepening Democracy in a Fragmented World.* New York: Oxford University Press.
UNDP. 2005. *Southeast Asia Human Development Report (SEAHDR). Regional Economic Integration and Regional Cooperation in Southeast Asia: Deepening and Broadening the Benefits for Human Development.* New York: Oxford University Press.
Viet Nam News. 2002a. "Enrolment Irregularities Bring on Suspensions at Dong Do University." *Viet Nam News,* January 14.
Viet Nam News. 2002b. "Police Grill Professor over Dong Do University Scandal." *Viet Nam News,* June 19.
Viet Nam News. 2002c. "Officials Fall in School Scandal." *Viet Nam News,* October 7.
Welch, Anthony. 1998. "The Cult of Efficiency in Education: Comparative Reflections on the Reality and the Rhetoric." *Comparative Education* 34 (2): 157–175.
Welch, Anthony. 2007a. "Ho Chi Minh Meets the Market. Public and Private Higher Education in Vietnam." *International Education Journal: Comparative Perspectives* 8 (3): 35–56.

Welch, Anthony. 2007b. "Blurred Vision? Public and Private Higher Education in Indonesia." *Higher Education* 54 (5): 665–687.
Welch, Anthony. 2009. "Internationalization of Vietnamese Higher Education. Retrospect and Prospect." In *Reforming Higher Education in Vietnam: Challenges and Priorities*, eds. G. Harman, M. Hayden, and T. Pham. Amsterdam: Springer.
Welch, Anthony. 2010a. "Vietnam, Malaysia and the Global Knowledge System." In *Higher Education: Policy and the Global Competition Phenomenon*, eds. L. Portnoi, V. Rust, and C. Bagley. New York: Palgrave Macmillan.
Welch. Anthony. 2010b. "Measuring Up? The Competitive Position of South-East Asian Higher Education." In *Quality Assurance and University Rankings in the Asia Pacific*, eds. S. Kaur, M. Sirat, and W. Tierney. Kuala Lumpur: University of Malaysia Press.
Welch, Anthony. 2010c. *Higher Education in Southeast Asia: Blurring Borders, Changing Balance*. London: Routledge.
Welch, Anthony, and Ka-Ho Mok. 2003. "Conclusion: Deep Development or Deep Division?" In *Globalization, Restructuring and Educational Reforms in Asia and the Pacific*, eds. K. H. Mok and A. Welch. London: Palgrave Macmillan.
Westcott, Christopher. 2001. *Combating Corruption in Southeast Asia*. Manila: ADB.
Wilson, Mary, Adnan Qayyam, and Roger Boshier. 1998. "World Wide America: Think Globally, Click Locally." *Distance Education* 19 (1): 109–123.
World Bank. 2000a. *East Asia: Recovery and Beyond*. Washington, DC: World Bank.
World Bank. 2000b. *Higher Education in Developing Countries: Peril and Promise*. Washington, DC: World Bank.
World Bank. 2006. *An East Asian Renaissance. Ideas for Economic Growth*. Washington, DC: World Bank.

Chapter 10

Higher Education in India: Emerging Challenges and Evolving Strategies[1]
Jandhyala B. G. Tilak

Introduction

After the introduction of neoliberal economic policies in India in the beginning of the 1990s that included globalization, there has been a significant change in public policy towards higher education. The immediate changes with long-term implications include reduction in public expenditure on higher education (as a part of overall reduction in fiscal deficit), increased cost recovery through students fees, student loans and other measures, non-recruitment of teaching faculty and other staff (as a part of overall policy of downsizing of the public sector), increased emphasis on private higher education, and initiating measures for the internationalization of higher education. As a result of some of these policies, there has been an erratic increase in student fees, unbridled growth of private higher education, increased levels of out-migration of students and scholars, flourishing of some areas of study and the demise of others. In short, there has been an overall neglect of Indian higher education. The situation is also characterized by the absence of clear, long-term policies.

The neoliberal economic policies pose new challenges to, and as some believe, offer new opportunities for higher education. It is now widely recognized that if India has to realize any gains from globalization, it is necessary to expand higher education quantitatively and in terms of quality and excellence as well. Globalization with a human face also requires policies of inclusive growth—equitable access to higher education. India has a vision of becoming an advanced country by 2020 and of achieving high and sustainable growth with equity, characterized by inclusive growth and reduction of poverty to negligible levels. Given the current growth rate of the economy—around 8–10 percent per annum during the second half of the present decade—the hopes of realizing this vision are not unrealistic. In this context, the role of higher education and knowledge is envisaged as transformer of the society into a knowledge society. Therefore, in the most recent years, the government has promised to pay serious attention to higher education. Following some of the recommendations of the National Knowledge Commission (2007, 2008) and the CABE Committee on Financing Higher and Technical Education (2005), the government of India in the Eleventh Five-Year Plan 2007–2012 (Planning Commission 2008) has outlined a few goals and strategies for strengthening higher education. They include expansion of higher education to double the enrollments and to reach a gross enrollment ratio of 15 percent by 2012 and setting up a large number of new universities and other institutions of higher professional and technical education. The plan also stresses strategies that focus on increased role of private sector, public private partnerships, internationalization of higher education, and so on. Higher education of excellence is currently the buzzword and the government is thinking of setting up world-class universities and some 'innovation' universities. The National Knowledge Commission, whose recommendations have been accepted by the government of India, also suggested major reforms in governance including setting up of an independent regulatory authority in higher education in place of many existing institutions. A similar suggestion of setting up a National Commission for Higher Education and Research was recently made by another committee appointed by the government of India, chaired by Yashpal. Efforts have also been initiated to develop a regulatory framework for internationalization of higher education. Draft Bills for (i) setting the National Commission for Higher Education and Research and (ii) Foreign Education Providers, along with a few other Bills for development of higher education such as (iii) for checking malpractices in higher education, (iv) for setting a National Authority for Regulation in Accreditation of Higher Education Institutions, and (v) for setting up a National Educational Tribunal have been prepared for placement in the National Parliament.

This chapter first reviews some of the recent developments in Indian higher education, and critically examines some of the above-mentioned proposals, in terms of their conceptual soundness, feasibility, and desirability, and their compatibility with the overall goal of inclusive growth.

Importance of Education

First, higher education is widely recognized as a public good, at least a quasi-public good, as it produces a huge set of economic, social, cultural, demographic, and political externalities. Higher technical education is associated, in addition, with technological and dynamic externalities. Second, education is also a merit good. The government of India has recognized postelementary education as a Merit-2 good, which needs to be financed considerably by the state (it recognized elementary education as a Merit-1 good). Third, education is an important investment both from social and individual points of view. Investment in higher education makes a vital contribution to accelerate the process and rate of economic growth through increasing human productivity. Higher education is, therefore, regarded as crucial to the development of the national economy and to compete in the global economy. Higher technical education is one of the most important components of human capital. It This is seen as "specialized human capital" (Schultz 1988), the returns on which are estimated to be very high. Increasing returns on total factor productivity are due to investment in specialized human capital formed through investment in higher technical and professional education, including science and technology; such human capital checks the general pattern of diminishing returns and even contributes to increasing returns. In short, higher education as a whole forms an important instrument for development, as it makes the difference between the rich and the poor nations and the rich and the poor people. Higher education also forms a unique investment that promotes growth and equity simultaneously and is perhaps one of the most important instruments for equity as it provides social, occupational, and economic mobility to the weaker sections of the society. After all, the promotion of equity is an important social function of universities, independent of other growth-promoting functions. Finally, the current discourses and debates on human rights are no longer confined to elementary education; they are being extended to higher education as well. After all, the *Universal Declaration of Human Rights of the United Nations* (United Nations 1948) does include higher education as an important human right, though qualified, in contrast to elementary education, which is recognized as an absolute human right. That higher education leads to a higher quality of life is also widely noted.

Higher education contributes to development by performing a few very important functions such as creation and dissemination of knowledge, supply of manpower, creation of knowledge workers in specific areas, inculcation of human values, bringing about attitudinal changes for modernization and social transformation, formation of a strong nation-state, and promotion of higher quality of individual and social life. It is widely recognized that these traditional functions of higher education are ever relevant for all societies—modern as well as traditional, developed as well as developing. These functions are performed through teaching, research, and extension activities; all the three are important facets of a sound higher education system and all the three need to be well nurtured and strengthened. Higher education in India has been performing some of these traditional functions. The policies of globalization introduced in India in the early 1990s further reinforce the need to develop a strong and vibrant higher education system for two reasons.

The institutions of higher education have to become centers of excellence and be internationally competitive. Global competition in higher education has put additional emphasis on the need for serious efforts to improve the quality of higher education. After all, only those societies that have strong and widespread higher education systems of high quality have been able to reap the gains of globalization, and those that have not made much progress in higher education have suffered severely. The very success of economic reform programs critically depends upon higher education. With increasing globalization and international competition, the need for more educated work force cannot be overemphasized. The government's reform programs cannot even take off properly if we have widespread illiteracy and ill-educated workforce. In this sense, higher education becomes "*even more important in the new context of a global economy*" (Stewart 1996, 331, original emphasis). Strengthening of higher education institutions (HEIs), even on a selective basis, may help in facilitating these institutions to compete with foreign institutions that are coming into India and even to force them to exit from India, if necessary. After all, many foreign universities are coming into India and other developing countries, where higher education systems are weak. Therefore, given the wave of globalization, increasing international competition, building of knowledge society, and increasing rates of international outflow of human capital, according a higher priority to higher education has become of paramount importance in countries such as India.

As inequity-enhancing aspects of globalization are very strong and they lead to progressive reduction in social opportunities (see Tilak 1992), it becomes imperative to pay serious attention to the improvement of access and equity in higher education as globalization progresses. Otherwise, large segments of young populations may become increasingly marginalized, and this would be a huge social loss.

It is increasingly felt that the emergence of the knowledge economy has brought into focus the interesting linkages between higher education, knowledge, and wealth creation. Knowledge is a driving force for enhancing the economic strength of a nation, which can be realized only if education and research in liberal as well as in professional disciplines are of sound quality. While technical education produces technical manpower, it is humanities, social sciences, languages, and natural and physical sciences that help in producing well-rounded citizenry. Given all this, the urgency to pay serious attention to higher education becomes all too apparent. However, the neoliberal policies that comprise stabilization and adjustment seemed to have gone against the growth of higher education in India (Tilak 2005).

Higher Education in India: Quantitative Explosion

First, it must be noted that India is a big country with more than one billion population. Higher education, like the rest of the education sector, is a concurrent subject—a subject on which the union (central) government as well as the state governments (there are 35 states and union territories) can formulate their own policies and programs as long as they do not conflict. In case of any conflict, the union government's policies prevail. Second, the system is characterized by a high degree of diversity. While a large number of universities are financed by state governments, there are a few universities funded by the central government through the University Grants Commission (UGC). Besides there are also a few private universities and institutions financially supported by the government, and some supported mainly through student fees. There are also a good number of institutions that are treated as "institutions deemed to be universities." There are a few that are set up essentially to meet the needs of minority populations. While many universities provide both general and professional education, there are also some which are exclusive in their coverage, providing either general or professional education— engineering, medical, agricultural, languages and linguistics and so on. In sum, HEIs include a variety of teaching and research institutions and universities—central, state, deemed universities (private and public), colleges (government, government-supported private, and totally private), national institutions of importance, research institutions, and other institutions of higher education. Third, the regulatory system is also too diverse with a variety of statutory and nonstatutory bodies. The main policymaking regulatory, coordinating, and statutory bodies of higher education include ministries (central and state) of education, the UGC, All India Council for Technical Education (AICTE), National Council for Teacher Education (NCTE), Medical Council of India (MCI), Bar Council of India (BCI), Indian Council of Architects, National Assessment and Accreditation Council, National Board of Accreditation, Association of Indian University, State Councils of higher education, and so on. Some of these bodies have regulatory functions in terms of recognition of degrees, curriculum, and licensing professional graduates to take up practice.

After independence, India had to start almost from scratch but over the years in the postindependence era, the country has made significant progress in education, (Tilak 2006a) and particularly the progress made in higher education is very impressive (Tilak 2008a). As indicated in table 10.1, on the eve of the heralding of the plan era in India, that is, in 1950–1951, there were 28 universities, less than 600 colleges with student numbers standing at less than a quarter million. During

Table 10.1 Growth of HEIs in India

	Colleges for			Universities[b]	Enrollment (in millions)
	General education	Professional education[a]	All colleges		
1857–1858	—	—	27	3	250[c]
1947–1948	—	—	496	20	0.2
1950–1951	370	208	578	28	0.2
1960–1961	967	852	1,819	45	0.6
1970–1971	2,285	992	3,277	93	2.0
1980–1981	3,421	1,156	4,577	123	2.8
1990–1991	4,862	1,765	6,627	184	4.4
2000–2001	7,929	2,223	10,152	254	8.6
2006–2007	11,458	9,650	21,108	511	15.6

Notes: "—" indicates that the data are not available.
[a] include engineering, technology, architecture, medical, education colleges, etc.
[b] include institutions deemed to be universities, institutions of national Importance, and research institutions.
[c] exact number, not in million
Source: Ministry of Human Resource Development (various years); UGC (various years).

the last 60 years after independence, higher education has expanded in India quite remarkably. According to the latest statistics available, in 2006–2007, there were about 500 universities including institutions deemed to be universities and more than 20,000 colleges offering general and professional education. Most of these colleges offer first-degree programs; some offer postgraduate programs. These figures do not include the vast network of approximately 300 specialized science and technology institutions, which include more than 200 specialized laboratories. These are in addition to industrial research and development laboratories in the private and public sectors. In professional education too, there has been the most spectacular achievement. Some of these institutions are regarded as institutions of world-class excellence. Today the Indian network of higher education systems is perhaps one of the largest in the developing world

The large network of education and research institutions has contributed to the rapid accumulation of specialized human capital. There has been an explosion in student numbers; the enrollments in higher education swelled from less than a quarter million in 1947–1948, that is, at the time of independence, to 15.6 million in 2006–2007. The output of these institutions is indeed impressive—in both quality and quantum. India has become one of the largest reservoirs of scientific and technical manpower in the world and is now able to "export" manpower, particularly in information and communication technology and related sectors. India's contribution in providing information technology manpower to the developed countries is now widely recognized. India today ranks fairly high in the size of its network of HEIs, enrollments therein, and the graduate manpower it produces, all of which contribute to the development of the domestic as well as international economy.

The massive expansion of higher education also contributed to the democratization of higher education. Presently the number of students from lower socioeconomic strata constitutes a sizeable proportion in the total enrollments in higher education. In the current system, approximately 40 percent of the enrollments in higher education is from the lower socioeconomic strata, in contrast with the extremely elitist system inherited from the colonial rulers. Women students currently form about 40 percent of the total enrollments. The emerging open learning systems, comprising traditional methods of correspondence courses and modern methods of distance education also contribute significantly to "massification" of higher education. These are no mean achievements for a developing country, though a high degree of inequalities does persist between several states, between several institutions of higher education, and between various groups of populations, besides different kinds of imbalances between different areas of study.

The number of teachers in HEIs has increased drastically over the last five decades. Until 2007–2008, more than half a million teachers were employed in HEIs in the country. But in 1980–1981, there were only about 250,000 teachers. In 1950–1951, there were barely 24,000 teachers. In 2007–2008, in all universities and colleges in India, nearly 50 percent of the teachers were lecturers/assistant professors. A quarter of all were readers/associate professors, followed by about 15 percent of senior lecturers/assistant professors, while full professors constituted about 8 percent of the entire teaching force. More than 80 percent of all teachers in higher education were employed in colleges, and only 16 percent were in universities. Within the universities, 21 percent were full professors, 32 percent were readers/associate professors, and 30 percent were lecturers/assistant professors. Most of the colleges offer undergraduate programs, while universities mostly offer postgraduate and research programs.

Over the years, the structure of teaching staff in several universities has been gradually changing from a typical pyramidal structure to a cylindrical one and then to an inverted pyramid, with a larger number of professors and associate professors and a smaller number of lecturers/assistant professors.

In brief, India has made significant strides in the development of higher education. First, after independence Indian education system at all levels was thrown open to all—rich, poor, and middle-income classes, men and women, rural and urban populations, backward and non-backward segments of the population. Second, as a consequence, there has been a veritable explosion in numbers of students, institutions, and teachers. Third, institutions of excellence, producing highly specialized human capital, have been developed. Finally, the country has developed the capacity to produce the second largest (next only to China) stock of educated and skilled manpower in the world, and the third largest reservoir of scientific and technical manpower.

Such an explosion in education has been inevitable as the provision of educational facilities in the pre-independence period was insignificant; with independence came an unquenched thirst for knowledge, resulting in a huge rise in social demand for higher education. Realizing that building up a new socioeconomic system in the postcolonial India required large-scale manpower with varied skills, the government embarked upon a significant expansion of the higher education system.

Problems and Challenges

While the strengths and achievements of higher education are significant, equally, if not more significant are the problems and weaknesses it is associated with. First, though India has one of the largest education systems, it is still inadequate for the country's needs. In all, nearly sixteen million young people were enrolled in the country's HEIs in 2006–2007, of whom about one-fifth were estimated to have been enrolled in technical education. Though the number of students seems large, the gross enrollment ratio (number of students as a percentage of the youth population of the age group 18–24) was just 12 percent, which is hardly adequate for a country that aims at transforming itself into an industrial tiger economy. The current level of higher education development is regarded woefully inadequate for the rapid and sustainable economic development of the country for facing global challenges including globalization and international competition, ensuring sustainable high levels of human development, building an equitable system of education that promises opportunities for all, and for creation of a knowledge society.

Second, though there are several universities and institutions of higher education of excellence, there are a larger number of institutions of substandard quality. Hardly does any Indian institution of higher education figure in the list of top-level institutions of the world, thus raising concerns about quality and standards of higher education in India. While the total quantum of output of the HEIs is one of the largest in the world, when quantum is adjusted for quality, and even with respect to indicators of quantity, India does not fare well compared with many developed and even developing economies. For example, India has the third largest stock of science and technology manpower (about 8–10 million scientists and engineers). But one has only to carefully examine their quality to explode the myth of the third largest stock of scientific and technical manpower in the world. Even this huge stock is not enough to match the requirements of the economy (Tilak 1997). Any standardized international comparisons of the stock of science and technology manpower would make the tall claims about size untenable. For example, for every one thousand of the population, there were only seven scientists/engineers in India at the turn of the twenty-first century, while in many other countries the corresponding figure is 10–30 times higher. The stock of graduate manpower is also made of first graduates. Postgraduates are few; and doctorates are fewer. This reflects to some extent the "quality" of the manpower India has.

Third, the growth in teachers has not kept pace with growth in demand for teachers caused by the growth in enrollments. As a result, the pupil-teacher ratio has deteriorated over the years. In 2005–2006, the national average was 26 pupils for every teacher in higher education. There are wide variations between several states with respect to the ratio: it ranges between 8 in small states and 54 in Uttar Pradesh, which is a large state. Though the pupil-teacher ratio is not a highly relevant parameter in higher education, the available data however does indicate the nature of the problem, at least to some extent.

An important problem for the academic profession is that there had been a de facto official ban on recruitment of teachers (and non-teachers as well) in many universities throughout the country. This followed the introduction of economic reform policies that required downsizing of all public sector units including HEIs. The block grants provided by the state governments to the universities have also remained virtually frozen for quite some time. Thus the depletion in the size of the faculty and the freezing of state grants have caused a serious damage to the morale and motivation of the teachers, the physical ambience of the universities, and the overall academic environment of the universities, because many departments and postgraduate centers of the universities are subcritical in the size of the teaching staff and their performance, as they offer few high-quality teaching and research programs. Universities had to resort to various methods, many of which may not necessarily be desirable, to confront the twin problems. Shortage of full-time faculty forced them to recruit temporary teachers with varied designations such as part-time teachers, guest teachers, contract teachers, and teaching assistants, at very low consolidated salaries, sometimes at one-fifth of regular teacher salary. The para-teachers in the school system have similar problems too. These teachers form 15–60 percent of the total staff strength in various universities in one of the states in south India. Many of them may not have the qualifications necessary for a regular university faculty member, but they seem continue in service for several years. Many of them are recruited to teach "self financing courses," which are not funded by the government but by student fees. Para-teachers are also recruited to teach regular courses of study. The long-term effects of all this on the quality of teaching and research in higher education could be devastating, if a sizeable system of higher education were to survive with the help of part-time contract staff (APSCHE 2005; Tilak 2006b). In many regards, the teaching profession is getting deprofessionalized. The role of higher education instruction is changing from knowledge creators and transmitters of knowledge to knowledge managers, networkers, and fund-raisers.

There is yet another important problem. With the introduction of cost-recovery mechanisms in higher education on the one hand, and growth of the private sector in the economy along with the opening up of the economy on the other, student demand for postgraduate and research courses—particularly in professional courses such as engineering and technology, and even in humanities, social sciences, and basic sciences—has been seriously affected. This is feared to pose serious problems in meeting the growing teacher demand in higher education. The recent measure of setting up 15 central universities also causes migration of quality teachers from the already depleted state universities to central universities. That many state universities have still not implemented new pay scales and other measures recommended by the central pay revision committee contributes to the migration further. All these developments might make the state universities which are in many ways already in a worse situation to be even worse off.

NCTE, in collaboration with the UGC and AICTE, is expected to ensure recruitment of properly qualified teachers in HEIs in India. The UGC sets guidelines for deciding the workload of every teacher and determining the number of teachers to be appointed in a given university/college. Teachers in higher education are also ensured promotions under the career advancement scheme, earlier known as the merit promotion scheme of the UGC, from the post of lecturer (assistant professor) to senior lecturer to reader (associate professor) and finally to professor, if they complete a minimum number of years of service at the given level and if their performance is satisfactory. Since this is subject to fulfillment of a bare minimum level of performance in teaching and research, it is widely feared that the scheme would be counterproductive and would adversely affect the motivation of the teachers to excel in their work. Nonetheless, the scheme has come to stay, as its withdrawal will incur the wrath of the teachers' unions. The recent pay revision committee of the UGC (2008) recommended its continuation, but with a few additional qualifications.

In order to ensure national standards of the teachers in higher education throughout the country, teachers in HEIs are recruited on the basis of a national eligibility test (NET) conducted by the UGC. Similar eligibility tests at the state level, namely the "state level eligibility test," conducted by state governments were introduced to ensure minimum uniform quality of teachers in HEIs. After all, teachers in HEIs do not receive any preservice training or even any substantial in-service training, unlike primary and secondary school teachers in India. In one of the most recent developments, in 2006, the NET as a minimum eligibility condition for recruitment as teachers, has been abolished with a view to easing the problem of teacher shortage in many areas. NET was relaxed for teachers who possess research degrees (doctoral and predoctoral). However, soon after the relaxation, it was found that the eligibility condition was too important to grant any exemptions. It has now been fully reinstated.

The teaching profession in India used to be accorded high respect and a high level of social status, though its salary levels were was far from encouraging. The National Committee on Teachers, constituted by the government of India (1985) had gone into several aspects relating to the teaching profession in universities and colleges. In recent years, significant increases in pay scales of teachers have been made, though many states are yet to implement the revisions. The pay revision committee has also recommended better/faster upward mobility of teachers and raised the retirement age. From the point of view of international comparisons, the salary levels seem to be low, but they are not bad in comparison with salary structures of others in the public sector in India and the relative purchasing power of the Indian rupee.

Policies of nonrecruitment of teachers and the growth of market forces have led to significant changes in research and teaching professions. The emphasis seems to be slowly shifting from scholarly research to economically productive knowledge creation, from scholarly research to project-based research, and from project-based research to consultancy. In the area of teaching, the shift is from promotion of scholarship to imparting of market-relevant, saleable, and employable information and skills.

Overall, there has been a steep decline in the status of the teaching profession in the country. Though in recent years, their economic status has improved, there has been a fall in their social status (see Basu 2005). Traditionally teachers in India were regarded as gods (Acharya Devobhava). This changed when teachers and students began to be treated as equals; and now the roles have became reversed with students being treated as gods. This role reversal is in much closer alignment with a market-based framework of education in which, customers are to be accorded number one priority. Both students and teachers, who used to be in the forefront of civil, social, and political movements in the country, seem to be slowly withdrawing into the background.

Fourth, the system is characterized by a severe degree of regional, social, and educational inequalities. Interstate variations in the development of higher education are glaring in India. Some states have expanded their higher education systems fast, but many are lagging behind. Development policies in higher education vary from state to state, particularly in terms of emphasis on provision of access to higher education, improvement in quality, funding, and so on, though most states follow the broad national policies and are in conformity with the policy guidelines periodically formulated by the apex education policy organizations such as the UGC, AICTE, and other similar agencies. There are, however, several other factors responsible for interstate variations. In addition to regional variations, the system is also characterized by a high degree of inequalities between social groups—caste, religion, gender, and inequalities between economic groups of population. While because of the initiatives and measures taken in recent years, a significant improvement in the situation regarding inequalities of gender and caste can be seen, regional inequalities persist. Inequalities between different economic groups of population are also strikingly high.

Fifth, enrollment rates have been uneven over the last half century. There were huge average annual growths of enrollments in 1950–1951 to 1960–61 (22 percent) and from 1960–1961 to 1970–1971 (25.1 percent). After that, average annual growths in the 70's and 80's dropped dramatically to 4.1 percent and 6 percent respectively. But the rate of growth in enrollments doubled between 1990–1991 and 2000–2001 (10.3 percent). Much of the growth has taken place between 1995–1996 and 2000–2001. The sudden rise in demand for higher education created the need for setting up of new colleges and universities in the following decade, that is, in the present decade. However, the growth in enrollments could not be sustained in the period 2000–2001 to 2008–2009 (3.7 percent). Further, a significant change in the demand for specific higher education subjects can be noted; for instance, there is an increased demand for professional courses such as engineering and information technology. The result is imbalance in educational development, with the flourishing of commercially viable disciplines on the one hand and an increasing neglect of the more traditional, scholarly disciplines, on the other. Most of the expansion in higher education has been in professional education, particularly in engineering education. The major part of the growth has been in computer science, electronics engineering, and other information technology-related disciplines. An equally important aspect of Indian higher education growth relates to an overall decline in postgraduate education and research-oriented programs.

Further, expansion during the last two decades has been mainly in the private sector (see table 10.2). There is a significant change in the current pattern of growth of HEIs in the country with an increasing number of private HEIs on the scene. There has been no noticeable growth in the number of public institutions (both universities and colleges) in the recent period. A large number of "institutions deemed to be universities" are being set up. "Institutions deemed to be universities" are a special kind of universities.

Table 10.2 Present Pattern of Growth of Higher Education in India

	Pattern of growth
Public universities	Not growing
Private universities	Emerging on the scene
Public universities—"deemed to be"	Not growing
State-supported private Universities—"deemed to be"	Not growing
Private universities—"deemed to be"	Growing rapidly
Colleges—public	Not growing
State-supported private colleges	Not growing
Private colleges—general	Growing rapidly
Private professional colleges	Growing very fast
Foreign institutions	Emerging on the scene

Quite a few existing institutions (like regional engineering colleges), and several de novo institutions were given the status of institutions deemed to be universities. A majority of the new institutions deemed to be universities are private HEIs. In fact, as setting up of private universities has been an unclear process with a Bill for setting up private universities pending with the Parliament for more than a decade and half, and as setting up of universities—public or private, requires approval by the National Parliament or State legislatures, many took this shortcut method of opening private universities as institutions deemed to be universities (Powar 2004). Institutions deemed to be universities can be set up without an approval by the Parliament or State legislatures; they are set up by an executive order of the government. Private bodies find this method attractive and easier, as such institutions also enjoy, additionally a greater degree of autonomy; and the government also finds it less cumbersome to allow setting up of new universities of this kind or grant the status of deemed universities to the existing institutions of higher education than to set up normal universities. As a result, a large number of private deemed to be universities came into existence during the present decade. Presently there are more than 100 such universities; and many of them have come up only in the recent years. In 2001–2002 there were only 52 such universities. Most of them are not comprehensive multifaculty institutions.

There were more than 21,000 colleges in 2006–2007, but nearly two-thirds of them are private colleges. There is a halt in the growth of private colleges that are financially supported by the government, as the resource-starved state governments have decided against allowing any more such colleges. In contrast, all over the country, there has been a proliferation of private self-financing colleges whose growth has been and unbridled.

To sum up, despite the massive growth in overall numbers, roughly 12 percent of the relevant age-group population in the country is presently enrolled in HEIs. Access and equity issues between socioeconomic and gender groups and between various states are quite pronounced especially in certain regions of the country. Despite some improvement in equity over the past few decades, higher education is still not accessible to the poorest groups of the population. There are marked variations between regions and institutions in quality, quantity, and equity dimensions of higher education.. Higher education needs to be empowered, as empowerment and empowerment alone helps in sustainable social, economic, and political development of the society and in some assurance of equity (Tilak 2004a).

Thus, given (1) the current level and status of higher education in the country, (2) the highly unequal system in general and in higher education in particular, (3) the relationship between higher education and development, (4) the rising aspirations of the people, (5) development goals of the country such as creation of a "knowledge society" and transforming itself into a developed economy, and (6) the introduction of policies of globalization to reap the benefits from the same, the need for according a high priority to higher education cannot be overstressed. The Indian government must recognize the need to expand higher education, to promote equity in the system, and to improve quality in higher education.

The attention paid to higher education was on a rapid decline until recently. The last two to three decades witnessed some disturbing trends. There has been a steady decline in the priority attached to higher education and budgets for higher education were subject to severe cuts. The cuts were clearly noted in relative terms—percentage of national income, percentage of total budgetary resources, and also in total and more particularly in per student terms in real prices (Tilak 2004b, 2005). The reduced levels of public funding were accompanied by increased levels of cost recovery with erratic and uncontrolled increases in student fees, introduction of self-financing courses, and increasing reliance on student loans. Public apathy to and the absence of clear policies have also contributed to unbridled growth of private institutions, particularly for-profit HEIs, and a rapid march toward vulgar forms of commercialization is clearly noticeable. Foreign education has also emerged as an important phenomenon with a large number of foreign education providers entering the scene with commercial motives. The system is also steadily becoming more deregulated, and the government is slowly and steadily withdrawing from its important responsibilities in policymaking, planning, coordination, regulation, and delivery.

All these developments can be attributed to three important and interrelated factors, namely the neoliberal policies introduced in the beginning of the 1990s, faulty assumptions on the role of higher education in development, and declining fiscal capacity of the government.

Recent Initiatives in Higher Education

There have been some interventions and initiatives taken by the Indian government to improve the status of higher education in the recent years. Some of these initiatives may result in strengthening the higher education system; others are viewed as problematic.

Assessment and accreditation program, an important initiative taken by the government in the recent years, can have a very positive effect on the quality of higher education in the country. It is indeed surprising that this was not taken up earlier. The assessment and accreditation program forced some HEIs to change and provoked significant reflection about many quality issues. After all, assessment and accreditation, an important instrument of maintenance of quality and standards in higher education, may help not only in identifying black sheep, but also in shining a light on star institutions (Tilak 2004a). But the process has been slow and only a small number of institutions are so far assessed and accredited so far, as only a few institutions seemed to have opted for it. There does exist much scope for improvement in the assessment and accreditation system and to make the process highly respected and valued by the universities and colleges. The assessment and accreditation by the National Assessment and Accreditation Council is not yet mandatory in India, though the current thinking is to make it compulsory for all institutions and to link it to funding also.

Following the resolve made in the *National Policy on Education 1986* (Government of India 1986), to encourage institutional innovations and experimentation, emphasis has been placed on increased institutional autonomy; and a good number of colleges have been given autonomy under the program of establishment of autonomous colleges to promote new methods of teaching, research, and learning (Tilak 2004c). Currently there are about 130 such colleges affiliated to 29 universities. Autonomy should, however, mean mainly academic autonomy to design new courses and curriculum, to promote quality and to make innovations, rather than financial and administrative autonomy. By granting autonomy, the role of government should not be minimized particularly in funding, planning and in providing a healthy sustainable teaching-learning environment.

Third, as resolved in the *National Policy on Education 1986,* a network of Academic Staff Colleges has been established in about 40 universities (at least one in each state). These provide an important platform for teachers in colleges and universities to refresh their knowledge and to reorient them to new methods of teaching and to emerging issues in their respective disciplines. They are also found to be important for motivating teachers in their research endeavors.

Fourth, in recent years, the UGC has given special focus to developing excellence in higher education. The UGC started a program to identify and support universities with potential for excellence, in order to improve excellence and quality in teaching and research activities in these institutions, which may influence the quality in other institutions as well. In addition, a program of supporting centers in universities with a focus on one given area of specialization in each university was launched. Centers/departments are identified as locations "with potential for excellence" for extrafinancial support by the UGC. Further—as a substantial part of higher education is imparted in colleges—the program for support for excellence has been extended to colleges; colleges with potential for excellence were identified for additional funding, with a view to achieving excellence in teaching activities and initiating research cultures in such institutions.

Fifth, the UGC has launched new funding programs, offering special funds to help two-tier and three-tier institutions to improve their infrastructure and to enable them to come up to the level of other institutions.

Sixth, a few important measures such as reservation policies in admissions to higher education have been introduced. These measures aim at promoting further access of the weaker sections—socially backward castes and religions—to higher education. In addition, new scholarship schemes have also been launched to promote postgraduate opportunities, particularly related to research studies.

But such initiatives are minimal and they barely have an effect on the enormous higher education system spread over such a large country. More sustained and concerted efforts are needed to promote access, quality, and equity in higher education.

The government of India has set up a National Knowledge Commission, as an advisory body to the prime minister; the commission has made certain recommendations, involving sweeping reforms of the higher education system. Some of these recommendations have been taken into consideration while making the Eleventh Five-Year Plan. The plan has proposed a massive increase in plan outlay

Table 10.3 Proposals for Expansion of Higher Education in the Eleventh Five-Year Plan

	New	Existing
Indian Institutes of Management	7	6
Indian Institutes of Technology	8	7
National Institutes of Technology	10	20
Indian Institutes of Science Education and Research	5	2
Indian Institutes of Information Technology	20	4
Schools of planning and architecture	2	1
Engineering & tech colleges	1,000	1,617
Polytechnics in each district	700	1,292
Research centers in frontier areas	50	—

Source: Planning Commission (2008).

to the tune of INR849,430 million (as compared to INR96,000 million in the Tenth Five-Year Plan). The ninefold increase is regarded as an "unprecedented increase in financial support for education in India." The Eleventh Five-Year Plan aims at increasing the enrollment ratio in higher education to about 15 percent in the next five years to be followed by a gradual increase in subsequent years. To reach the 15 percent ratio, the enrollments need to be doubled and they should increase at an annual growth of 9 percent in general higher education and 15 percent in higher professional/technical education. The plan has also envisaged a large-scale expansion of the system. The National Knowledge Commission has recommended setting up of 1,500 universities, 50 major universities, new central universities (at least one in each state), 14 world- class universities, and so on. Though it is unlikely that the country plans to establish 1,500 universities in the near future, already 15 new central universities, some institutes of technology and of management were established in 2009; there are plans for establishing 374 new colleges in all low enrollment ratio districts. There are proposals to establish many other kinds of professional institutions as well. Besides, the National Knowledge Commission has recommended that "knowledge cities" and "knowledge networks" be created. Proposals for expansion of other institutions are listed in table 10.3.

The expansion of higher education institutions in India is long overdue. But will expansion efforts be sustainable and are there no alternative models of university development (Tilak 2008b)? Problems of shortage of high quality faculty are already being felt in the existing institutions. Long periods of underfunding of higher education, a virtual ban on recruitment of faculty, and other similar measures have resulted in the accumulation of such problems. All of a sudden, once funds are made available, it may be possible to set up many central universities and technical institutes, but it may not be easy to staff these institutions with high-quality faculty, unless new and innovative methods are devised to attract good faculty. Otherwise there is a danger that these institutions will be planned and designed to be developed on a very small scale, with a very small number of faculty and student numbers, offering a few specialized, if not market-oriented, programs as a result of which they may turn out to be privileged and elite institutions. Alternatively, these institutions will be allowed to grow into large institutions in terms of student numbers but with small faculty, or large numbers of low-quality faculty. Both are serious dangers that need to be avoided. The question of sustainability or their "viability" assumes importance, as the location of the central universities and other institutes, including world-class universities, it appears, is being decided more on political considerations than on educational and other relevant scientific and objective considerations. Further, all the central universities and other central HEIs, though being set up on regional considerations, need to be designed to work truly as national HEIs, with students and faculty drawn from all parts of the country and all socioeconomic strata, thus truly representing national diversity, an essential characteristic feature of good national HEIs. Finally, surprisingly the resources allocated in the plan for massive expansion are far from adequate. In fact, the allocations from the budgetary resources may meet only about 10–12 percent of the requirements. How will the gap be filled? The government proposes to rely on new modes of development, particularly public-private partnerships to set up some of these institutions, but such models do not necessarily work in the area of education for the benefit of the larger society. Earlier experience shows that public-private partnerships models yield negligible additional resources. Moreover, public-private partnership in education is an incompatible partnership, as the objectives and interests of the public and private sectors are different and they are unequal in power, resulting in distortions in educational agenda, research priorities, and research findings (Tilak 2007a).

While the system does require massive expansion, the plans to achieve this may seem ambitious. Further, establishing world-class universities from scratch may not seem conceptually sound, nor will it be easy, given that it takes several years (even be decades, if not centuries) to develop a world-class university. World-class universities can be either developed by nurturing the existing universities, or can be the long-term goal of newly established universities. The former route may seem easy, but in many cases, institutional habits, cumbersome governance structures, and bureaucratic management practices stand as formidable stumbling blocks. There can be a third alternative of merging some of the best existing institutions, to maximize on collective institutional synergies to obtain world-class status. Mergers, as a strategy, not only ensure economies of scale, but also enrich the academic environment (Salmi 2009).

Another major recommendation that the National Knowledge Commission makes is the establishment of an Independent Regulatory Authority for Higher Education (IRAHE) holding all powers and responsibilities, and a redefined, reduced role for the UGC, AICTE, MCI, BCI and other such bodies. It clearly argues for the abolition of the AICTE, and limiting the role of the MCI, BCI, and the like to work as professional associations, conducting nationwide examinations to provide licenses. The commission also suggests the establishment of a Central Board of Under-Graduate Education and State Boards of Under-Graduate Education. How far are these proposals desirable and feasible for implementation? Of late, it has actually become very fashionable to suggest setting up new bodies rather than strengthening and restructuring the existing ones. After all, the suggested structure of governance of the IRAHE—starting from setting it up by an act of the parliament, the appointment of the chairperson and members, their tenure, and so on— is more or less the same as that of the UGC. The UGC and similar bodies were all set up with noble ideas but they were not allowed to function autonomously; they were given limited funding and were subjected to all kinds of avoidable interventions and distortions and now we say that they have become defunct and should be replaced or revamped (Singh 2004). If the UGC was not provided with sufficient funds, how could it adequately fund various universities, command respect from universities, and perform its functions properly? If the UGC has deteriorated over the years, then how do we ensure that the IRAHE will not deteriorate to the same level of the present UGC in years to come? The rationale for establishing the IRAHE and the mechanism that will ensure its superior functioning compared to that of the UGC is not clear. Instead of arguing for the setting up of another organization, one might favor strengthening and even revamping the UGC to ensure its autonomy and efficient functioning as was originally conceived to enable it maintain the quality and standards in all levels and types of higher education. In fact, the UGC may be entrusted with the larger responsibility of coordinating the development of the entire higher education system in the country, with the help of other bodies.

Recently, another committee has made a similar suggestion for the establishment of a National Commission of Higher Education and Research as an umbrella body of higher education (Government of India 2009). The proposed commission is to replace several existing bodies such as the UGC and the ACITE. However, while the National Knowledge Commission has argued that the IRAHE should be essentially a regulatory body serving as a single window to facilitate easy entry and exit of private institutions, and should promote private and international education, the recent committee headed by Yash Pal has argued that such a body should mainly ensure defragmentation of knowledge and decubicalization of higher education and promote academic innovations. This is indeed worth examining. As already mentioned, a draft Bill to set up the National Commission for Higher Education has already been approved by the Cabinet.

Finally, some efforts have also been initiated to provide a regulatory framework for the growth of private sector in higher education. In addition to the existing rules and regulations, many states have made legislations in the recent past for setting up private universities. At the national level, a revised bill for the establishment of private universities, in place of a bill which is pending before the parliament, is likely to be taken up soon. Similarly to promote the internationalization of higher education (i.e., to enable regulated entry of foreign universities into India and to enable Indian institutions to go offshore) (Tilak 2007b), a framework of rules and regulations is formulated in the form of a draft Bill which has already been approved by the Cabinet for finalization and placement in the Parliament. Regulations for both private institutions and foreign institutions may face stiff resistance from the pubic, as it is widely feared that these regulations allow growth of more private and international institutions in India, which maynot necessarily be good for the development of a strong higher education system.

Conclusion

India recognizes the need to expand higher education to meet the challenges of globalization, which impose additional demands on higher education. As Kalam (2003) noted, "empowerment of higher education" is the critical need of the hour. Higher education needs to be empowered as its empowerment alone helps in sustainable social, economic, and political development of society. The empowerment of higher education should include (1) provision of a basic minimum level of physical infrastructure facilities to all the colleges and universities (a crash project like the operation blackboard project in primary education may have to be launched), (2) recruitment of good quality teachers in all institutions, and further enhancement of their quality, and above all, (3) sound public policies particularly relating to funding, management and governance.

In the era of globalization, it is important to ensure that HEIs do not become commercial enterprises but remain as centers of learning. It is equally important to deliberately protect the idea that the university is a place where scholars from various corners of the country and the world come and live together, discuss and debate various social, political, economic, and scholarly issues.

The plans for higher education expansion have to be carefully prepared and they should be in the public sector. The system is already more privatized than in countries such as the United States. Hence there is need to restrict the growth of the private sector. With respect to internationalization, it is necessary to be careful and selective, and not to open the doors for unrestricted entry into higher education. The promotion of internationalization should primarily be for academic purposes and not for monetary gains. Costs of open international trade in higher education can be high. Keeping in view the goals regarding inclusive growth, reliance on cost recovery measures such as student fees and loans has to be minimized. Only an effective scholarship scheme and not loans, along with a highly subsidised public education can promote equity in the system. At least a minimum assured portion of the budget has to be allocated to scholarships that will promote excellence (merit scholarships) and equity (merit-cum-means scholarships). Similarly, a minimum portion of the budget has to be set aside for research. Presently very small amounts are allocated to research and scholarships. A large part of the higher education system requires sizeable investment in infrastructure development. One of the crucial policies should be relating to teachers, their recruitment, pay conditions, and their professional development. Ban on recruitment of teachers will prove to be very costly.

The government has long resolved to allocate 6 percent of national income toward education and a quarter to higher education. This should ease the financial problems of higher education to a great extent by reducing the need for severe cost recovery measures, privatization, and reliance on foreign education providers. Public investment should simultaneously focus on quality, quantity, and equity in higher education, as the three are closely related. Public investment policies should also aim at a balanced development of all layers of education, as they are interdependent with very close linkages. Finally, adhocism which seems to be the current common practice must be replaced with a clear, coherent, and unambiguous long-term policy and a perspective plan for higher education in the country..

Higher education develops and nurtures values. With the demise of value-oriented programs such as the National Social Service, National Cadet Corps, and other extension activities universities seem no longer concern themselves with social issues. It is important that special efforts are made to preserve and promote values such as a thirst for knowledge, critical thinking, search for truth, and more importantly to inculcate universal human values such as peace, tolerance, nonviolence, love, patriotism, and social welfare through education. These values may, in the final analysis, reflect the true quality of our higher education. The inculcation of these values is perhaps more important in the era of globalization, when national and traditional values are being rapidly replaced by global, and most prominently Western and market-oriented values. These are the educational and human values that Jawaharlal Nehru, the first prime minister of India, expected our universities to provide, when he observed, "A university stands for humanism, for tolerance, for reason, for the adventure of ideas and for the search for truth. It stands for the onward march of the human race towards even higher objectives." (Nehru 1950, 118)

Note

1. This is a revised version of the paper with the same title, presented at the Symposium on Positioning University in the Globalized World: Changing Governance and Coping Strategies in Asia, Hong Kong, December 10–11, 2008.

References

Andhra Pradesh State Council of Higher Education (APSCHE). 2005. *Report of the High Power Committee on Rationalization of Staff and Financing Universities in Andhra Pradesh.* Hyderabad: Government of Andhra Pradesh.

Basu, Kaushik. 2005. "Teacher Truancy in India: The Role of Culture, Norms and Economic Incentive." *Indian Economic Journal* 53 (2): 3–12.

CABE: Central Advisory Board for Education. 2005. *Report of the CABE Committee on Financing of Higher and Technical Education.* New Delhi: Central Advisory Board of Education, Ministry of Human Resource Development, Government of India http://www.education.nic.in/cabe/Report%20CABE%20Committee%20on%20Financing%20 Higher%20and%20Technical%20EducationL.pdf

Government of India. 1985. *Report of the National Committee on Teachers II.* New Delhi: National Institute of Educational Planning and Administration.

Government of India. 1986. *National Policy on Education 1986.* New Delhi: Government of India.

Government of India. 2009. *Report of "The Committee to Advise on Renovation and Rejuvenation of Higher Education."* New Delhi: Ministry of Human Resource Development. http://education.nic.in.

Kalam, A. P. J. Abdul. 2003. "University Education and National Missions." Address presented at the Golden Jubilee Celebration, University Grants Commission, Vigyan Bhavan, New Delhi, 28 December 2003. http://presidentofindia.nic.in.

Ministry of Human Resource Development. Various Years. *Selected Educational Statistics.* New Delhi: Ministry of Human Resource Development.

National Knowledge Commission. 2007. *Report to the Nation 2006.* New Delhi: Government of India.

———. 2008. *Report to the Nation 2007.* New Delhi: Government of India.

Nehru, Jawaharlal. 1950. *Independence and After: A Collection of Speeches, 1946–1949.* New Delhi: Government of India.

Planning Commission. 2008. *Eleventh Five Year Plan 2007–2012.* New Delhi: Government of India.

Powar, K. B. 2004. "Deemed to be Universities: Their Genesis and History, Present Status and Future Prospects." *Higher Education Policy and Practices* 2 (1): 12–18.

Salmi, Jamil. 2009. *The Challenge of Establishing World-Class Universities.* Washington, DC: World Bank.

Schultz, Theodore W. 1988. "On Investing in Specialized Human Capital to Attain Increasing Returns." In *State of Development Economics,* eds. G. Ranis and T. P. Schultz. Oxford: Basil Blackwell.

Singh, Amrik. 2004. *Fifty Years of Higher Education in India: Role of the University Grants Commission.* New Delhi: Sage.

Stewart, Frances. 1996. "Globalization and Education." *International Journal of Educational Development* 16 (4): 327–333.

Tilak, Jandhyala B. G. 1992. "Education and Structural Adjustment." *Prospects* 22 (4): 407–422.

———. 1997. "Human Capital for Development and the Development of Human Capital in India." *Anvesak* 27 (1&2): 75–124.

———. 2004a. "Quality Higher Education and Sustainable Development." In *Quality Higher Education and Sustainable Development: NAAC Decennial Lectures* (pp. 77–104). Bangalore: National Assessment and Accreditation Council.

———. 2004b. "Absence of Policy and Perspective in Higher Education." *Economic and Political Weekly* 39 (21): 2159–64.

———. 2004c. "Autonomy in Higher Education in India: Old Wine Fails to Attract—A Review of Growth, Problems and Prospects of Autonomous Colleges." *IASSI Quarterly* 23 (2): 129–157.

———. 2005. "Higher Education under Structural Adjustment." In *Financing Higher Education in a Global Market,* eds. S. O. Michael and M. A. Kretovics. New York: Algora Publishing.

———. 2006a. "Education: A Saga of Spectacular Achievements and Conspicuous Failures." In *India: Social Development Report,* ed. A. Kundu. New Delhi: Oxford University Press Council for Social Development.

———. 2006b. "On Reforming Higher Education in Andhra Pradesh." *University News* 44 (31): 1–3.

———. 2007a. "Knowledge Commission and Higher Education." *Economic and Political Weekly* 42 (8): 630–663.

———. 2007b. "Internationalisation of Higher Education—GATS: Illusory Promises and Daunting Problems," *Journal of Indian School of Political Economy* 19 (3) (July-Sept): 371–418

———. 2008a. "Transition from Higher Education as a Public Good to Higher Education as a Private Good: The Saga of Indian Experience." *Journal of Asian Public Policy* 1 (2): 220–234.

———. 2008b. "Towards a National University System." *Seminar* 587: 66–68.

United Nations. 1948. *Universal Declaration of Human Rights*. New York: United Nations.

University Grants Commission (UGC). Various Years. *Annual Report*. New Delhi: UGC.

———. 2008. *Report of Pay Review Committee*. New Delhi: UGC. http://www.ugc.ac.in/.

Chapter 11

Governance and the Governance of Higher Education in Vietnam

Jonathan London

Introduction

As recently as the late 1980s, Vietnam was among the poorest countries in East Asia. Since the late 1980s, Vietnam has developed a rapidly growing market economy. Poverty has declined sharply, while incomes and living standards have increased considerably if unevenly across different geographical regions and segments of the population. Through inward investment and exports of primary goods and manufactured items and the expansion of bilateral and multilateral ties, nominally socialist Vietnam has become increasingly enmeshed in the processes and institutions of global capitalism. In late 2008, Vietnam's average Gross Domestic Product (GDP) per capita surpassed US$1,000, indicating that the country had joined the ranks of the world's lower middle-income countries. Intent on avoiding a "middle-income trap," Vietnam's leaders have charted strategies designed to promote rapid industrialization in such a way that promotes the Communist Party of Vietnam's (CPV) professed commitment to social equity.

In many respects, Vietnam's economic prospects appear promising. However, recent economic turbulence—emanating first within and then from outside Vietnam—have exposed economic and social vulnerabilities (London and Van Ufford 2008; Pincus 2009). Vietnam has a small economy that is largely dependent on trade. The country's infrastructure is overloaded and many new investments in infrastructure defy economic logic. Perhaps most ominously, Vietnam lacks an adequately skilled labor force, and sustained shortages of skilled labor will almost certainly limit the pace and scope of Vietnam's industrialization. To industrialize rapidly and in a way that promotes broad, equitably shared benefits, Vietnam needs more, better, and more relevant higher education. But at present, Vietnam's higher education system is woefully inadequate to the country's needs. What is to be done?

After decades of neglecting and mismanaging higher education, many of Vietnam's leaders appear to have woken up to its importance. Vietnam's government has since 2005 been urgently seeking to reform the country's higher education system. Limits on public investments in higher education in Vietnam stem from the country's developing-country status (i.e., there are simply limited economic resources available) and the sometimes-mystifying spending priorities of the country's political leaders (e.g., approved plans for some 20 international shipping ports along the coast). Of course, there are things in higher education that money cannot help but not buy outright, including ideas, good intellectual debate, motivated students, and effective, if not "good," governance.

International experience suggests that "good governance" in higher education is a critical if not a sufficient condition for the development of an effective higher education system (World Bank 2000), where good governance refers broadly not only to responsive and efficient institutional arrangements, but also (sometimes) neoliberal (i.e., market-promoting) governance. The government of Vietnam has indicated that it recognizes the importance of governance in higher education. But in Vietnam, governance and the governance of higher education have special meanings and complexities owing to the specific features of Vietnam's social and political economy and its higher education system. This chapter clarifies the meanings, attributes, and dynamics of governance in Vietnam and its higher education system, especially in light of recent efforts by the state to reform the governance of higher education from the top down.

This chapter consists of three sections. The first section considers governance in Vietnam in broad terms, examines recent fundamental changes in the governance of education, and explains the significance of the skills gap Vietnam now faces and its relevance to the governance of higher education. The second examines the organization of higher education, recent trends in higher education, and recent efforts to reform the higher education system and higher education governance from the top down. The final section examines three analytically distinct yet empirically overlapping dimensions of higher education governance. These include *systemic governance*, which refers to the governance of the entire higher education system including its relation to other major social institutions and processes; *external governance*, which refers to relations between higher education institutions (HEIs) and supervisory agencies; and *internal governance*, which refers to the internal operation of HEIs. The analysis is based on discussions with policy makers, educators, and other stakeholders in Vietnam and a consideration of relevant English and Vietnamese literature on the subject.

State Governance in Vietnam

In Vietnam, governance is almost exclusively understood in conventional terms, for example, as "state governance."[1] The label state governance tells us too little.

For the distinctive feature of state governance in Vietnam is its occurrence within the framework of democratic centralist political institutions and other institutional legacies of state socialism. This means that many (but certainly not all) aspects of state governance in Vietnam are centralized and hierarchical and are subordinated to the organizational activities and political decisions of the CPV, which has ruled North Vietnam since the 1940s and 1950s and the entire country since 1975. In formal organizational terms, attributes of Vietnam's party-state are summarized in the slogan "the Party Leads, the State Implements, the People Inspect" (cf. Porter 1993). The functional organs of Vietnam's state are commanded by the party apparatus; while the so-called mass organizations (e.g., labor unions, the women's union, the Vietnam Fatherland Front—all of which are subject to party control) are supposed to inspect the state's activities. The party, state, and mass organizations are organized in a hierarchical manner extending from the central government in Hanoi to thousands of administrative units, including thousands of localities and either state-run or state-affiliated work units.[2] All local state agencies and state organizations—including state-organized mass organizations, schools, and even student groups—are interpenetrated with political hierarchies of the party. In formal organizational terms, the CPV is a hierarchy par excellence.

A distinction is commonly drawn between formal and informal governance, where the former refers to principles enshrined in laws or codes while the latter refers to "institutionalized rules" such as customs. In any social context, governance occurs through combinations of formal and informal institutional arrangements. The formal organization of state governance in Vietnam is hierarchical, but it should not be confused with the way the governance actually occurs. In Vietnam, authority relations and social activity are organized in hierarchical and centralized ways in some respects but in competitive and decentralized ways in others. At the national level, political power in Vietnam is diffused within a factionalized but stable political coalition (see Malesky et al. forthcoming). Though state governance in Vietnam exists within the framework of democratic centralism, it is more decentralized and competitive and (in these respects) more pluralistic than is commonly assumed.

Market Transition: Toward Pluralistic and "Good" Governance?

Pluralist notions of governance, which view the state and its agencies as one among many types of actors that coordinate social activity in a society rose to prominence in the 1990s, when many observers claimed the power of states was in certain decline (for an extreme example, see Ohmae 1995). This sentiment was echoed in many writings on "transitional" (e.g., formerly state-socialist) countries, where the transition to market modes of economic coordination was predicted to weaken the power of the state. This did not occur in Vietnam. On the contrary, the CPV has since the late 1980s used market-based strategies of economic accumulation to promote its core political aims through a political economy best described as market-Leninist (London 2009). Nonetheless, Vietnam's transition from centrally planned state socialism to a state-dominated market economy has altered the governance of social life in Vietnam in profound ways.

In the late 1980s, Vietnam's semi-autarchic and state-socialist economy was dominated by agriculture. Over 50 percent of Vietnam's workforce remains in agriculture, as does a large proportion of the country's poor. But Vietnam today is an increasingly globalized market economy specialized in the export of labor-intensive manufactured items, primary commodities, and tourism.

A second way in which governance in Vietnam has become more pluralistic concerns the prominent role of international organizations in shaping the course of the country's institutional changes. International development organizations such as the World Bank, Asian Development Bank, and the United Nations have, along with a host of bilateral donors, provided Vietnam's state substantial capital and continuous doses of technical assistance to achieve development goals.[3] In its own way, each of these organizations advocates various forms of "good governance."

A final general change in governance is related to welfare. In the past the state was, in principle, the guarantor of economic security and essential social services. State socialism failed to deliver on the economic security it promised (Vietnamese often resorted to dealing with illegal markets and informal networks to get by); essential social services were offered at very basic level and in a way that privileged urban and state-affiliated segments of the population (London 2003). The economic growth associated with Vietnam's market transition has certainly improved welfare, however unevenly.

Since the mid-1990s, the state has offered increasing yet still-limited degrees of protection from market forces, such as various social insurance schemes and fee exemptions for basic public services (including certification of poor persons). Nonetheless, many facets of the provision and payment for essential social services have been commodified. In the past, social inequalities were mediated largely through relations with bureaucratic allocative institutions. Today, social inequalities in Vietnam are mediated by one's position in the emerging market economy, even as that market position is itself heavily contingent on one's relation with the state.

The Governance of Education in Transition

Education has been celebrated as one of the great successes of Vietnam's process of renovation, or *đổi mới*. Until the 1990s, the development of education and higher education faced severe resource constraints. Education in many localities took place under makeshift conditions and the Vietnamese academic year was among the shortest in the world. Less than 10 percent of Vietnamese advanced beyond secondary education. Over the last two decades, however, there has been a change which is reflected in school enrollments surging at every level of education. For example, by 2008, an estimated 57 percent of Vietnamese were completing upper secondary education, compared to just well below 50 percent about a decade ago.[4] Once-wide disparities in enrollment levels have declined across regions, income groups, and (to a lesser extent) ethnic groups. Remarkably, one finds no major discrepancies in the educational achievement of boys and girls at any level of education, including tertiary education. Total (public and private) spending on education has increased continuously; education spending as a share of the state budget has reached 20 percent.

Indicators of progress mask important problems, however. Although enrollments have increased across all levels, enrollment has grown much slower among poorer segments of society, and ethnic minorities in particular. There is massive unevenness in the quality and accessibility of education across regions. Vietnam's state budget is still broadly redistributive, but the scope of redistribution has not been sufficient to address the comparatively greater needs of poor provinces. In poor zones, education still takes place under threadbare conditions, while the inability or failure of the state to adequately fund education sector wages over the course of the 1990s contributed to the proliferation of private extra study courses offered after school hours by "public" teachers. Enrollment figures showing rough parity among boys and girls mask other (sometimes severe) forms of gender discrimination. Preschool enrollments are improving but remain lower among the poor and minority groups, who show up at primary school already at a disadvantage and are the groups least likely to advance through the education system. Household expenditures on upper secondary education (including costly, informal, and the so-called extra study sessions, with public school teachers after school hours), can run as high as US$100 per month, which is an extraordinary amount of money even for middle-income Vietnamese. Presently secondary education fees (all told) can be higher than the cost of tertiary education and represent one of the largest household expenditure items. Moreover, the commercialization of education has led to rampant cheating, often organized and tolerated in exchange for bribes to exam proctors.

Changes in the governance of education can be seen with respect to the state's role in the provision and payment for education and, but much less so with respect to the role of the central state in educational administration. Under state socialism, the governance of education—and the provision and payment for all formal education—took place through state channels. Vietnam's education bureaucracy was highly centralized, and policies regarding funding, staffing, curricula, and norms were centrally determined and administered. Vietnam's state has maintained a dominant role in the provision of education and the state has increased its investments in education continuously; they now amount to 20 percent of the state budget. However, institutional responsibility for the payment for education has changed fundamentally. A series of policies known in Vietnamese as "socialization" (*xã hội hóa*) have actually shifted institutional responsibility for the payment of education onto households and the society. Primary education is available to all children free of charge, at least in principle. In reality, households sending children to primary school must still make payments to the school, but just not for tuition per se. Students must pay tuition and other school charges at all other levels of education, including formal and informal fees, some of which are technically illegal.

A second major change in the governance of education concerns the state's efforts (halting and in some respects reluctant) to expand what is in Vietnam called non-public (*ngoài công lập*) education at all levels of education, except primary education. In some instances, the state has opened up so-called semi-public slots or classrooms in nominally public schools, allowing students with lower academic results to pay several times more tuition for the chance to study, while contributing to school revenues. There are, in addition, "people-founded" schools (the word private is less favored by state officials), which operate with relative autonomy from the education bureaucracy. Sometimes the state provides basic infrastructure such as roads and sewer links, while investors provide funds for school construction and manage school affairs. The upshot of these developments is that, though the state retains an important role in the provision and payment for education, education has become increasingly commodified and the quality and amount of education children receive beyond a basic level (or in preschool) is often contingent on households' ability to pay out of pocket.

Vietnam's Emerging Skills Gap: The Governance Connection

In 2009, a featured article run by Reuters news agency reported how, in 2008, 2000 of the "best and brightest" from five of Vietnam's best known universities were invited to test for an interview with Intel Corp at its new US$1 billion assembly testing facility, on the outskirts of Ho Chi Minh City (Ruwich 2009). As the article notes, the Intel investment was "more than just another big project... [it] would put Vietnam on the global tech map and help a rising star in the manufacturing world move closer to its dream of advancing up the value chain." But, as the article continues,

> [T]he results from Intel's test cast a spotlight on one of Vietnam's biggest barriers to achieving that dream: its inadequate and inflexible higher education system. A fraction of the students passed the written exam, covering physics, electrical engineering, maths and other topics. They were given an English test and just 40 made the final cut.

The above story is emblematic of a systemic problem with Vietnam's higher education system concerning the education-skills nexus, or lack thereof. Vietnam has a highly literate workforce that remains cheap relative to other countries in East Asia, including China. Unlike China, Vietnam has failed to invest adequately in higher education and without more adequate knowledge and skills, Vietnamese will be hard-pressed to move into the production of more advanced and value-added goods and services, let alone advance to the kind of "knowledge economy" its leaders fancy. Higher education does not merely concern international competitiveness. Without improvements in the quantity and quality of higher education (and lower levels of education), Vietnam's education system is likely to perpetuate existing regional, as well as income- and ethnicity-based inequalities. In addition, without changes in the way the educational incentives work, higher education is likely to remain a labyrinth in which struggles for resources and the politics of status and party rank will trump the pursuit of knowledge and the development of national capacities of sciences, social sciences, and humanities. Ultimately then, higher education governance in Vietnam cannot be responsive to the country's developmental needs.

Higher Education in Vietnam: Organization, Trends, and Rescue Efforts

Vietnam's higher education system has seen important changes in its scale, organization, and governance. In this section, an introduction to the organization of the education system and recent expansions in its scale is followed by an examination of recent efforts by the state to reform the governance of education from the top down.

The Organization of Higher Education

Contemporary Vietnam's higher education system traces its roots to the development of a state-socialist economy in the north of Vietnam in the early 1950s and its extension south of the 17th parallel after 1975. In 1954, the University of Hanoi was reestablished (from its previous colonial form) with 40 teachers and 500 students, most of whom were Viet Minh intellectuals (Marr 1981). The university was mostly concerned with training doctors and teachers. In the late 1950s, Soviet assistance was used to establish 13 new universities under various functional ministries of government, while in the 1960s all tertiary education was shifted from French to Vietnamese. Marr (1988) notes that, by 1974, tertiary students in the (northern) Democratic Republic of Vietnam numbered some 54,000, down from 69,000 in 1970, though some 10,000 students a year were being accepted in Eastern European universities during this period. As of 1974, it is estimated that about 85,000 people in Vietnam had tertiary degrees, while the figure was roughly 70,000 in the south.[5]

Vietnam's higher education system was modeled on the Soviet system in which universities and colleges were mainly devoted to teaching, whereas research was done in specialized research institutions. With the exception of teacher training, social sciences, and a range of other fields of study, universities, professional schools, and research institutes were organized under the authority and within the economic plans of specific functional ministries (the so-called line ministries, e.g., the ministries of construction, agriculture, health, and police). The Ministry of Higher Education and Professional Schools, which was a separate entity from the Ministry of Education until 1993, maintained managerial authority over universities and colleges with more explicitly educational and teaching missions (e.g., teaching, social sciences). However, the Ministry of Higher Education and Professional Schools also performed certain regulatory functions across the higher education system, including the validation of curricula, program design, and enrollment levels. Similarly, research institutes were managed largely within functional ministries, excepting certain fields such as education and social sciences.

The erosion of state-socialist economic institution over the course of the 1980s hastened the search for new institutional arrangements for financing education. In the early 1990s, state retrenchment in education had catastrophic effects. Teachers went months without pay. Enrollments fell rapidly—by 40 percent in secondary education in some areas—and did not recover until the mid-1990s. Beginning in the late 1980s, the government had begun authorizing and promoting the development of semipublic higher education (same education, higher fees), as well as "people-founded" universities and colleges, that is, self-managing, self-financing institutions that are permitted to make use of state assets. Vietnam's higher education system now includes "public" (*công lập*) institutions, "people-founded" institutions, and the incipient presence of foreign higher education providers.

Vietnam's public universities remain the core of the higher education system. In 1993, the government of Vietnam began to reorder higher education by declaring the establishment of five "new-style" universities, including two "national" universities, in Hanoi and Ho Chi Minh City, and three regional universities in Hue, Da Nang, and Thai Nguyen. Each of these universities was actually amalgam of smaller preexisting schools and research institutes. But these universities combined teaching and research activities—in line with higher education as organized in much of the world—and were meant to be a model for future universities (Hayden 2006, cited in World Bank 2008). Under the new model, universities would offer bachelor, master, and doctoral degrees, and sometimes associate degrees also.[6] The higher education system comprises universities, colleges, and research institutes as well as an array of supporting bureaucratic institutions at the national and local levels. Most such colleges are teacher training schools or they offer other professional education and have small enrollments of approximately d 1,500 (World Bank 2008, 7).

In 2004, the government undertook expansion of higher education and established nine additional universities which, in addition to the five listed above, were labeled "key" universities and were to be the foundation of the new higher education system.[7] Further, under the new order, colleges (*cao đẳng*) were to perform functions similar to those of "community colleges" in North America; that is, specialize in professional education (including teacher education) and grant the equivalent of associate degrees.

Recent Trends and the State of Higher Education in Vietnam

Generally, higher education in Vietnam is substandard and compares poorly with that in most other countries in East and Southeast Asia. As of 2009, Vietnam still lacked a single university of international standing, notwithstanding current plans for increased investment and the establishment of a number of elite "medallion" technical universities.

The scale of higher education in Vietnam has grown rapidly. By 2009, there were over 1.7 million students in tertiary education, roughly double that of the number enrolled in 1999 and more than ten times that of the 162,000 enrolled in 1993. Gross enrollment in tertiary education (i.e., the proportion during this period) has increased from 2 to more than 13 percent. By 2008, roughly 400,000 students were enrolled in colleges or college-equivalent programs alone. Demand for higher education outstrips supply, even as the number of schools has increased sharply. Only 10 percent of students pass the national education exam. Between 1999 and 2008 the number of universities more than doubled from 69 to 160, while the number of vocational schools (colleges) nearly trebled from 84 to 209 (MOET 2008).

Between 2000 and 2007, the national budget for higher education increased more than fourfold (MOET 2008). Still, public spending on tertiary education remains at barely more than 1 percent of GDP, and combined spending on training and tertiary education amounts for less than a quarter of the entire education spending. Private (household) spending has grown continuously. However, the accessibility of education is of special concern to those who wish Vietnam to develop into an equitable society. Examples of promoting accessibility include controls on tuition costs, targeted subsidies, and scholarships.

While inequalities are moderating, sharp inequalities remain. As of 2004, enrollment rates among students from the richest quintile of Vietnam's population are roughly four times that of the poorest while ethnic minorities, who accounted for 13 percent of the total population and 39 percent of those below the poverty line accounted for just 4 percent of tertiary enrollment. Regional unevenness is another concern. As of 2005, the Red River Delta (led by Hanoi) and the Southeast (led by Ho Chi Minh City)—Vietnam's second and wealthiest regions—accounted for 60 percent of all universities and 67 percent of all enrollment. Gross tertiary enrollment in each of these regions was roughly three times that of the country's poorest region, the Northwest. Across rural areas, but especially remote regions, there are few outlets for higher education and most schools that do exist tend to offer training that is incommensurate with ongoing processes of economic diversification or the skills that need to be taught if these regions are to avoid lagging further behind. That said, there have been recent increases in scholarships for eligible and officially certified poor students and students from households of valued political constituencies, such as war veterans.

As things stand now, staff qualifications remain low, on average, while many staffs are engaged in teaching part-time students in special nondegree programs. As of 2008, roughly 55 percent of Vietnamese academic staff had postgraduate qualifications, and most of these (73 percent) were at the master's level (MOET 2008). Less than 1 percent of academic staff in Vietnam consists of full professors, which partly reflects the state's desire to limit pay promotion and spending on higher education. In some universities, more than 60 percent of academic staff consists of bachelor degree holders. It is not uncommon for recent graduates of undergraduate programs to go up to the front of the class and lecture the class, a practice some Vietnamese have referred to as "eating rice with rice" (ăn cơm với cơm).

Efforts at Top-Down Systemic Reform: Resolution 14 and Its Aftermath

After long neglecting higher education, Vietnam's leaders have recognized its critical importance, from economic, social, and even political viewpoints. In the last ten years, efforts to reform higher education in Vietnam has gained momentum. Successive prime ministers Phan Văn Khải and Nguyễn Tấn Dũng have convened blue-ribbon commissions, held meetings with the leaders of elite universities around the world, and enlisted the support of diverse partners, ranging from World Bank, bilateral donors, foreign universities, to prominent individuals.[8] Vietnamese intellectuals at home and abroad have weighed in energetically. The appointment in 2007 of Minister of Education Nguyễn Thiện Nhân to the post of deputy prime minister has given education and higher education greater political prominence.

There have been special efforts to address problems in the governance of higher education. Party organs and state agencies (including MOET) have generated a number of important policy documents that embody this aggressive reformist agenda. Many of these documents resemble "wish lists" of achievements and priorities that are characteristic of so many policy documents in Vietnam, with little said about how these achievement goals will actually be reached, and even less to be said about ambiguities or contradictions the new policies will inject into current authority relations. However, other policies evidence a serious engagement with new ideas, call for specific measures to be taken, and are very ambitious in their scope. Among the most important of documents as Resolution 14 of 2005 on the "Fundamental and comprehensive renovation of university education in the period 2006–2020," which identified general and specific aims for higher education in Vietnam.[9] Resolution 14 states its general aim as the following:

> To fundamentally and comprehensively renovate university education, bring about fundamental changes in the quality, effectiveness and scale, meet the requirements of industrialization and modernization of the country, of international integration, and the educational demands of the people: By 2020, higher education in Vietnam (should) reach an advanced level in the region and approach advanced levels in the world; have the capacity to compete on a high level, adapt with a socialist orientated market mechanism.

Resolution 14 seems to grasp these points, as its specific aims include the following:

- Fully work out the national network of university education, establishing stratification with respect to functions, training missions, system of qualifications, professional coverage, and geographical distribution in a way appropriate to the aims of "socializing" education and advancing the general socioeconomic development of the country and localities;
- Establish research and professional education streams; ensure internal consistency of the different programs in the system; establish and perfect measures to ensure quality and accountability through accreditation schemes; establish some universities up to international standards;
- Increase the scale of training, achieve a ratio of 200 students for every 10,000 population by 2010 and 450 per 10,000 by 2020; of that ensure 70–80 percent are following professional education, and that roughly 40 percent of all students are outside the state system;
- Develop a cadre of teachers and education managers of sufficient quality, ethical standards, and professional commitment, with high levels of qualification, advanced methods of teaching and management; ensure student/teacher ratios in the entire system is not beyond 20. By 2010, 40 percent of teachers will have

a master's degree and 25 percent a doctoral degree, with the corresponding figures of 60 percent of masters and 35 percent of doctors by 2020;
- Decisively increase the scale and effectiveness of research and technology in the universities. The largest universities must be the strongest centers for research in the entire country, with revenues from their scientific and technological activities and production and service activities of 15 percent at minimum by 2010 and 25 percent by 2020;
- Develop the university education policy in a way that ensures the autonomy and social responsibility of the universities, management of the state, and the supervisory and evaluative of society with respect to university education.

The impacts of Resolution 14 have been mixed. The resolution drew a great deal of attention and served to energize national debates on higher education. The issuance of the resolution was followed by a flurry of announcements, decisions, and (even) practical steps, including the establishment of a "Steering Committee for the Renovation of Higher Education." The committee is to be headed by the deputy prime minister, a position that is now occupied by the current minister of education.[10] One lightening-rod issue has been whether or under what conditions Vietnam should seek to develop an international standard university (it presently lacks it) that would be the apex institution of Vietnam's higher education system, with debate centering on whether such a university would draw resources away from the rest of the system. In 2006 the prime minister decided to build one or more "international standard" "technical universities." There have been sharp increases in funding for some national universities, but not others (Hồ et al. 2008).

However, like previous efforts to reform higher education (an earlier reform effort in the 1990s contained much of the same rhetoric as Resolution 14), the aims of the resolution have faltered in the face of the usual political obstacles including political sensitiveness about the much-needed curricular reform and the associated reluctance of MOET and other central government agencies to cede substantive authority to universities. disseminated a new strategic plan for education, for the years 2009–2020 which ignored and even contradicted the recommendations of Resolution 14. MOET has also confronted difficulties in drafting new officials to lead its higher education departments, and those who have been selected have no background in the field. An analysis of systemic, external, and internal facets of governance in Vietnamese higher education permits a better appreciation of problems in Vietnam's higher education system and the prospects for achieving reforms as specified in Resolution 14 and other documents.

Higher Education in Vietnam: Systemic, External, and Internal Governance Issues

By systemic governance, I refer to the broad relation between higher education, the state, and other major social institutions and processes, including "the market." External governance refers to relations between HEIs and supervisory agencies.

Internal governance refers to the governance of individual HEIs, and includes consideration of such institutions internal operations and external links. In what follows, I examine the governance of higher education in Vietnam from each of these perspectives.

Systemic Governance I: Provision and Payment for Higher Education

With respect to the provision and payment for higher education, systemic governance has indeed moved from a purely hierarchical model of state governance to a somewhat more pluralistic arrangement, in which markets and networks play increasingly important roles.

Facing limited public spending, HEIs have survived by expanding their own revenue base, primarily by expanding enrollments of semipublic and short-course students. Notably, roughly half of all full-time enrollments in public universities are "semipublic" enrollment, that is, students who are admitted under a higher tuition fees regime. As of 2008, full time students accounted for only 46 percent of all enrollments at Vietnamese universities; over 48 percent of enrollment is in short-term, nondegree training courses.[11] At four of Vietnam's flagship universities, Hanoi National University, Ho Chi Minh City National University, the University of Hue, and the University of Da Nang, short-course enrollment as a proportion of total enrollment is at 57, 55, 72, and 47 percent of all enrollments respectively (Vũ 2008).[12]

Another way to increase the availability of higher education has been the expansion of the role of nonstate educational institutions (i.e., people-founded and private schools). Of 369 colleges and universities in 2009, 64 were nonstate, accounting for 17 percent of all schools and 12 percent of tertiary students. By 2020, government targets stipulate that nonstate providers of higher education will account for 40 percent of enrollments, though this target is unlikely to be met without significant relaxations in enrollment caps or the mass entrance of foreign education providers. The World Bank has urged the government of Vietnam to permit larger nonstate institutions. It has become progressively more involved in advising higher education governance; indeed, Vietnam represents the World Bank's first ever "development policy lending operation" in higher education. In the late 1990s, the World Bank committed over US$80 million to a higher education reform project that was largely regarded as a failure. A second round of higher education reforms had tangible results. In 2009, the government announced plans to build four "international standard" universities, with a loan of US$400 million from the World Bank and Asian Development Bank. These will be Vietnam's first public nonprofit and foreign-managed universities (Trần 2009).

The increasing incidence of partnerships with foreign institutions and domestic as well as foreign businesses shows the growing significance of market and network governance. Several universities in Vietnam have developed exchange programs for income students from overseas as well as "sandwich programs" in which foreign institutions deliver instruction for higher fees within a Vietnamese public university, followed by an optional year of overseas studies by Vietnamese students.[13] The government sees cooperation with foreign universities as a way to defray costs, increase technological transfers, and gain economically.[14] The government is promoting collaboration between universities and businesses, and is encouraging universities to expand such partnerships. In a trip to Singapore in 2007, a delegation of Vietnam higher education officials devoted much of their questioning to the commercial activities of universities in Singapore. Commercial aspects of higher education have come to the fore in recent debates over whether or under what conditions some public universities ought to be privatized or "equitized," through the sale of "shares" to individual investors (for example, see Bùi 2008).

Systemic Governance II: Higher Education and the Economy

Vietnam needs not just more higher education, but also greater interconnectedness between higher education and the economy. Clearly, industrialization will entail major changes in occupational structure and in the structure of demand of skilled labor. As of 2005, 57 percent of the workforce was in agriculture, which accounted for just 20 percent of GDP, while 70 percent of those with higher education in Vietnam worked in education or civil service jobs (World Bank 2008). In future years, the proportion of workers in industry and services will increase, as will the industrial and services shares of GDP. Ensuring an adequate numbers of workers in these fields with adequate skills will require realignments of resources, academic programs, curricula, and pedagogical methods. International experience suggests ways to maximize resources through pluralistic governance arrangements, for example pooling resources to establish regional research facilities available to several universities in a given region.[15]

As they stand, present patterns of specialization and training are skewed, with quite low enrollments in hard sciences and (until recently) engineering. By contrast, as of 2005, nearly half of all tertiary students were enrolled in the two disciplines of education and economics/business (World Bank 2008, 15). There remain relatively few opportunities for graduate studies in Vietnam, and 35 percent of enrollment in graduate programs is in the fields of medicine and pharmacy. There is a movement to promote more and more diverse forms professional education. Existing professional and vocational education schemes often produce graduates with inadequate or inappropriate skill sets. Though there are examples of new and innovative schemes,[16] it is unclear whether these will be replicated or scaled up.

It is equally clear that higher education graduates require more than just specialized knowledge. Indeed, international experience shows that *general education* is frequently neglected in professional schools, even as such education is precisely what is needed if students are to learn new skills or specializations in the future.[17] This suggests a new pedagogy that moves away from rote memorization to active, problem-based learning. As one observer put it, "encyclopedic knowledge transfer is no longer appropriate" (Oosterlinck 2004, 123). Yet, a standard university education in Vietnam stands in contradiction to these ideals. Vietnamese university curricula are centrally approved and there is little flexibility for individual universities, let alone instructors to modify them. A full-time Vietnamese student spends in studying nearly double the time a student in the United States does (Vũ 2008). The content of compulsory class time is also of dubious value. As of 2008, one half of students' compulsory general education hours and 14 percent of total class hours were accounted for by five courses in state ideology (Marxist-Leninist Philosophy, Marxist-Leninist Political Economy, Scientific Socialism, the History of the CPV, and Ho Chi Minh Ideology [Vũ 2008]).[18]

External Governance

Questions concerning external governance of higher education in contemporary Vietnam concern the relations between HEIs and various supervisory agencies, including the prime minister's office, MOET, Ministry of Planning and Investment (MPI) and the Ministry of Finance (VMOF), as well as other functional ministries. In Vietnam, universities and national research institutes are accountable to the prime minister, whereas colleges (called *cao đẳng* or "higher grade" schools, and which are mostly teacher-training colleges and other specialized schools) are accountable to the authority of provincial governments (i.e., Departments of Education) and MOET.[19] In Vietnam, there is considerable talk about the need to expand HEIs' autonomy. To this day, however, it is central state agencies that dictate and, in many respects, micromanage the affairs of HEIs.

In Vietnam it is MOET that provides the general curriculum and curricula for all disciplines. Decisions about instruction taken by individual institutions require approval from MOET. Personnel management occurs under the supervision of MOET and relevant overseeing functional ministries. Rectors are appointed by MOET or overseeing functional ministries, with or without the involvement of individual institutions. MOET retains control over curricular matters in all non-public universities and colleges. Admissions levels are determined by MPI and MOET in accordance with MOET exam rules. Nonstate universities are managed under MOET guidelines; they can plan subject to MOET consent, and may except students on the basis of exam results, though they are subject to caps on admissions. External auditing and accreditation agencies in Vietnam are in their early stages of development. Vietnam's National Universities, supposed bastions of autonomy, do have managerial autonomy from MOET, but their leadership, planning, and oversight are closely overseen by the office of the prime minister.

Internationally, there is increasing agreement that ministries of education should occupy a stewardship or orchestrating role in the field of higher education. That is, ministries should provide broad policies and regulations, ensure accountability, but should not interfere directly in the business of educational institutions. As Rhodes (2006, p.214) suggests, this is not about taking power away from the education ministry, it is about freeing the central ministry to think about and focus upon strategic matters.[20] One way of stating this principle is "nose in, hands out." MOET's roles would include perfecting the overall "architecture" of higher education, fulfilling certain regulatory roles, and providing "public goods" for the enhancement of higher education overall.

Critics of MOET suggest the development of the higher education system has been adversely affected by the resilience of excessive centralization and "controlism" (chủ quản), which is perhaps best described as a conservative management disposition that seeks to maintain central dominance and adherence to old management practices. They charge that pressures for the maintenance of centralization have worked against meaningful reform, including decentralization proposals emanating from the central state. Within HEIs, administrators and educators complain that central control constricts the space available for schools and educators to respond to local needs (including the needs of employers) and to innovate. Most advocates of higher education reform in Vietnam agree in principle that MOET should retain a regulatory role, but that universities should be granted greater autonomy, allowing individual institutions more leeway in taking initiatives and responding to local needs as they see fit, provided that education providers meet quality standards.

To support quality improvements, MOET can help develop systems of quality assurance, help to establish (but not directly oversee) academic accreditation boards, and sponsor programs, processes, and events that promote the development of higher education overall (e.g., programs that help universities tailor their curricula to the national interest or the needs of local employers).[21] Vietnam is just now developing a system of accreditation and presently even people-founded schools are subject to core curricular and staffing norms of the MOET. There are also concerns about the transparency of decision making regarding the establishment of new universities.

Internal Governance

Rhodes (2004, 11), the former president of Cornell University, cites five fundamental powers of the university should not be eliminated, modified, or reduced. These include the following:

1. The power to select, amidst, instruct, and certify or graduate students in fields that are represented by the institution;
2. The power to select what to teach and how to teach;
3. The freedom to study, explore, and publish on any topic;
4. The power to accept funds and create partnerships; and
5. The autonomy of the institution and the independence of its governance.

As Rhodes (2004, 11) emphasizes, "Any erosion of any one of those responsibilities seems to me to threaten the idea of the university." Measured against these norms, the internal governance of tertiary institutions in Vietnam looks quite different. Many aspects of internal governance in Vietnam are limited by external institutional constraints, as detained above. On the other hand, there is a movement toward greater financial decentralization, which will give educational institutions greater operational discretion, particularly with respect to the organization of their noncore revenue-enhancing operations and the management of finances. Yet most Vietnamese institutions of higher education have little experience in governing themselves.

Given the limited resources, little training, and few opportunities, it is not surprising that few Vietnamese academic staffs are involved in research activities, and very few publish in international journals. While Vietnam's central government has expressed its intent to promote more research, it is difficult to see how a vibrant research culture will emerge without significant changes in the academic governance of the higher education system. But change is difficult to imagine when hiring and promotion within virtually all universities remain primarily based on seniority, political considerations, or other nonacademic criteria, rather than professional skill or achievement.

Another basic limitation on following international governance norms arises out of institutions' lack of control over their curricula, limited time for research, complex terms of hiring, and the consequent unattractiveness of higher education as a career. Although some schools have developed new curricula under pilot programs or through joint degree programs with foreign partners, curricular matters remain largely under the authority of MOET. Academic staffs are expected to log long classroom hours. Though recent decrees on administrative decentralization confer greater discretion with respect to the management of human resources, it is in practice very difficult for any organization in Vietnam to fire staff outright, while all newly hired staffs still need to be vetted by the Ministry of Home Affairs. Universities do not decide on the qualifications or suitability of their faculty. Such a system of hiring and promotion provides a compelling reason for talented individuals to exit or avoid the higher education system altogether. This includes staffs with master and PhD degrees returning from overseas, who dread being "robots" delivering precooked materials. That faculties (let alone individual staff) are not given autonomy to develop their programs of instruction exacerbates high faculty turnover. International experience suggests advancement systems that recognize excellence in research and teaching should be developed.

A final concern about academic governance is related to commercialization. While Vietnam requires higher education that is responsive to markets, dependence on external revenues promotes commercialization and can lead HEIs to forget their primary mission (Zemsky and Duderstadt 2004). An interesting example of the ambiguities involved is found in the case of the recently established FPT University in Hanoi, a venture of Vietnam's largest information technology corporation. Established as a people-founded institution, the school must abide by the general curricular guidelines of MOET, including the standard general education program. However, the school has apparently received permission to develop its own curriculum, which is reported to have been supplied by Microsoft Inc., which has close ties with FPT's founder and CEO. Arrangements like this raise interesting questions about the academic purpose of higher education.

Public investments in higher education in Vietnam are coordinated principally by three agencies, MPI, the MOF, and MOET. As of 2005, public HEIs were receiving nearly 70 percent of their revenues through the state budget, whereas tuition accounted for roughly 26 percent. By contrast, 90 percent of semipublic universities revenues and 82 percent of "people-founded" universities' revenues came from tuition and other student fees (2005 also saw the elimination of the semipublic category, as all such schools were reclassified as either people-founded or public)

(World Bank 2008, 49). A 2005 decision required semipublic institutions to either revert to public status or become "people-founded." The dynamics of financial governance differ for these two categories of institutions.

Within public HEIs, there is increased reliance on nonbudgetary sources of revenue increases. Under Decree 43, issued in 2004, HEIs along with other public service delivery units are encouraged to promote nonbudgetary sources of revenues through the promotion of new services, while maintaining their chief educational and research functions. Perhaps unsurprisingly, one of the most important risks facing higher education in Vietnam is commercialization. Already, many universities in Vietnam derive substantial shares from revenue from "sideline businesses" (Hồ Vũ Ngọc Khuê 2010). Recent moves toward making universities even more financially autonomous have generated concerns that universities are becoming excessively business-oriented. Already, commercial enterprises established within universities are among the fastest growing forms of business in Vietnam. The commercialization of higher education risks exacerbating educational inequalities across income groups, which are already most pronounced in higher education. To see the dangers of rapid expansion, Vietnam needs look no further than its recent past.

A final dimension of internal governance concerns the responsiveness of HEIs to local needs. In Decree 14, there is a call, repeated in more recent documents, to have universities to move toward a system accountable directly to boards of governors rather than the MOET. To ensure that higher education responds to social needs, some have advocated a regional system of governance whereby universities are accountable to a regional board of governors that ensures HEIs are meeting their general and specific obligations. It is important to consider the form and function of the boards of governors to study the differences and similarity between these and boards of trustees arrangements in other countries such as the United States.[22] Given the nature of Vietnam's political institutions, one could easily imagine this type of system falling into the same problem of top-down chủ quản problems, but only on a regional level.

Conclusion

This chapter has sought to demonstrate that caution is appropriate when extending contemporary academic and policy notions of governance to an analysis of higher education in Vietnam, owing to the special features and meanings of governance in Vietnam. I have suggested that Vietnam's efforts to remake its higher education system in the interest of promoting industrialization, modernization, and political stability may produce results desired by the country's leaders. But it is feared that the messy, opaque politics of higher education in Vietnam as well as the tensions and contradictions that characterize Vietnam's particular brand of market-Leninism may undermine the reforms' overall efficacy and their contributions to a more internationally competitive Vietnam.

In Vietnam today, there is great concern as well as debate about the future of the country's higher education system and the way to address perceived inadequacies in accessibility and quality, apart from the concern about the relevance of higher education. This chapter has sought to highlight attributes of governance in Vietnam and in its higher education system. Vietnam's higher education system was initially designed to supply a small coterie of scientists and intelligentsia for the needs of state-socialist planned economy. It is now being reformed into a mass education system with the ability to meet the needs of an internationally oriented market economy. Many of the obstacles Vietnam faces concern not resources but governance. "Controlism," perverse incentives that reward quantity over quality, and commercialization, all threaten the efficacy of present reform efforts. There is considerable disunity among education officials about how best to reform the governance of higher education in Vietnam.

Notes

1. It is telling that the English word governance is most frequently translated into Vietnamese as *quản lý*, or *điều hành*, two terms for "management," even in documents which were prepared by foreigners and which attempt to promote a more pluralistic notion of governance. See, for example, the translated and English versions of the 2005 Vietnam Development Report (World Bank 2005a, 2005b).
2. Vietnam's localities consist of 63 provinces and cities, hundreds of districts, over 10,000 precincts and communes, and tens of thousands of hamlets, and urban neighborhood blocks.
3. According to data from Vietnam's Ministry of Planning and Investment (MPI), the amount of Official Development Assistance committed to Vietnam averaged roughly 15 percent of annual GDP for the period 1993 to 2003, while disbursed Official Development Assistance for the period 2004 to 2007 rose from US$1.1 to 1.4 billion per annum (OECD 2009). Often, grant and loan capital are contingent on the acceptance of technical assistance, though Vietnam's state has been effective in resisting calls to privatize the economy.
4. According to MOET of Vietnam.
5. Marr (1988) offers a detailed discussion of tertiary education in Vietnam during the 1970s and 1980s. Between the 1950s and the 1980s, some 200,000 Vietnamese received training in the Soviet Union, Eastern Europe, and China, though not all or even a majority received tertiary degrees. Most of this training was in the natural sciences, engineering, and medicine (Marr 1981, 18). The CPV's military victory resulted in the immediate overhaul of curricula and the closure or seizure of universities run by private and religious organizations.
6. But the meaning of "university" needs to be treated with caution. In what is a truly confusing practice, a large Vietnamese university (*trường đại học*) can sometimes contain a number of schools which call themselves universities (for greater prestige value) even though they are formally a part of another university.
7. According to Decision 1269/CP-KG, as related in World Bank (2008).
8. In 2005, PM Phan Văn Khải's trip to the United States in June of 2005 included meetings with the presidents of Harvard and MIT, as well as Professor (and former Dean) Henry Rosovsky, a leader of the Taskforce on Higher Education, a panel of experts assembled by UNESCO, and the World Bank.
9. Resolution 14 was issued on November 2, 2005.

10. This committee would comprise 11 members from across different sectors; the state function of this committee was to guide MOET and other ministries with specific and detailed schemes, programs, and solutions for each task group to map out the renovation process.
11. Roughly half of these students are involved in part-time study programs designed for people still at work (tại chức) and half of which is "other," including various forms of distance education.
12. By 2004, each of these universities had over 50,000 students; Ho Chi Minh City National University and the University of Hue had over 80,000 students each.
13. One such example is the program at Hanoi University with LaTrobe University of Australia. The university's Web site has advertising from the Gap Inc.
14. Numerous foreign universities (including many from the United States) are anxious to establish operations in Vietnam (Overland 2009).
15. There is much talk about how, given expected changes in the labor market, emphasis in higher education in Vietnam should be on professional education for the service sector as well as high-tech fields. Yet if sustainability and poverty reduction are important aims (not just competitiveness), agricultural and life sciences should deserve more attention. Perhaps the land grant option (on a smaller scale) is a viable mechanism for the establishment of agriculture-oriented universities. These universities can also provide valuable extension services (discussed further, below). One of the great successes in the history of higher education has been the development of Land Grant universities in the United States, which began with the United States' Land Grant Act in 1862. As Hasselmo (2004) explains, the Land Grant Act was an act of the federal government, which donated several states and territories 30,000 acres (each) of public lands for each senator and representative based on the 1860 census. Proceeds from the sale of these lands were invested in a perpetual endowment that would support colleges of agriculture and mechanical arts in each of the states and territories.
16. One promising effort to address this problem is a large Vietnam-Netherlands project on Professionally Oriented Higher Education, which ran from 2005 to 2009, and which aims to ensure that that teachers and students in professional education programs have appropriate knowledge, skills, and experience. To this end, universities participating in the scheme were encouraged to develop close and sometimes collaborative relations with employers. Under the project, participating institutions conducted and disseminated results of surveys of employers' needs and used these to develop competency profiles for different occupations. The universities were assisted to develop and implement "industrial attachment" schemes, which encourage university students take six months to one year while in university to work at an outside enterprise, before returning to school for a final year. Whether this model will be scaled up remains to be seen.
17. To ensure students develop skills for lifelong learning the Taskforce on Higher Education and Society has suggested that higher education systems need to (1) produce a body of students with a general education that encourages flexibility and innovation, thus allowing the continual renewal of economic and social structures relevant to a fast-changing world; (2) teach students not just what is currently known, but also how to keep their knowledge up to date, so that they will be able to refresh their skills as the economic environment changes; (3) increase the amount and quality of in-country research, thus allowing the developing world to select, absorb, and create new knowledge more efficiently and rapidly than it currently does; and, (4) provide increasing numbers of students, especially those from disadvantaged backgrounds, with specialized skills, because specialists are increasingly in demand in all sectors of the world economy (World Bank 2000, 10).

18. According to Vũ's (2008) analysis, Vietnamese university students' study program is often more than twice as long as a student's in a U.S. university, not including 165 hours of defense and 175 hours of physical fitness training, or the time that all students (as well as staff and administrators) must also devote time to Party and (Communist Party) Youth Union activities.
19. The Ministry of Labour, Invalids, and Social Affairs has authority over vocational education schools, which are not considered in this analysis.
20. Specifically, de Rooij (2005) suggests six important roles for an education ministry in a decentralized education system. These include (1) cooperation with other ministries in a way that does not obstruct change; (2) well-developed monitoring and evaluation capabilities; decentralization and autonomy should not mean MOET loses power but that MOET can focus on strategic issues; (3) the development of quality enhancement systems; (4) awareness-raising activities on the importance of higher education, including systems and institutions to guide students at local level for further training opportunities; awareness raising will also help facilitate the link between education providers and employers; (5) establishment of and support for high quality institutions for training teachers and professors; and, (6) promotion of variety and flexibility within higher education, orchestration within and between regions; diplomas should have *national* not just regional value.
21. Arguably, Vietnam's National Academy of Science and its National Academy of Social Sciences and the Humanities are well suited to contribute to the development of accreditation mechanisms, but accreditation needs to be depoliticized and subject to strict principles of accountability and integrity.
22. In the United States, the board of trustees is the most important institution for the governance of individual universities. Presidents of universities reports to the board of trustees, which at once assumes legal responsibility for the institution and protects and advances the university's interest in the face of interference. Boards of trustees can include past leaders, eminent scholars, and prominent businesspersons.

References

Bùi, Trọng Liễu. 2008. "Vì sao không nên cổ phần hóa đại học công? [Why Shouldn't We Equalize Public Universities?]." *Diendan Forum*. Bourg-La-Reine, France: Diendan Forum. http://www.diendan.org.

Các Nhà Tài Trợ Tại Việt Nam. 2005. "Quản Lý và Điều Hành: Báo cáo Phát trien Vietnam 2005 [Governance: Vietnam Development Report 2005, Vietnamese version]." *CNTTTV*. Hanoi: Vietnam Donors Group.

De Rooij, Peter. 2005. "Vietnam and Profession-Oriented Education." Paper presented at a seminar on Instruments and Conditions for a Profession-Oriented Approach in Higher Education, Hanoi, April 22, 2005.

Hasselmo, Nils. 2004. "The Research-Led University and the Wider Community." In *Reinventing the Research University*, eds. L. E. Weber and J. J. Duderstadt. London: Economica.

Hayden, Martin. 2006. *Harmonizing the Regulatory Framework of Higher Education: Institutions in Vietnam and Overcoming Current Organizational and Institutional Barriers to their Academic and Economic Development*. Washington, DC: World Bank.

Hirst, Paul. 2000. "Democracy and Governance." In *Debating Governance: Authority, Steering, and Democracy*, ed. J. Pierre. London: Oxford University Press.

Hồ, Tú Bảo, Trần Nam Bình, and Trần Hữu Dũng. 2008. "Đề án cải cách giáo dục Việt Nam [A Proposal for Reforming Education in Vietnam]." *Thời Đại Mới (New Era)* 13. http://www.tapchithoidai.org.

Hồ, Vũ Ngọc Khuê. 2010. "Market-Led Globalization and Higher Education: The Case of Đà Nẵng University." In *Education in Viet Nam*, ed. Jonathan London. Singapore: ISEAS Press.

London, Jonathan D. 2003. "Vietnam's Mass Education and Health Systems: A Regimes Perspective." *American Asian Review* 21 (2): 125–170.

———. 2009. "Vietnam & the Making of Market-Leninism." *The Pacific Review* 22 (3): 373–397.

London, Jonathan D, and Paul Van Ufford. 2008. "Food Prices, Vulnerability, and Food Security in Vietnam." *A UN Perspective*. Hanoi: UNICEF Vietnam.

Lowndes, Vivien, and Chris Skelcher. 1998. "The Dynamics of Multi-Organizational Partnerships." *Public Administration* 76 (2): 313–333.

Malesky, Edmund, Regina Abrami, and Yu Zheng. Forthcoming. "Accountability and Inequality in Single-Party Regimes: A Comparative Analysis of Vietnam and China" *Comparative Politics*.

Marr, David G. *Vietnamese Tradition on Trial: 1920–1945*. Berkeley: University of California Press.

Mayntz, Renate. 1993. "Governing Failures and the Problems of Governability: Some Comments on a Theoretical Paradigm." In *Modern Governance: New Government-Society Interactions*, ed. J. Kooiman. London: Sage.

Ministry of Education and Training (MOET), Vietnam. 2008. *Số liệu thống kê giáo dục đào tạo năm học 2007–2008 (Education Statistics for the 2007–2008 Academic Year)*. Hanoi: MOET. http://www.moet.gov.vn.

Organisation for Economic Co-operation and Development (OECD). 2009. *Query Wizard for International Development Statistics*. Paris: OECD. http://www.oecd.org.

Ohmae, Kenichi. 1995. *The End of the Nation-State: The Rise of Regional Economies*. New York: Simon & Schuster.

Oosterlinck, Andre. 2004. "The Modern University and Its Main Activities." In *Reinventing the Research University*, eds. L. E. Weber and J. J. Duderstadt. London: Economica.

Ouchi, William G. 1991. "Markets, Bureaucracies and Clans." In *Markets, Hierarchies and Networks: The Coordination of Social Life*, eds. G. Thompson, J. Frances, R. Levacic, and J. Mitchell. London: Sage.

Overland, Martha Ann. 2009. "American Colleges Raise the Flag in Vietnam." *Chronicle of Higher Education* 55 (36): A1.

Pierre, Jon. 2000. "Understanding Governance." In *Debating Governance: Authority, Steering, and Democracy*, ed. J. Pierre. London: Oxford University Press.

Peters, Guy. 2000. "Governance and Comparative Politics." In *Debating Governance: Authority, Steering, and Democracy*, ed. J. Pierre. London: Oxford University Press.

Pincus, Jonathan. 2009. "Sustaining Growth in Difficult Times." *ASEAN Economic Bulletin* 26 (1): 11–24.

Rhodes, Frank H. T. 2004. "Reinventing the University." In *Reinventing the Research University*, ed. L. E. Weber and J. J. Duderstadt. London: Economica.

———. 2006. "Governance of U.S. Universities and Colleges." In *Reinventing the Research University*, ed. L. E. Weber and J. J. Duderstadt. Paris: Economica.

Porter, Gareth. 2003. *Vietnam: The Politics of Bureaucratic Socialism*. Ithaca: Cornell University Press.

Rose, Richard. 1978. *What is Governing? Purpose and Policy in Washington*. Englewood Cliffs, NJ: Prentice Hall.

Ruwich, John. 2009. "Firms struggle to hire skilled professionals in Vietnam." *Reuters News Agency*, May 13. http://www.reuters.com.

Streek, Wolfgang, and Philippe C. Schmitter, eds.1985. *Private Interest Government: Beyond Market and State*. London: Sage.

Thompson, Grahame, Jennifer Frances, Rosalind Levacic, and Jeremy Mitchell. eds. 1991. *Markets, Hierarchies and Networks: The Coordination of Social Life*. London: Sage.

Trần, Thị Hà. 2009. "400 triệu USD xây dựng bốn trường ĐH 'trình độ quốc tế'" [US$400 million for the Construction of Four 'International Level' Universities]." *Tuổi Trẻ Cuối Tuần Online* (*Youth Weekly Online*), May 6. http://www.tuoitre.com.vn.

Vũ, Quang Việt. 2008. "Giáo dục Việt Nam: Nguyên nhân xuống cấp và các cải cách cần thiết [Vietnam's Education: Causes of Decline and Essential Reforms]." *Thời đại mới* [*New Era*] 13. http://www.tapchithoidai.org.

Weiss, Thomas G. 2000. "Governance, Good Governance and Global Governance: Conceptual and Actual Challenges." *Third World Quarterly* 21 (5): 795–814.

Williamson, Oliver E. 1985. *The Economic Institutions of Capitalism: Firms, Markets, Relational Contracting*. New York: Free Press.

World Bank. 2000. *Higher Education in Developing Countries: Peril and Promise*. Task Force on Higher Education and Society. Washington, DC: World Bank.

———. 2005a *Quản lý và Điều Hành: Báo Cáo Phát Triển Việt Nam 2005* (Management: Viet Nam Development Report 2005). General Report of Donors, Donors Consultative Conference. Hanoi: World Bank.

———. 2005b. *Governance: Viet Nam Development Report*. Washington, DC: Poverty Reduction and Economic Management Unit, East Asia and Pacific Region, World Bank.

———. 2008. *Vietnam: Higher Education for Skills Development*. Education Sector Review. Washington, DC: World Bank.

Zemsky, Robert, and James J. Duderstadt. 2004. "Reinventing the Research University: An American Perspective." In *Reinventing the Research University*, eds. L. E. Weber and J. J. Duderstadt. London: Economica.

Notes on Contributors

ABDUL RAZAK AHMAD is Associate Professor at Universiti Pertahanan Nasional Malaysia, Kuala Lumpur, and was previously with the Governance Section, Ministry of Higher Education Malaysia. Abdul Razak is a law graduate and has reviewed extensively the University and University Colleges Act and public university constitution, particularly those relating to governance and autonomy. Abdul Razak is now working on international terrorism.

STEPHEN J. BALL is the Karl Mannheim Professor of Sociology of Education the Department of Educational Foundations and Policy Studies, Institute of Education, University of London, and he is a Fellow of the British Academy. Stephen Ball's work is in the field of "policy sociology," the use of sociological theories, and methods to analyze policy processes and outcomes. Specific research interests focus upon the effects and consequences of the education market in a variety of respects including the impact of competition on provider behavior, the class strategies of educational choosers, the participation of private capital in education service delivery and education policy, and the impact of "performativity" on academic and social life. His most recent books are *Education Plc.* (Routledge, 2007) and *The Education Debate* (Policy Press, 2008).

SHENG-JU CHAN is Assistant Professor in the Graduate Institute of Education at the National Chung Cheng University, Taiwan. Prior to that, he has also taught at the National Chiayi University, Taiwan since 2006. Chan received his PhD from the Institute of Education, University of London in 2006 and served as international alumni ambassador for the institution. His areas of special interests are higher education policy, comparative education, and higher education management. He is author of more than a dozen publications in Chinese and currently conducts a commissioned research regarding national university merger policy for the Ministry of Education in Taiwan.

JOHN N. HAWKINS is Professor Emeritus and Director of the Center for International and Development Studies at the Graduate School of Education and Information Studies at the University of California, Los Angeles. He was Dean of International Studies at UCLA, and has served as a Director of the UCLA Foundation Board, and is currently a Director of the East West Center Foundation Board. He is co-editor of Palgrave Macmillan's *International and Development Education* Book Series, has served as President of the Comparative and International Education Society, and

Editor of the *Comparative Education Review*. He is a specialist on higher education reform in the United States and Asia and the author of several books and research articles on education and development in Asia. He has conducted research throughout Asia since 1966 when he first visited the People's Republic of China and Japan.

WILLIAM YAT-WAI LO is Instructor, Department of Applied Social Sciences, the Hong Kong Polytechnic University; and currently is a PhD Candidate, University of Bristol, UK. He has published articles in several scholarly journals such as *Higher Education* (forthcoming), *Policy Futures in Education*, *International Journal of Educational Management*, *Asia Pacific Journal of Education*, and *Journal for Critical Studies of Education*. He is Associate Editor of *Journal of Asian Public Policy*.

JONATHAN LONDON directs the Vietnam Project at the Southeast Asia Research Centre, City University of Hong Kong, where he is also Assistant Professor in the Department of Asian and International Studies. London has authored scholarly articles on contemporary Vietnam's education and health systems and is completing a book on Vietnam's welfare regime. He holds a PhD in Sociology from the University of Wisconsin-Madison.

KA-HO MOK is Associate Vice President (External Relations) and Dean of Faculty of Arts and Sciences of the Hong Kong Institute of Education (HKIED). Before joining the HKIED, he was Associate Dean and Professor of Social Policy, Faculty of Social Sciences, University of Hong Kong. He is now Visiting Professor of the Graduate Education and Centre for East Asian Studies, University of Bristol, UK. He also served as Associate Dean of Faculty of Humanities and Social Science at City University of Hong Kong before taking up the position at the University of Bristol. Mok obtained his doctorate degree from London School of Economics and Political Science, University of London. He has published extensively in the fields of comparative education policy, policy studies, and governance and social development in contemporary China and East Asia. He has also worked with UNICEF and World Bank as international consultant.

JUN OBA is Associate Professor of the Research Institute for Higher Education (RIHE), Hiroshima University, Japan. His current research focuses on changing university governance and diverse staff issues. He has published extensively in the field of higher education. Recent journal publications appear in *Higher Education*, *Policy Futures in Education*, *Higher Education Research in Japan*, and the *Journal of Comparative Asian Development*.

BYUNG-SHIK RHEE is an Assistant Professor of the Department of Education at Yonsei University, Seoul, Korea. He previously served as a visiting scholar in Higher Education Research Institute at the University of California, Los Angeles. He has served as advisory member of Presidential Committee on Education Innovation and Education Policy Committee of Korean Ministry of Education. He holds a PhD in Higher Education from the University of Michigan. His current research interest is in college impact, institutional performance, college student assessment, and organizational behavior and management in higher education institutions.

MORSHIDI SIRAT is the Director and Professor of the National Higher Education Research Institute (IPPTN) based at Universiti Sains Malaysia. Since 2008, Morshidi was appointed as Dean of Research, Platform for Social Transformation Research, Universiti Sains Malaysia. Morshidi is currently coordinating the APEX University Research Agenda (AURA), a project which monitors and reports the impacts of APEX on the university community and system. Morshidi has published widely on state-university relationship in Malaysia.

JANDHYALA B.G. TILAK is Professor at the National University of Educational Planning and Administration, New Delhi. He has a PhD from the Delhi School of Economics. Professor Tilak had taught in the Indian Institute of Education and the University of Delhi, and as a Visiting Professor at the Sri Sathya Sai University, Hiroshima University, and Virginia University. An economist of education, Tilak was also on the staff of the World Bank, Washington, DC. He is the author of 10 books and more than 250 research papers in the area of education and development studies and recipient of several honors, including the Swami Pranavananda Saraswati Award of the UGC for outstanding research in education and the Dr. Malcolm Adiseshiah Award for contributions to development studies.

ANTHONY WELCH is Professor of Education, Faculty of Education and Social Work, University of Sydney. His numerous publications include studies of reforms, principally within Australia, and the Asia-Pacific Region. Professor Welch has consulted to international agencies such as UNDP and the *Commonwealth of Learning*, governments in Australia, Asia, as well as within Europe, and to U.S. institutions and foundations. He has been Visiting Professor in the United States, United Kingdom, Germany, France, and Japan. He was recently selected as a Fulbright New Century Scholar (2007–2008). His most recent books are *The Professoriate: Profile of a Profession* (2005), *Education, Change and Society* (2007), and *The Dragon and the Tiger Cubs* (on China's relations with Southeast Asia, forthcoming). His forthcoming book on Southeast Asian higher education will appear in 2010, and he is also completing further joint work on internationalizing Chinese universities, and directing the ARC project, *The Chinese Knowledge Diaspora*.

RUI YANG worked at a Chinese university for nearly a decade before commencing doctoral studies at the University of Hong Kong in 1996. He received his PhD from the University of Sydney in 2001. He has taught and researched at Universities of Shantou and Hong Kong in China, and Universities of Western Australia and Monash in Australia. He is now Director and Associate Professor, Comparative Education Research Centre, Faculty of Education, University of Hong Kong. He has written extensively in the field of comparative and international education. His current interest is focused on comparative and global studies in education policy, higher education internationalization, cross-cultural studies in education, and education policy sociology.

Index

Academic freedom 6, 8–9, 42–43, 85, 90, 98, 120, 133, 136, 139, 141–144, 150
Accountability 6, 8–9, 11, 22–23, 26–27, 32–34, 38–39, 44–45, 69, 72, 75, 77, 83, 93, 104–107, 112, 114, 118, 120, 135, 142, 145–146, 148–153, 162, 202, 206, 212–213
Accreditation 43, 111, 167, 172, 175, 183, 190, 202, 206–207, 212
Asia-Pacific 10, 20, 30–31, 34, 39, 41–42, 45, 217
Autonomy 5–6, 32, 34, 40, 42–43, 55, 59, 69, 72, 75, 78, 86, 89–90, 98, 100, 111–112, 114, 120, 126, 128–130, 132–137, 139–152, 169, 182, 184, 187, 190, 198, 203, 206–208, 212, 215

Centralization 34, 43, 45, 116, 134, 144, 149–150, 162, 169, 207
China 5, 9, 11, 18–22, 26–27, 30, 36, 38–40, 44–46, 49–68, 82, 121, 142, 151–152, 154–155, 177, 198, 210, 213, 216–217
Commercialization 3, 9, 35, 63, 103–104, 107, 109, 183, 197, 208–210
Corporatization 3–4, 6–8, 10, 49, 82–83, 113–114, 116–118, 135, 146, 148

Decentralization 2, 38, 40–41, 43–45, 50, 52, 56, 63, 65, 77, 80, 116, 149, 162–163, 169, 207–208, 212
Demographic 70–71, 78, 153, 159–160, 172
Deregulation 6, 27, 70, 71, 77, 80, 104, 140, 144–147, 149
Devolution 7, 15, 63, 95, 134, 144, 147, 162–163

East Asia 13, 26–27, 38–39, 45–46, 66, 99, 119, 158, 170, 193, 198, 214, 216
Enrollment 5–6, 33, 35, 49–50, 52–54, 56–59, 61, 69–71, 73, 94–95, 109, 142, 157, 160–162, 165–167, 172, 176–178, 181, 185, 196–197, 199–201, 204–205
Entrepreneurialism 6, 49, 67, 103–106, 111–112, 115, 118–119
Evaluation 5, 15, 73, 76, 79, 90, 92–95, 97–102, 125, 136, 141–142, 145–147, 165, 212

Globalization 1, 4, 7, 9–11, 14–15, 25–27, 29, 32, 38, 40, 44–46, 49–50, 52, 62, 64–65, 67, 104, 120–122, 125, 140, 145, 148, 151, 160–161, 170–171, 173–174, 177, 182, 188–189, 213

Heterarchies 2, 4, 13–18, 23
Hierarchies 2, 15, 195, 213–214
Higher education reform 5, 7, 29, 31, 45–46, 66–69, 72–73, 78, 80, 82, 115, 118–119, 134, 147, 151, 162, 204, 207, 216
Hong Kong 6, 10, 19, 21, 38–39, 45–47, 63–64, 66–67, 82, 103, 105–107, 109–111, 113, 115–123, 189, 216–217
Human resource 5, 33, 42, 60, 71–72, 81–82, 89–90, 101, 130, 146, 169, 175, 189–190, 208
Hybrid 2, 4, 13, 17–18, 21, 23, 25, 40, 81, 127

Incorporation 4–5, 7–8, 15, 25, 67–68, 73–75, 77–83, 85–87, 90–93, 96, 98, 100–101, 117, 130, 154

Index

India 7, 20, 23, 30, 36, 45, 58, 64, 128, 171–185, 187–191, 217
Inequalities 8, 60, 176, 180–181, 196, 198, 201, 209
Innovation 10, 15, 17–18, 73, 87, 116–117, 122, 130, 146–147, 152, 158, 172, 184, 187, 211, 216
Internationalization 7–8, 41–42, 44, 65, 117, 125–126, 170–172, 187–188, 217

Japan 5, 7, 21, 30, 38, 44, 46, 67–68, 74–75, 77, 81–83, 85, 87, 89, 91–93, 95–102, 126, 139, 150, 159, 216–217

Knowledge economy 22–24, 38–39, 42, 122, 137, 174, 198
Korea 3, 5, 8, 21, 30, 38–39, 46, 67–83, 101, 216

Liberalization 5, 30, 141, 144

Malaysia 3, 6–7, 9, 19–20, 40, 101, 110, 125–135, 137, 149, 151, 153–155, 157–164, 169–170, 215, 217
Managerialism 17, 42, 103–104, 106, 111–112, 115, 117, 121, 142, 148–151
Marketization 3, 8, 10, 25, 38, 46, 52, 63, 77, 80, 82, 111, 122, 146–147, 151

National universities 5, 67–69, 71–81, 83, 85–87, 89, 91–102, 150, 152, 200, 203, 206
Neoliberalism 3, 6–7, 22–23, 31, 43, 64, 83, 121, 136, 142, 147–149
Network 2, 11, 13–14, 16, 19, 22, 24–27, 37, 45, 54, 61, 115, 125, 154, 176, 179, 184–185, 196, 202, 204, 213–214

Ownership 24, 51, 75, 114

Private universities 41, 55, 112, 155–156, 160–161, 169, 174, 181–182, 187
Privatization 2–4, 7–10, 26, 35–36, 38, 40, 43–45, 99, 110, 142, 153, 167, 169, 188
Provision 2, 8–9, 15, 20, 34, 51, 54–55, 78, 109–111, 114–115, 119, 129, 131–135, 144, 146–147, 154–155, 159, 177, 180, 188, 196–198, 204

Public sector 2–4, 7–8, 10, 13, 15–19, 22–27, 43, 70–71, 78, 99, 104, 141–142, 153, 161–162, 164, 167, 171, 176, 178, 180, 188
Public universities 21–22, 36–37, 44, 59–61, 82, 95, 100–101, 113–114, 126, 128–131, 133–135, 137, 139, 142, 144–146, 156, 181, 200, 204–206, 208, 212

Quality assurance 8–9, 19, 23–24, 43, 79, 103, 105–107, 112–114, 116–117, 122, 146, 165–166, 170, 207

Regulation 3, 8–9, 18, 41, 43, 70–72, 83, 106, 131, 135, 139, 141–142, 144, 151, 155, 163–164, 166–167, 172, 183, 187, 206

Singapore 6, 14, 19–23, 38–41, 47, 66–67, 82, 101, 103, 105, 107, 109–119, 121–123, 149, 151, 166, 169, 205, 213
Southeast Asia 6–7, 9, 15, 18, 23, 42, 153, 155–164, 166–170, 200, 216–217
State building 3, 10

Thailand 6, 8, 20, 120, 137, 153, 158–161, 164, 168
Transnational 2, 4, 7, 14, 18–19, 21–25, 112, 115, 117, 123, 163–164, 167

United Kingdom 3, 8, 18, 20–21, 27, 67, 96, 128, 148, 217
United States 3, 5, 8, 18, 21, 30, 36–38, 42–45, 58, 62, 68, 78, 91, 96, 98, 148, 158, 188, 206, 209–212, 216–217
University governance 1, 4, 6–9, 38, 54, 82, 86, 91, 94, 103–104, 115, 118, 125, 135–136, 139–141, 144, 146–147, 149, 151, 216

Vietnam 6–7, 20–21, 153–154, 156–157, 159–162, 164–166, 168–170, 193–214, 216

World-class 1, 4, 8–9, 11, 30, 70, 72, 112, 115, 117, 126–129, 135–137, 145, 151–152, 157, 172, 176, 185–186, 190

GPSR Compliance

The European Union's (EU) General Product Safety Regulation (GPSR) is a set of rules that requires consumer products to be safe and our obligations to ensure this.

If you have any concerns about our products, you can contact us on

ProductSafety@springernature.com

In case Publisher is established outside the EU, the EU authorized representative is:

Springer Nature Customer Service Center GmbH
Europaplatz 3
69115 Heidelberg, Germany

www.ingramcontent.com/pod-product-compliance
Lightning Source LLC
LaVergne TN
LVHW011816060526
838200LV00053B/3800